PUNISHMENT
WITHOUT
CRIME

PUNISHMENT
WITHOUT
CRIME

The True Story of a Man Who Spent Twenty-four
Years in Prison for a Crime He Did Not Commit

by ISIDORE ZIMMERMAN
with Francis Bond
introduction by Drew Pearson

Clarkson N. Potter, Inc./Publisher New York

92341
Z74p

© Clarkson N. Potter, Inc., 1964
Library of Congress Catalog Card Number: 63-19897

Manufactured in the United Sates of America
First Edition

This book is dedicated to the memory of my beloved Mother, who always believed in my innocence, but who did not live to see that dream come true . . . to my wonderful Father, who spent his life savings to help make that dream a reality . . . to my loyal family and in-laws who never gave up, and to the following: the late Herbert H. Lehman, Maurice Edelbaum, Ruth Bradley, Harry H. Lipsig, Charles Bernard, Drew Pearson, Clarkson N. Potter, Francis Bond, Johnny Carson, Art Stark, Roy Cameron, Stu Billet, and the staff of "Who Do You Trust," ABC-TV Network, Woody Woodbury, Jennie Grossinger, Rabbi Sol H. Oster, Reuben and Helen Wishnia, Isidore Olshon, Anthony Molese, Teamster's Local #138, William Slevin.

And to all the others, too numerous to mention here, my deepest thanks! Without their help, this book would still be a part of my second dream.

CONTENTS

INTRODUCTION

by Drew Pearson

For a man who spent twenty-four years in prison, nine months of the time on death row, Isidore Zimmerman is an amazingly unembittered man.

You would think that one who had watched the barber shave his head for the electrodes on what was to be his last day would be vengeful and vindictive or at least a little dramatic about it. Isidore Zimmerman is not. You would think also that he would like to brag a bit or at least talk about ordering a steak dinner with two kinds of dessert on that last day, and having the phonograph records he wanted played all day long.

In his book Zimmerman has written: "I knew I was never going to see another sunrise. I walked to the "dance hall" in a dream. I was ready to go, as ready as you can be. But I didn't want to go: the pastureland could wait. Act like a man, I told myself, and try to think of those who have gone before me, like men . . .

"My father and two brothers came up to say good-bye. Mamma didn't come; it would have been too much for her. She was home, in the kitchen, praying for me before two candles. We had three hours together. It was more than enough to make arrangements for my funeral, to give them the last messages I thought out for the family.

"I think Papa believed me when I told him I had lost my fear of dying . . . 'Tell them I died a good death with expectations of a better world,' was what I said to sum it all up. The last embrace; tears; and they'd go through one door and I'd go through another, and I knew I'd never see them again."

Suddenly the principal keeper was there with a message from Governor Lehman. "I am advising you officially that your sentence is commuted," he said; "the Governor is granting you executive clemency."

But Isidore Zimmerman didn't believe it. Furthermore he didn't care. "For nine long months, I had been rehearsing my death, dying a little every day, dying a little more every night, while just up the hall from my cell they were killing men. I knew my role as victim too well, knew it by heart, couldn't back down now. 'I don't want clemency,' I heard myself saying.

" 'You have nothing to say about it,' the keeper replied. 'You are being transferred out of the death house to B Block. Get yourself ready.' "

Today, twenty-four years later, Isidore Zimmerman nurses no grudges. He is an amazingly tolerant man. He has not even complained that society failed to step forward following his release from prison to offer him a job. He went to Freedomland to ask for one, thinking that there might be something healthy and even newsworthy about a man who had been erroneously denied his freedom for twenty-four years finally getting economic freedom at Freedomland. He was hired at the top, but kicked out by the personnel director below. He went to Palisades Park. The answer was: "We don't hire your type of man . . ." "But I was exonerated." ". . . Sorry." That was that.

The Vice-President of Chemstrand accepted him, but the girls beside whom he was to work threatened to quit. The owners of two restaurants accepted him, but the kitchen unions balked. "We don't want any ex-cons here," was the reply wherever he turned. Even the New York State Employment agency failed. He went on television, offered to do anything, sweep floors, anything. He got friendly letters, but no job. Finally the Teamsters Union and the Embassy Grocery Cor-

poration at 407 Greenwich Street came through. He became
a warehouseman.

Yet Zimmerman remains philosophical about the present as
well as the past. His story is dramatic, tragic, full of pathos,
but it is not bitter.

Many people will read that story with interest and incredulity.

J. Edwin LaVallee, the warden at Dannemora, will read it
with interest though not much incredulity. He is the warden
who considered all inmates animals. And Robert E. Murphy,
chief keeper at Greenhaven, will read it with interest and
possibly some remorse. He is the warden who confined Zimmerman for an entire year without food. "Get your friends to
feed you," Murphy decreed, after his prisoner had refused to
eat one prison dish. (His friends in prison *did* feed him.)

And John Flynn, now President of the City Council at Platts-
burg, N.Y., will read it with satisfaction, because he, as
assignment officer at Dannemora, befriended Zimmerman.

But the two men who should read this story with greatest
interest are Thomas E. Dewey and Edmund P. Brown.

Brown will read it because as Governor of California, he
experienced the excruciating pain of making the decision regarding the death sentence of Caryl W. Chessman. Half the
world watched and much of it criticized as he parried the
problem of what was best for humanity and what was the
letter of the law in this famous case. From this soul-searching
he emerged more convinced than ever that capital punishment
was a mistake.

Tom Dewey will read this book because it was during his
days as crime-busting District Attorney of New York that
Zimmerman was given the death sentence. Being human,
Dewey will doubtless look back and ask himself how his staff
could have made such a gruesome mistake. He may even do
some soul-searching regarding those days when ambition was
interwoven with the zeal of the prosecutor and when he was
hell-bent not only on crime clean-up but for higher office.

This link between duty and ambition is present in the breasts of most public prosecutors. It is part of our system. We cannot blame Dewey that he was out to make headlines; that the more convictions his staff got, the greater his chance of going on to Albany or Washington. But we can blame ourselves that the process of criminal review is not perfected enough to prevent a man from spending twenty-four years in prison before the slow-grinding machinery of justice rectifies the mistake. And we should blame ourselves that we have not banned capital punishment, so that those who suffer from judicial error can be saved before it is too late.

It may be unfair to ask why Thomas E. Dewey, as Governor, released Lucky Luciano from his 30 to 50 years' imprisonment as leader of Murder Incorporated, and let him quietly sail back to Italy; whereas in contrast he did not take the trouble to probe the record of a teen-ager given the death sentence for rather a tenuous connection with the 1937 murder of a New York cop. This, I repeat, may be an unfair question. Nevertheless, it will be asked. Furthermore it was an unfair world in which young Zimmerman grew up in those difficult, depression-ridden days on the East Side.

The crime for which he was given the death sentence was the holdup of an all-night gambling joint at 144 Second Avenue in which a policeman, Michael J. Foley, was killed. For his murder at 3:20 A.M. on Saturday, April 10, 1937, five boys, all in their teens or early twenties, were given the death sentence.

Isidore Zimmerman, only one of the five alive today, was not present at the holdup. He was convicted on the ground that he had supplied the murder weapon. The evidence was tenuous. But in that day of popular furor over the death of a policeman and passionate determination of Dewey's young prosecutors, evidence did not have to be copper-riveted.

During the trial, Harry Levy, a practicing member of the New York bar who donated his free time to helping those in trouble, worked with Miss Ann Goldstein, a social worker on the East Side, and Hyman Liebowitz, another dedicated lawyer, to ascertain the truth regarding Zimmerman's guilt. They interviewed Danny Rose, one of the holdup gang, who turned state's evidence.

"Rose told me very definitely, very positively and conclusively, that Zimmerman knew nothing at all about the whole thing," Levy later testified. Liebowitz confirmed this.

"I asked Rose what connection Zimmerman had with the crime," Levy testified. "He told me positively that Zimmerman had no connection whatsoever with the crime. He outlined for me the story of what had transpired on the night of the murder. . . . I pressed him a number of times on the connection Zimmerman had with the case. He repeated time and time again that Zimmerman had absolutely nothing to do with it."

Before the trial Levy approached the office of District Attorney Dewey, talked to a Mr. Mendelson in the Homicide Bureau and to a Mr. Sarafite, deputy to prosecutor Jacob Rosenblum who handled the trial. However, the prosecutor's office did not even bother to make a written record of the conversations.

James Murray, Zimmerman's defense attorney, in examining Levy at the trial asked: "Did he [Mr. Rosenblum] call a stenographer?"

"No."

"Did he take your statement down in writing?"

"No."

"Did you give him an address?"

"I did, and I gave my telephone number."

"And that was to someone representing Mr. Dewey's office, is that right?"

But Levy was vague on the dates, and apparently Dewey's office was not particularly concerned over statements about the innocence of one of the defendants.

On the witness stand Danny Rose reversed himself and said that Zimmerman supplied the gun; and Levy had not thought to put Rose's earlier statement in writing. On such tenuous oversights and on such determination by prosecutors do the lives of men sometimes hang.

When the jury brought in its verdict of guilty, District Attorney Dewey issued a public statement: "Robbery with a gun and murder are at last becoming unsafe in New York City. There have been eight convictions for murder in the first degree in the county so far this year as compared with two convictions for murder in the first degree for the entire year of 1937."

It was a great day for Tom Dewey's batting average! But it was not a great day for a nineteen-year-old boy who then began twenty-four years of punishment without crime.

"For Harvey, Hutch, and Dominick, it was over," said Zimmerman after three of the East Side boys had been electrocuted. "But for Chaleff and for me it was just beginning, and it would never end as long as I drew breath. The score for Foley's death hadn't been evened, hadn't even begun to be evened. Two or three cells away, the nightmare started up again: mumble, wail, shriek, mumble. I was awake, and yet I was living a nightmare, someone else's nightmare that shouldn't have been mine. Because I remember it, after all my terror and my tears and saying good-bye to life, that it had all been for nothing: I was innocent. Harvey, Hutch, Dominick, were dead. I wasn't dead, no. But every day from now on they'd bury me a little more, and in the end it would be just the same for me. Harvey, Hutch, Dominick, would be buried dead. Me, they were burying alive. And I could live to be a hundred."

"You can give a prisoner a pardon; but you cannot give him back a moment of his imprisonment."

GEORGE BERNARD SHAW

CHAPTER 1

THE CRIME

IN THE BEGINNING was the gun: a black .38 provided by Smith & Wesson. It belonged to Salvatore, whose son Ralph fired two rounds from it into his bedroom wall and passed it on to Danny. Danny offered the gun to Philip. From Philip they said it went to Beany; from Beany to Popeye; and from Popeye to Hutch and Harvey.

Hutch and Harvey had ideas. So did Sonny, and Little Benny and Little Chemey. For them the manipulation of firearms was the logical means to social status and economic security. The ideas were wrong, but demonstrating the error proved to be costly: at the lowest estimate two lifetimes, four lives and a classic miscarriage of justice.

———————

The establishment occupying the second floor of the dingy tenement at 144 Second Avenue was variously described as "cafe," "coffeehouse," "teahouse," "waiters' club," "restaurant" and "gambling joint." A loft-type room some hundred feet long fragmented by occasional partitions running almost the length of the building; circular wooden tables among clusters of wooden chairs; globe suspension lamps shedding a harsh white light from the fretted yellow ceiling to wooden floors devoid of carpeting; metal coatracks on casters ranged

1

along the walls for the customers' convenience; a massive cast-iron stove; a garish mural along which stylized Egyptians marched in procession, turning their profiles to the Ninth Street windows. To the left of the entrance—one flight up from the street—a massive partition screened the cardtables from view; to the right, near the end of the long room, a food counter and behind it the kitchen—steam table, broiler, coffee urns, wooden icebox—and a corridor to the right leading to doors marked "Ladies" and "Men." But at the Boulevard Restaurant, known informally as "Willie the Dutchman's," ladies were a rarity. It was men who kept the Dutchman open till all hours: taxi drivers on the night shift, sailors on shore leave, drifters, grifters, unemployed dishwashers, cardplayers, insomniacs and police officers.

In uniform and out, the police paid periodic visits to the Dutchman's in line of duty: when you bring together men and cards and money, your chances for trouble are promising. And the Lower East Side of the city of New York provided a climate in which trouble could flourish. In March of 1937 a holdup of the Boulevard by persons unknown had brought its perpetrators some fifteen hundred dollars. It was natural for the police to suppose that one successful robbery would inspire a repeat performance at a later date, and natural for them too to keep close watch on the Boulevard.

The supposition on which detectives of the Ninth Squad were operating was solidly grounded. A group of young men —the youngest seventeen, the oldest twenty-seven—conceived the idea of "knocking over the Dutchman's." Weapons were required and acquired: the .38 Smith & Wesson test-fired into the bedroom wall, a .32 pistol, and another .38 reputedly not in working order. Conferences on strategy and tactics were held—in a candy store at 218 East Broadway, in a restaurant directly across East Broadway on the corner of Clinton, and in a taxi parked in front of the restaurant. At 2:20 A.M. on Saturday, April 10, 1937, a six-man task force armed with three pistols and observing the military precaution of dispersal was on the march north up the east side of Second Avenue to

"take" the Boulevard Restaurant. The forces deployed: Dominick Guariglia, Arthur Friedman, Joseph Harvey O'Loughlin,
Philip Chaleff, Benjamin Ertel, and Isidore Perlmutter.

———

John R. Gallagher, detective, Shield No. 1153, has been
attached to the Ninth Squad of the New York Police Department over ten years. For eight of those years he has known
Detective Michael J. Foley, and for five of the eight served
shoulder to shoulder with him in the jungle of the city. The
danger they have shared has brought each man to esteem the
other, and either man's life may depend on that esteem. On
the night of April 9, 1937, their joint tour of duty begins
routinely in plain clothes at 6:00 P.M., and according to the
assignment chart hanging on the wall in the Ninth Squad
offices at 321 East Fifth Street, it will extend to 8:30 A.M. on
the morning of the tenth: a policeman's lot is not an easy one.
The night is clear and cool. The two police officers work their
way up Second Avenue to St. Marks Place, check the restaurant at No. 9, near Third Avenue, where they speak briefly
with the owner. At a leisurely pace they head back downtown,
toward Second Avenue. It is nearly three in the morning; they
are interested in loiterers, night owls, insomniacs, strollers.
After five they will head farther downtown to Stanton Street,
to keep an eye on the clothing stores until half-past six or
seven, when the city comes awake to another day. At Ninth
Street they cross Second Avenue and head for the Boulevard
Restaurant, where they are accustomed to drop in two or three
nights a week. Seventeen steps up the street: a landing and a
door opening into the Dutchman's. Over the tables hangs a
thick pall of cigarette smoke; there is a continuous murmur
of conversation, laughter, calls for waiters, counsel to cardplayers, comment on the cards. A score of spectators are
grouped around a single table where two first-rate pinochle
players are locked in combat. Behind the partition to the left
where the bigger money games are usually held a game of
klabiatsch is under way. But this Saturday night at the Dutch-

man's is calm—there are no more than fifty or sixty customers in the long, low-ceilinged room. Gallagher and Foley work their way down toward the food counter, the kitchen: nothing to report. They are on their way to the door when Samuel Cooperstein, the "Dutchman," puts down his pinochle hand and hails them. To Cooperstein the familiar faces of the detectives are welcome, for his memory of the March holdup is as vivid as it is unpleasant. "How about some coffee, boys?" he asks.

It is shortly after three in the morning, and the two police officers have more than five hours' tour ahead of them. The lure of the coffee is not easy to resist. Foley and Gallagher sit, flanking the Dutchman, at a table on the Ninth Street side of the room, diagonally opposite the entrance. Cooperstein orders, "Two coffees and one milk here." Before the waiter is out of earshot he countermands, "No, make it two milks and one coffee."

Twenty-five feet across the room the door from the landing opens to admit a man with a .32 pistol in his hand. Behind him, almost on his heels, another man, unarmed, who shouts out, "This is a stickup. Everybody up!" Together the two bear sharply right, head up toward the food counter and the kitchen. A third man, pistol at the ready, takes up his position at the door without advancing farther into the room. A fourth —blue-eyed and sandy-haired, holding a black .38 with a brown grip—advances to the table where the Dutchman is seated between the two police officers, unrecognizable in their plain clothes. "All right, you bastards, in back with the rest," he raps out, indicating the rear of the restaurant where the bulk of the Dutchman's customers have frozen into immobility.

The April night is cool enough for Gallagher to have worn his topcoat. During the late night hours he carries his weapon in an outside pocket: a Smith & Wesson .32 Long. Detective Foley carries his revolver, a .38 Banker's Special, in a clip holster attached to his trouser band. Both Foley and Gallagher reach for their guns.

The infernal machine is wound up. Before it runs down it will take four human lives. Before it runs down it will bury two men alive, one for his life and one for a quarter of a century. And for the families of those it will maim or destroy—wives, mothers, brothers, fathers—the machine, even twenty-five years later, has not yet ground to a stop.

======

According to the records Dominick Guariglia is seventeen. His close-cropped hair frames a baby face, sallow of complexion, which impresses with its appearance of youthfulness. But appearances can be deceptive. From the age of fourteen, when he began to deliver papers to the neighborhood newsstands, Dominick has been a working man. In the walk-up apartment at 219 Henry Street, which he shares with his parents, five sisters, and a brother, no one can afford the luxury of idleness, and childhood is a disability that interferes only briefly with the business of earning a living.

One job succeeds another. He gives up delivering papers to shine shoes, walking the streets of the East Side with a battered shoeshine box in his hands. In 1937 a shine costs a nickel —not enough to earn a man's keep whatever the tips he is lucky enough to get, and not enough shines in the day if the man has to attend school, like Dominick. When he reaches 7A, Dominick at sixteen turns his back on Public School 147 to go to work full time. A better job has turned up: the Victoria Doll Company on Greene Street near West Houston needs the kind of skill he can furnish, packing dolls, stacking cartons, delivering orders. School has become an extravagance.

He can read and write; his parents, good Catholics, have seen to it that he received religious instruction; and the laws of New York oblige him—since he has quit school before the age of seventeen—to continue his studies outside of working hours at a "continuation school." A new opportunity arises: Danny Tricarico, his brother-in-law, owner of a delivery truck, needs a helper. Dominick quits the Victoria Doll Company to work for Danny, but in a few months' time this job too evapo-rates, though not before he has acquired professional experi-ence. Now he is able to hire on as a trucker with Daniels & Kennedy down on South Street. Here too the work leaves something to be desired. The truckers report evenings to de-liver Home Relief parcels to the poor, and if extra men are needed they are engaged on the spot. Work is available—or not—much as it is on the docks at a "shape-up": if you're there, if your face is familiar, if there's enough to go around, if you're lucky. All too often Guariglia is not lucky. He craves steadier employment, and finds it briefly as a hat cleaner in a little shop two blocks from his apartment on Henry Street, between Scammel and Jackson, but that job too has its draw-back. By March of 1937 Dominick has begun to work in a flower shop on Bleecker Street, cutting flowers, wrapping flow-ers, delivering flowers. The Easter holidays confer a seasonal prosperity on the florist. Dominick works for a few weeks with the conviction that he has found his way at last, and then, reporting for work one morning, learns to his dismay that the boom is over: no further need for his services.

A man without a job is only half a man. Dominick turns to the church of his faith in the person of Father Knight, the parish priest, to help him find work. "Father Knight says he would try his best," recalls Guariglia. "He wrote out a letter and he gave me the letter, and I went to the place where the address was on Varick Street and they gave me a test, some kind of test to read and to answer questions. I took the test and I failed. Then later on they sent me another postal card and I took another test and I failed again. Then I didn't go no more."

Twice a week Dominick reports, in search of work, to the parish boys' club that Father Knight directs. No luck. The Guariglias are drawing Home Relief. It occurs to Dominick to ask the Relief investigator for a WPA job. He learns he is ineligible because his father is already employed by the WPA.

On the morning of April ninth Dominick arises around seven. "My mother gave me fifteen cents to went [*sic*] looking for a job. I went on West Houston Street, on Greene Street, Bleecker Street, all around the West Side. I used to look for signs, and sometimes I went to the elevator boy and asked him if there were any jobs, he told me no." After a morning wasted pounding the pavement Dominick returns to Henry Street and lunches. Shortly afterwards he is visited by one John Harvey O'Loughlin—nicknamed Harvey—whom he has known to speak to for about three months. Harvey, also unemployed, invites Dominick to the movies. By four that afternoon he is back in the Henry Street apartment, where he stays until seven in the evening. "I went down in the poolroom and I stood in the poolroom until about half-past nine, ten o'clock."

The poolroom is on Henry Street between Clinton and Montgomery, about five doors from Dominick's apartment. By ten that evening he is on his way to Muskin's Restaurant on East Broadway and Clinton, a block and a half distant. Though he recalls leaving Muskin's for good around half-past two in the morning, he has not remained continuously in the restaurant. He may have gone for a walk around the block; he may have taken a stroll as far as the park on Hester Street; he may have had a soda at Tobias Hanover's candy store just across Broadway from Muskin's; he may have had a cup of coffee with O'Loughlin—he is certain he had coffee with someone that evening—but he can't be sure.

Around one o'clock in the morning Guariglia looks up from his table in Muskin's to see an unwelcome face: "Little Benny" Ertel, an acquaintance of some five or six weeks. Dominick has lost money to him in a poolroom card game and deferred payment. "He started asking me about three dollars I owed him, and I told him I didn't have any three dollars to pay him, that I went looking for a job, that I couldn't find it; that I would pay him back as soon as I get it. He started hollering at me and then he says, 'Don't forget to pay me back.' And then he went away."

Ninety-odd minutes elapse. Little Benny returns to Muskin's and calls Dominick out for a conversation on the sidewalk. "He told me he wanted me to carry guns for him . . . that I looked like a young boy, a kid . . . that nobody would suspect me of carrying guns." At first Dominick refuses flatly. "I told him I didn't want to carry guns for him, and he said, 'All you got to do is carry the guns and we will call the three dollars even that you owe me, and you will get a few dollars.' " Little Benny is insistent, persuasive; Dominick accompanies him to 221 Henry Street, next door to his apartment. "We went downstairs, down in the basement in a toilet, and he took out a bag behind the toilet bowl and he took out three guns." Dominick puts one gun in the right and one in the left pocket of his coat and the third under his belt. Little Benny and Dominick walk together to East Broadway and Clinton, then up to Eighth or Ninth Street, where they consult in a darkened hallway with O'Loughlin and two others: Isidore Perlmutter, nicknamed "Little Chemey," and Arthur Friedman, a thin-faced, sharp-nosed young man known around the neighborhood as "Hutch" or "Hooch." In the hallway Little Benny recovers the pistols from Dominick, distributes them: one to Friedman, one to O'Loughlin, one for himself. Around the corner on Second Avenue stands the Boulevard Restaurant.

On the way from the Henry Street basement where the guns were hidden, Dominick has been protesting to Little Benny. " 'Must I carry them? I don't want to carry them.' So he told me, 'Come on, you little wop bastard, what are you ascared of? All you got to do is carry them.' " In the hallway, after the weapons have been distributed, Benny changes his tune. " 'You got to come.' He says, 'We need somebody else to look out the window.' . . . So I told him I didn't want to go. So then he says, 'I'll blow your brains out if you don't come.' "

The task force emerges from the hallway, turns the corner, and finds itself before the entrance to 144 Second Avenue. Little Benny is eager. Opening the door from the street, he pushes Arthur Friedman, who is carrying one of the pistols, toward the stairs. "Hurry up, hurry up," he repeats. Behind Friedman on the narrow stairs comes Guariglia, unarmed; Little Benny has told him he will be free to go as soon as his job as lookout is over. Seventeen steps up from the street

Guariglia pushes open the door of the Boulevard Restaurant, hard on Friedman's heels. He advances into the room six feet. Then, in his recollection, the shots begin.

———

Arthur Friedman is twenty. He is another of those for whom schooling is a luxury; his Austrian-born mother, Yetta, cannot recall the age at which he quit school to work—fourteen? fifteen? His father Morris, a native of Romania, is living in retirement after more than twenty-five years as an employee of the Department of Sanitation, and it devolves on Hutch and his mother—whose other two sons, Max and Benjamin, have families of their own to support—to keep the pot boiling in the tiny kitchenette of their apartment on Madison Street.

Arthur—Hutch or Hooch to his friends—gives his occupation as "laborer," but by 1933, when he is only twelve, it has occurred to him that there are easier ways than labor to make a living. The Bronx County Court records a conviction for unlawful entry and another for attempted burglary in that year, but sentence is suspended. In any event, work is hard to find. Doubly handicapped by a police record and the lack of a high-school education, Friedman is all the more inclined to look for consolation elsewhere. The matter of his nickname reflects his philosophy: there are those who lay it to his fondness for "hooch," that is to say whiskey; and there are those —friends of Arthur's—who will concede that on occasion Hutch has looked to marijuana to make the world more livable. There are those too who will contend that Friedman derived little benefit even from his brief course of studies at Public School 65, on Grand Street, for reasons quite beyond his control. At the age of seven he was struck by a delivery truck. His injuries: a fractured right foot, the loss of five teeth, and a brain concussion, the gravity of which may have contributed to impair his intelligence.

On the night of April 9 Arthur Friedman meets a friend, Abe Kirschner, on the sidewalk in front of Louis Golden's Bar and Grill on East Broadway and Clinton Street, opposite

Hanover's Candy Store and up the block from Muskin's Restaurant. Together they enter the bar, and in the space of forty-five minutes Arthur has four shots of whiskey to Abe's two, but Abe is drinking beer for a chaser. Around eleven, the two emerge from Golden's to meet friends, Joseph Reibach and Isidore Meichenbaum, and the group proceeds a block down Clinton and half a block up Henry Street to Artie's Poolroom.

Hutch and Abe seek out a pool racker named Popeye Cooperman; Cooperman provides six marijuana cigarettes, for which Hutch pays a dollar, and the Friedman-Kirschner-Reibach-Meichenbaum quartet then walk to a deserted stable in an uninhabited loft building on Division Street, a quiet dead end. There, in the course of forty-five minutes, each one smokes a marijuana cigarette. As Kirschner recalls the effect of the drug: "It made you jolly, it made you powerful, you could swim from here to Europe—do anything." Friedman's euphoria takes the form of dancing, singing, joking with the others: Meichenbaum, a hat blocker who has known Friedman for some six years, recalls that Hooch was "kissing everybody, jumping around, happy." Both Meichenbaum and Friedman, elated, declare under the influence of the marijuana that they can "beat Joe Louis." Toward midnight the group disperses.

In Yetta Friedman's recollection her son Arthur had left the apartment at 206 Madison Street, after a six o'clock dinner, around eight in the evening. "I gave him a good supper. He don't eat. I give him plenty eat." By eleven that evening she and her husband are in bed. On Arthur's return shortly after midnight: "He came home and he went to my bed and he kiss me; he wake me up. I said, 'What do you want?' He told me, 'Give me eat, Ma, I am hungry.' When he kiss me I felt like from his mouth was like liquor . . . I went up from my bed and I give him eat, and he ate and I stay in the kitchen and I look on him, he was all upset; I couldn't tend to him. He was like falling from his feet. I tried to keep him up but I couldn't. He was dancing, singing. I didn't know what he was doing. He was taking me around and kiss me, and . . . when he eat, I give him, I tried to sit him and he can't sit."

Friedman's mother has one concern: to get her son to bed. "He act dancing, singing. I didn't see from him . . . never [sic] what I saw from him this night . . . I made the bed. I please him, 'Go in the bed, sleep,' but I couldn't hold him in . . . He was falling from the feet, he didn't know what he talk to me even the night." Fifteen or twenty minutes later Hutch is up again. "Here, I made the bed for you," says Mrs. Friedman. "And he said, 'No, I want to go for a walk'; and he went for a walk."

By now it is shortly after 1:00 A.M., Saturday morning. Boruch Dworkin, who drives his cab nights for the Yellow Taxi Company, has backed his hack around the corner of Clinton Street into East Broadway and occupies the taxi station directly in front of Muskin's Restaurant. He notices Friedman standing in front of Muskin's window and recalls having seen him half a dozen times earlier that evening. Dworkin will head for the barn around three, when the street lights go off. Meantime fares are few and far between, and he absents himself from the vehicle as his fancy dictates: a phone call, a drink of water, a turn on the sidewalk to stretch his legs. Returning to the cab after one such absence, he finds six of the neighborhood crowd occupying the back seat and both jump seats: O'Loughlin, Little Benny, Popeye Cooperman, Philip Chaleff, and two individuals known as Chester and Smitty. They are listening to the car radio and talking among themselves. Though Dworkin knows most of them only by sight, he is philosophical about their occupation of his cab. There they stay while Dworkin, who will have no fares for the remainder of the evening, walks off to buy a paper.

About 1:30 A.M., Little Benny, whom Dworkin knows by sight as he does O'Loughlin and Friedman, leaves the cab. "He walked over and started talking to Hooch," recalls Dworkin, but he is unable to hear their conversation. Thereafter "Hooch went away. He walked up Clinton Street . . . going north . . . Benny remained standing in front of Muskin's. Then Harvey got out [of the cab] and started talking to Benny. Then Benny went away up Clinton Street. Then Harvey walked back to the cab and just looked in and listened to the music for awhile, and walked back." Then Philip Chaleff— nicknamed "Sonny"—left the cab. "He was talking to Harvey there for awhile and then the two of them walked away. They turned the same corner, up Clinton Street."

It is shortly after 2:00 A.M. on Saturday morning. Dworkin, unaware, has witnessed the departure of the task force, now on the march north up Clinton to take the Dutchman's. And Hutch Friedman's next public appearance will be at the Boulevard Restaurant with a .32 caliber pistol in his hand: first man through the door.

———————————

Joseph Harvey O'Loughlin is generally known as "Harvey": twenty-two years of age; sandy blond hair; a wiry, muscular frame; a touch of the stubbornness reputed to be Irish, and to go with it, though he is American-born, a touch of the brogue. The fourth of six children, he recalls his parents calling it quits when he was only six. It was then that his mother Ellen left his father, since deceased. She was three months' pregnant with Harvey's younger brother, now fifteen. Since then Ellen has reared her family as best she could, and it has never been easy. From 1921 till 1929 she did the housework of the Henry Street Settlement House for a weekly wage of around fifteen dollars. Thereafter, for another six years, she worked as janitor in the building where she lives with Harvey at 255 East Broadway, supplementing her meager income by cleaning a doctor's office located in the same building.

Harvey is another for whom schooling is out of the question. At the age of seventeen he leaves Public School 147 before graduation to look for work, first as a messenger boy for the Postal Telegraph Company—two years—then as helper on a truck for the Gem Trading Company—one year—and finally, on the advice of his uncle, hiring on with Daniels & Kennedy, a trucking company at 290 South Street that delivers Home Relief parcels. After a year and a half on the night shift there he transfers to the WPA, which employs him at present as a

pick-and-shovel worker on various hospital construction projects—Bellevue, Gouverneur, Sea View, Welfare Island—and
on the Willard Parker Park.

But beginning in the late summer of 1934 Harvey takes on
problems compared to which his daily pick-and-shovel ordeal
must seem pleasurable. He meets a pretty Jewish girl
named Ida Weiss; they fall in love, and from both sides—the
O'Loughlin and the Weiss—there begins bitter family opposition to the marriage. Devoutly orthodox, Ida's mother re-
sents and resists the idea of a Roman Catholic son-in-law. Her
resistance continues even after the foreseeable—Ida's preg-
nancy—and to such effect that it is only a month before their
son's birth that the young couple can muster the resolution
to marry.

Harvey recognizes the child for his own; there is never any
doubt that he will. He does his best to be a good father. But
the O'Loughlins are as militantly Catholic as the Weiss family
is militantly Jewish, and Harvey and Ida are continually being
whipsawed between two irreconcilable opposites. Harvey, secretly feeling his son should be brought up in the Catholic
faith, has him baptized unknown even to Ida. Ida takes similar steps, without advising her husband, for the child to be
admitted to her faith.

On Ida O'Loughlin's return from the hospital after the birth
of the baby, she sets up housekeeping with her mother-in-law
for two or three months, until the couple, with the help of the
Home Relief services, can be located as a family unit in their
own quarters at 168 East Broadway. Harvey is drawing relief
checks; but even later, when a WPA job brings him $60 a
month, the marriage is in jeopardy. The constant pressures
he and Ida must endure over the religious issue would make
their happiness together problematic even without financial
difficulties. When their son is barely a year old, Ida takes him
with her to live with her mother. Harvey, left to himself, stores
the furniture in the basement and goes back to live in his
mother's apartment.

On the evening of April 9, Ellen O'Loughlin takes the eve-

ning meal with her son sometime between seven and eight.
Dinner over, he reads the paper for an hour and leaves. (Unknown to his mother, Harvey is again out of a job. To
conceal the fact he spends the early part of the afternoon
watching a film at Loew's Canal in the company of Dominick
Guariglia, and the remainder of the working day with his
wife and child, whom he has been seeing secretly.) Harvey
drops by Artie's Poolroom and meets a friend with whom he
is in the habit of visiting a tavern on Madison Street. They
drink—several rounds—and then head back to the poolroom
where the friend, having business to transact, leaves Harvey
but promises to return. By nine-thirty or ten he is back. Together they drop into the Madison Bar and Grill on the corner
of Madison and Clinton; more drinks, and drinks thereafter at
still another place on East Broadway; but by now Harvey is
refusing the drinks his friend continues to offer. A walk in the
fresh air, he feels, is preferable.

"We walked up along First Avenue, looking in hat shops,
shirts. I know we came back about half-past twelve or a quarter to one . . . in Muskin's, and he bought me a sandwich
and coffee, and we have a habit of doing the crossword puzzle
in Muskin's . . . and I stood in that place about a quarter to
two." Harvey has no more to drink in Muskin's, nor does he
remain continuously at his table doing crossword puzzles. "I
was in and out . . . then I met some party and I took a walk.
I went to Ninth Street and Second Avenue. It was . . . about
half-past two, rather twenty-five minutes to three, and we
started out . . . We went upstairs into the premises. Some
person was behind me. The person that was behind me walked
halfway . . . into the room, when I moved, when I was struck
with a bullet. Coming out, as I was struck, I heard a lot of
other shots. I . . . was coming out the door, and I was shot in
my left arm. I come downstairs. I got on the landing here. I
picked my hat up . . . and the person that came in back of me,
I felt somebody holding me up coming out of the premises,
and he helped me along and around to the corner . . . to
Eighth Street and First Avenue."

Ellen O'Loughlin recalls: "In the early morning hours someone came knocking at my door and asked me did O'Loughlin live here. I said Yes, and I opened the door . . . I guess probably it was a detective and . . . I got all excited. He says . . . 'Are you the mother of Joseph O'Loughlin?' I said yes . . . 'What's the trouble?' He says, 'Well,' he says, 'there is some boy after coming in to Gouverneur Hospital,' he says, 'and I think that he is Joseph—' "

Philip Chaleff, whom his friends call "Sonny," is different from the others. For one thing he is older, twenty-seven on the eleventh of March. For another, he has some of the advantages that education is presumed to confer on innate intelligence. At the age of six he is enrolled in Rabbi Jacob Joseph's School—a sort of parochial institution—at 167 Henry Street, where, as a certificate of graduation attests, he masters not only English—always a problem to his Russian-born father Louis—but Hebrew as well. And if Sonny, at the age of fourteen, quits De Witt Clinton High School in the middle of his second term, it is less by choice than by the dreary necessity familiar to so many families on the Lower East Side. Times are hard, and the tinsmith's trade exercised by Louis Chaleff is barely adequate to the wants of his wife, his son, and three daughters. Philip Chaleff must go to work.

He has already served a sort of apprenticeship during the period at De Witt Clinton, selling candy evenings in the local theatres. He continues this work at night, and in the daytime hires on as messenger boy and assistant shipping clerk for a medical book concern, Hochel, Incorporated, on Fifth Avenue. But his native abilities take him further: first to A. B. Braham & Company, investment brokers at 50 Broadway, where he remains some eighteen months as an office clerk and messenger, entrusted on occasion with the delivery of stocks and bonds to the bank; and then, making the move on his own, to Ira Haupt & Company of the New York Stock Exchange, where he works posting stock record books. When the

market crashes in November of 1929, Sonny Chaleff finds
himself out of work.

The promising beginning is going by the board. Chaleff
addresses himself to a blur of jobs, odd jobs, part-time jobs,
stop-gap jobs. For a time he sells newspapers; for a time he
takes a delivery route for the *East Side Home News*. In March,
1930, he is employed as an usher at Loew's Delancey and
working on occasion as a relief cashier; but four months later
circumstances have forced him to relinquish the post. Three
times already Chaleff has been hospitalized in a state of
diabetic coma, but when, during the first week in August, he
enters Beth Israel Hospital for extended treatment, it has become clear that for the rest of his life he will suffer from
chronic diabetes.

Philip Chaleff is different from the others: older and presumably wiser, better educated and presumably more intelligent. But his physical handicap and all it entails—a special
diet, insulin injections twice a day, special exercises—handicap him further in the crucial matter of earning a living. If in
1937 he lists his occupation as "clerk," his employment seems
altogether casual. On the morning of Friday, April 9, for
example, he can afford the luxury of arising at eleven-thirty,
of going for a stroll after breakfast and a bath, of sitting in
the park, and, while a light spring rain falls on the city streets,
of spending some two hours in Hanover's Candy Store across
the street from Muskin's Restaurant. Next he can pay a leisurely visit to the apartment of his friends Israel and Leah
Lepson, a married couple living in Knickerbocker Village.
Chaleff is on the best of terms with them. He has known Israel
nearly fifteen years; he is godfather to the Lepsons' child,
and often spends the night in their Monroe Street apartment.

On this rainy Friday afternoon Chaleff cuts his visit short
well before dark, for it is his habit, in observance of the Jewish
Sabbath, to take the evening meal with his parents. But he
has made a date to take Mrs. Lepson to the films that evening,
and around quarter-past eight Leah Lepson, accompanied
by Philip Chaleff, leaves her husband Israel with the baby in

their apartment and walks to Loew's Canal, a movie house
near the Chaleff apartment. From about eight-thirty on they
watch a double feature: *Penrod and Sam* and *Parole Board*.
At the end of the last feature Chaleff and Mrs. Lepson walk
down to Hanover's Candy Store, on East Broadway and Clinton, where they arrive sometime between eleven-thirty and
midnight.

As Chaleff recalls it: "At the candy store there was some
drinks ordered. I don't drink soda myself; I just had some
plain water and Mrs. Lepson had a soda. The radio was
going, listened to the radio. There was some fellows standing
and playing the pinball machine, and I walked over for a
minute or two and watched them." After thirty to forty minutes in Hanover's, Sonny escorts Mrs. Lepson to the bus stop
at the corner of Madison and Clinton, returning about one to
the candy store, and Leah Lepson, according to her own and
to her husband's recollection, gets back home to Knickerbocker Village at approximately the same time.

One o'clock, or shortly after, is closing time for Tobias
Hanover. After five minutes' sidewalk loitering in front of the
candy store Chaleff crosses East Broadway, settles with some
acquaintances—Chester, Smitty, Fat, Popeye—in Dworkin's
cab. "I sat in the taxicab listening to the radio when Harvey
came over to the taxicab, opened up the window and asked me
if I wanted to take a walk. I got out of the taxicab and started
walking with Harvey . . . until I reached the corner of Ninth
Street and First Avenue." There, in the middle of the block,
Chaleff encounters another acquaintance, Isidore Perlmutter,
nicknamed "Little Chemey," and they begin to walk west on
Ninth Street in the direction of Second Avenue. "While walking . . . [Chemey] . . . called my attention to some fellows
coming out of a hallway. He said, 'Do you know any of them
fellows?' I said, 'No,' and at that time Harvey dropped in the
back . . . and started to walk with [Chemey] and me . . ."
The group that has emerged from the hallway is walking west
on Ninth Street, ahead of Chaleff, O'Loughlin, and Little
Chemey.

"When I got to the corner of Ninth Street and Second Avenue [Chemey] said to me, 'Are you going upstairs?' I said, 'For what? . . . I didn't start walking to go up anywhere. I started out to take a walk.' And he said, 'Well, they are going upstairs to do something.' I said, 'I don't know what they are going upstairs for, but I'm not . . .' " The appeal for Chaleff's participation becomes more precise: "Somebody asked me to go upstairs, and when I did come upstairs, if everybody had their hands up in the air to go through their pockets. I said, 'I don't do them things and I am not going upstairs!' "

But some of those in the group preceding Chaleff have already started up the steps leading to Willie the Dutchman's. "I got a hold of Little Chemey . . . I asked him if he's going upstairs and he said yes. Well, I grabbed him by the arm and I didn't allow him to go upstairs, and I told him, 'You're coming back to the corner with me,' and with that I started to walk. When I passed that building and I was about four or five doors away . . . I heard some noise, the sound of shots; but at that time I didn't know it was the sound of shots; it sounded like automobile backfire to me. I stopped and stood there for about a minute . . . when . . . I saw Harvey come running towards me, and Harvey said, 'Go on home,' or 'Take a walk; turn around and take a walk.' "

Chaleff is old enough to have learned prudence. With Little Chemey on his arm he walks the twenty-five or so blocks back to the corner of East Broadway and Clinton. Muskin's Restaurant is open till 6:00 A.M. that Saturday morning. Chaleff loiters there until closing time, and on his way home buys the morning papers. Then, "I waited till my father left for synagogue and lied down in his bed."

———

Max Gevirtz is a waiter at Willie the Dutchman's. Tonight he is off duty, but the lure of the cards is too strong. From ten o'clock on he has been watching the play, wandering from table to table. By 3:00 A.M. he has settled, like a score of other spectators, two tables from the dumbwaiter, close to the kitchen, where an ask-no-quarter pinochle game is under way between Michael Semenik—known as "Mike the Polack"—and John Storch—known as "Missis." Mike, like Max Gevirtz, is an off-duty waiter who works as an "extra" at the Dutchman's when the crowd is heavy; like Missis he is a strong player, and the two-handed game, some two hours old, has drawn more than its share of side bettors and kibitzers.

Gevirtz, standing behind Missis, has a view straight down the long room to the partition opposite the kitchen. Looking up as the cards are shuffled, he registers the presence of Detectives Gallagher and Foley, whom he has seen before in the Boulevard; notices Samuel Cooperstein—Willie the Dutchman—leave his own game at another table with Leo Fink, a window washer, to approach the police officers; and turns his interest again to the Semenik-Storch game.

Max Rockower, taxi driver and merchant seaman, is in the Dutchman's for coffee, half hoping to pick up a fare that will take him in the general direction of Brooklyn, where he shares an apartment with his sister. His coffee has grown cold, and there are no fares in sight, but for the last thirty minutes he has been keeping score for the pinochle game between the Dutchman and Leo Fink. The Dutchman recalls: "They [the two policemen] walked all the way up to the showcase and stopped there for a minute, and I said to Fink, the fellow I was playing with, 'Just wait a minute, please,' and I put the cards on the table, and just as a courtesy I got up and I walked down with Detective Gallagher and Detective Foley and asked the gentlemen if they wanted to have some coffee . . . They sit down at . . . about the second table facing the door on the Ninth Street side . . . I said, 'Gentlemen, will you get some coffee and milk?' And they sit down and I remember Mr. Gallagher asked for a large glass of milk. I called the waiter and asked him to bring over coffee and milk. All of a sudden I seen two fellows rushing towards the kitchen. I couldn't say where they came from. They must have come from the entrance, from the door."

Mike Semenik is looking over his cards. It is 3:20 A.M. "I

heard somebody walk in and holler 'Stickup,' see. In the same time start shooting match, see. I don't know who was in that, you see, because I was by the wall. People fall down on the floor and covered themselves, under the table, and press me to the wall, and I was sitting like now, was looking . . . and I see two fellows walk in to the counter—there is a counter in the restaurant what is keeping cake and everything there. And at the same time they jump into the kitchen, I notice that it is a strange two fellows."

Gevirtz recalls: "I couldn't hear . . . and I fall on my knee, because I stood up there and I have seen the two fellows, a short and tall fellow, running into the kitchen . . . The taller fellow had a gun." The tall man is Arthur Friedman; the other Dominick Guariglia. As they head for the kitchen only their backs are visible to the Dutchman. Gevirtz continues: "I cannot describe them; just one looked a little smaller than the other . . . And as they been rushing through I heard Detective Gallagher mumbling 'M-m-m, M-m,' and all of a sudden I heard—I seen . . . Detective Mike Foley . . . going for his side; and all of a sudden I heard shots and I dropped under the table . . . I was so amazed this very minute that I really didn't know what is what."

Harry Gold, kitchen man at the Dutchman's, is taking his coffee break alone at the table by the telephone booth, just to the right of the kitchen entrance. "And I see two fellows rushing in, one without the gun and one fellow with a gun the back of him . . . and I hear firing a shot. The first shot was fired I stretched myself out under the table, and then, after the shooting was over, you see, Gallagher rushed into the kitchen and bring them two fellows out . . . back them up the other way." Four tables from Foley's, Rockower, the taxi driver, sees the Dutchman rising to his feet. "When things quieted down I started to get up, and after I get up I seen Detective Foley, bleeding, holding his hand on his side." Foley has begun to die.

Guariglia and Friedman, thoroughly cowed, hands above their heads, herded back from the kitchen under Gallagher's gun, are the first casualties of the expeditionary force. Gevirtz recalls Foley, sagging in his chair, holding his gun on the pair. "He said to them, 'I would give you a better chance than you gave me.'" Gold: "I find Foley sitting on the chair, holding his gun in his hand and hollered out to the boss, 'Search them fellows.' And I say, I told him, 'You were shot?' 'Yes.' He was bleeding in his hand, blood is coming from his trousers, and tell me, 'Pick up my holster.'"

Six blocks from the Boulevard Restaurant William J. Steffens, Patrolman, Shield No. 6152 of the Ninth Precinct, is recording the messages received by his radio patrol car. At the wheel is Patrolman Hertz, also of the Ninth Precinct. Seventeen years of police work have only sharpened Steffens' sense of urgency when the familiar Signal 30—felony in progress—comes crackling over the line. Hertz takes less than sixty seconds to cover the distance to 144 Second Avenue. Neither man knows more than the minimal information—Signal 30— radioed out from the Precinct on the receipt of a telephone call—from Gallagher—for reinforcements; neither man, weapon at the ready as he races up the stairs, knows what is waiting on the other side of the Dutchman's door.

Fast as they are, Steffens and Hertz are late. When Signal 30 goes out over the air at 3:23 A.M., there is another patrol car from Ninth Precinct less than a hundred yards from the Boulevard Restaurant, with Eugene Callahan, Shield No. 16942, at the wheel, and Anthony Pignatelli recording. On the sidewalk outside the Dutchman's they meet two men who inform them of the holdup still in progress. Neither Pignatelli nor Callahan knows that Foley and Gallagher are upstairs, well in command of the situation by this time; their reaction is the same as that of Steffens and Hertz, arriving scant seconds behind them. Callahan: "There was a fight in there; there were a group of men . . . seemed to be beating a couple of men. So somebody hollered to us, 'Here they are, officer, two stickup men.' So we pushed our way through the crowd and I found . . . Guariglia and Friedman laying on the floor." Callahan and Pignatelli advance on the two men; then Calla-

han hears Detective Gallagher's voice from behind him saying, "O.K., it's O.K., Cal . . ." Steffens, arriving next, sees
Callahan and Pignatelli in the process of stemming an assault
by the outraged patrons of the Boulevard on Guariglia and
Friedman: "They were grabbing hold of everybody and separating them, trying to stop this fight. I chipped right in trying
to push everybody into the corner . . . In the meantime there
was plenty more cops coming in there and we got everybody
over into a corner . . . I think Callahan and Pignatelli picked
them fellows up [Guariglia and Friedman] . . . There was
quite a lot of excitement going on there. I think they held on
to them. They said they were the guys that done the job up
there . . . The first recollection I have of Gallagher was hearing his voice hollering 'Hold them.' " Harry Gold, the kitchen
man: "Then was a whole tumult; the police come up [uni-
formed patrolmen]. I rush in with them in kitchen [*sic*] and
look for them guns. We looked over all the place and we could
not find them. Then . . . I noticed the biggest fellow had flour
on his sleeve. I rush over myself in the kitchen where the bag
of flour was, just put my hand on the bag of flour, I find the
gun there, pull the gun out and hand it over to the police;
and then they making me mark my initials, they went in the
kitchen, put the gun on the table and make me mark my initials on every cartridge and the gun."

Max Rockower, the taxi driver in search of a fare to Brooklyn: "Gallagher come up and . . . asked me to take Foley to
the hospital, which I took up Foley and carried him down
into the car and rushed him right to the Post Graduate Hospital. When I got in there . . . in that hospital, I placed Foley
on one of these wheeling tables and nobody was there, and I
started in raising a riot in there to get a little attention there.
Then the attendant or intern . . . the attendants and nurses
start coming running out, and started taking off his clothes
there and giving him an injection."

At the Boulevard, Patrolman Callahan recalls seeing Foley
carried downstairs by four men, one of them Rockower. Callahan, weapon at the ready, has taken over the custody of

Guariglia and Friedman. "After Detective Foley was carried out of the house, Detective Hill and myself took the two of them to the Ninth Precinct station house in a cruiser radio . . . patrol car. We took them upstairs to the Detectives' Squad office . . . and I stayed there with them in company with Detective Hill until about 6:00 A.M. that morning."

Patrolmen Steffens and Hertz take advantage of the presence of other police officers to institute a search of the premises. "It is quite a long place. We walked all the way into the interior. We searched the kitchen there, looking in all the utensils and closets, for anybody may be hiding; and then we went up one flight of stairs and we found a fellow hiding up there . . . one of the customers . . . After about ten minutes I drove . . . Detective Gallagher . . . up to the Post Graduate Hospital where Detective Foley had been removed to in the meantime. I stayed up there about ten or fifteen minutes and then drove him back again to 144 Second Avenue."

At approximately the time of Foley's entering Post Graduate Hospital—about three-thirty—another patient is being admitted for emergency treatment about a mile from the Dutchman's, at Gouverneur Hospital: John Harvey O'Loughlin. If he is dazed, in a state bordering on shock, it is for good reason: two police bullets are lodged in his body, one in the left arm, and one on the left side, between the third and fourth ribs.

O'Loughlin's recollections are cloudy. He remembers following two men up the stairs of the Boulevard Restaurant, being followed by a fourth, recalls walking halfway into the room with a pistol in his hand, and then shots, flame. "I felt myself shot, I seen a man jump up in front of somebody else and they kicked the tables away, I seen the tables being thrown over . . . the only thing I had in mind was safety, to get out of the place . . . It was a matter of seconds. As soon as I got shot in the chest I was struck with fear; and as I was going to go out of the door, I must have been . . . two or three steps away from the door when I was shot in the arm . . . coming out of the door I stopped to look for my arm, because the bone was broke and it was hanging, and I felt something hit me along the side of the thigh, and I discovered that it was my arm and I held it up." Now Harvey recalls stopping on the stairs to pick up his hat, which has fallen to the floor, and being helped by someone "coming out of the premises." The someone is Little Benny. "He helped me along and around to the corner . . . and he put me in a taxicab and told me to give him my gun, which I did, and he went outside and . . . he came back with a cab driver, and . . . he then instructed the cab driver to take me to Gouverneur Hospital and the cab driver did, and I remember being on the steps of the hospital; I was bleeding a lot and getting weak . . . I think an orderly helped me . . . I was taken into the Emergency Ward and put on a table and they start cutting my clothes up."

Dr. Eugene Iseppettini, the house surgeon on duty, treats Harvey for gunshot wounds, orders a blood transfusion and the application of a Jones arm splint to the fracture arm, transfers him to the 26-bed ward known as Male Surgery East, where he is placed in a bed three feet from the head nurse's desk. Harvey, on the critical list, is given a "fair chance" of recovery.

Thirty-six hours later, after X-rays and additional blood transfusions, John Harvey O'Loughlin is transferred, under the guard of two police officers and a hospital orderly, by ambulance to a semi-private room in the prison ward of Bellevue Hospital. His prospects are not encouraging, and the last rites of the Roman Catholic Church are administered to him.

At 1:00 P. M. on Saturday afternoon Mayor La Guardia and Police Commissioner Lewis J. Valentine visit Michael Foley's bedside. Preparations are under way for the police officer to receive a second blood transfusion. Both La Guardia and Valentine have publicly expressed their sympathy to the wounded man's wife, May, of 116 East 92nd Street, and to his brother Charles; but Foley requires more than sympathy, more than transfusions. By eight-forty that evening he is dead.

Of those responsible for his death the police are satisfied already to have in custody O'Loughlin—in the "cage" at

Bellevue Hospital—and Guariglia and Friedman—in cells at the Tombs Prison, where both are held without bail pending a hearing set for April 23. That there are more than three participants in this felony crime the police are certain. To determine their identity and apprehend them involves a point of honor, a matter of patience, and—occasionally—a stroke of luck. The fourth man swims into the net of his own volition. On April 15, Philip Chaleff, his attorney Milton Lerner at his side, walks into the District Attorney's office, there to protest his innocence for some three hours before confessing to participation—unarmed—in the holdup of the Boulevard Restaurant. With or without Chaleff's cooperation, the investigators had already begun, thanks to statements made by Guariglia, to turn their attention to him. By now they are aware that six men at least are to be brought to justice. On Friday, April 23, however, the New York County Grand Jury is content to indict only five men for the crime which has led to the death of Michael Foley: O'Loughlin, Guariglia, Friedman, Chaleff, and "John Doe"—that is to say, someone whose exact identity the police are either unwilling or unable for the moment to reveal.

————

The spectacle of men capitulating to their own folly is always depressing. The folly here was a criminal undertaking (therefore a priori foolish, if only in terms of the odds automatically against success), poorly—if at all—planned (there must be a kind of ungrudging admiration extended even by the police for the intellection necessary to a coup like the Brink's robbery or the Boston mail truck operation in July of 1962), and not so much executed as spasmodically improvised in a series of desperate half-reflexes on the part of ignorant young men so dismally equipped for the pursuit of happiness that they felt it natural to stake and to lose, first their liberty and then their lives.

But there is another side to their folly, committed out of mindlessness: it can cost an innocent his life—a police officer like Detective Foley lives, draws his paycheck, and on occasion dies by it. Every day of the week, every month of his thirteen years with the New York Police Department, Foley's wife May knew as well as her husband the gamble they were taking when he said good-bye and left for work. It was, quite simply, that she might never see him alive again. After eleven years of marriage they have finally lost their gamble. "My husband never told me anything that could worry me," says the widow, trying not to cry. "He took everything quite naturally and shared all but his troubles with me." That is his epitaph. Detective Foley, dying, leaves a widow and a seven-year-old daughter. All their grief can do nothing to alter the unalterable.

It is a truism that the police are not inclined to tenderness with the murderers of policemen. By sundown of April 10, 1937, every member of the New York Police Department has an overriding concern, simultaneously professional and personal: rapid and terrible justice for the parties responsible. When Magistrate Michael Ford, ordering his prisoners Guariglia and Friedman held without bail on Monday, April 12, two days after Foley's funeral, predicted, "These boys are on their way to the electric chair," he was faithfully reflecting that concern, shared, moreover, by the vast majority of the public. Guariglia must feel it too. On the steps of the Felony Court building at 32 Franklin Street he tries to leap the balustrade into the stairwell. Detective Nicholas Santamorena, to whom he is handcuffed, thwarts not only this blind attempt at escape but another one as well, on the way to the Tombs. Friedman too must know it. Why else, at his arraignment in Homicide Court, would he kick at and knock down a press photographer except out of rage and fear for the future? And yet in the course of the retribution that is to follow—that must follow, in a society under rule of law—there will also be, regrettably, injustice done.

By order of Police Commissioner Valentine, Detective Foley was accorded an inspector's burial. Attendance was compulsory for all six deputy police commissioners and all deputy

inspectors of the uniformed police. The funeral cortege set
out from Foley's home at 166 East 92nd Street—where final
rites had been held at 10:00 A.M. on the morning of Wednesday, April 14—and proceeded downtown to the Church of
Saint Ignatius Loyola at Park Avenue and 85th Street for a
Solemn Requiem Mass. The Police Department band, ninety-
eight strong, led the procession; 117 uniformed police marched
behind the hearse, on the heels of the Police Commissioner;
and groups of uniformed police stationed along the route
stood smartly at attention as the convoy passed.

At the Requiem Mass celebrated in Foley's memory by
the Reverend Francis Donovan assisted by Charles Gallagher
and Thomas Delahanty, Father Joseph A. McCaffrey, senior
chaplain of the New York Police Department, pronounced
the eulogy: "I never knew a man who faced death with less
fear than Detective Foley. He was a martyr to his duty, an
honor to the Police Department and a credit to the city of
New York." Mayor Fiorello La Guardia declared, after the
ceremony of interment that afternoon in Saint John's Cemetery, Brooklyn: "We are going to do everything that is hu-
manly possible to apprehend criminals and convict them . . . I
attended the funeral of this brave police officer to express the
appreciation of the people of this city . . . The people of this
city are behind the police force in its battle against bandits,
criminals, racketeers and gangsters . . . The police have orders
that when they see a criminal with a gun they are to be quick
on the trigger, and the results are showing it."

The indictment issued by the Court of General Sessions
of the County of New York accuses the defendants of murder
in the first degree, committed as follows: "The said defendants
in the County of New York aforesaid, on the tenth day of
April, in the year of our Lord one thousand nine hundred
and thirty-seven, with force and arms, in and upon one
Michael J. Foley, in the peace of the said people then and
there being, wilfully, feloniously and of their malice aforethought did make an assault, and a certain pistol, then and
there charged and loaded with gunpowder and one metal

bullet, which said pistol they, the said defendants in their right hands then and there had and held, to, at, against and upon the said Michael J. Foley then and there wilfully, feloniously and of their malice aforethought did shoot off and discharge; and the said defendants with the metal bullet aforesaid, out of the pistol aforesaid, then and there, by force of the gunpowder aforesaid, shot off, sent forth and discharged as aforesaid him, the said Michael J. Foley then and there wilfully, feloniously and of their malice aforethought did strike, penetrate and wound, giving unto him, the said Michael J. Foley, then and there with the metal bullet aforesaid, so as aforesaid discharged, sent forth and shot out of the pistol aforesaid, by the said defendants in and upon the body of him, the said Michael J. Foley, one mortal wound, of the breadth of one inch, and of the depth of six inches, of which said mortal wound he, the said Michael J. Foley, did then and there die."

The language of the indictment, for all its convolutions, cannot distract the understanding from its terrible hard core of truth: that a human life was taken and taken senselessly.

The first indictment, #212947, filed on April 23, 1937, names as defendants to the charge of first-degree murder Dominick Guariglia, Joseph Harvey O'Loughlin, Arthur Friedman, Philip Chaleff, and Benjamin Ertel.

In the indictment superseding, #212947½, filed on June 21, 1937, there are modifications. Two individuals still at large are named: Benjamin Ertel, known as Little Benny, and Isidore Perlmutter, known as Little Chemey. Mentioned in the indictment as being in custody are Dominick Guariglia, Joseph Harvey O'Loughlin, and Philip Chaleff. Also mentioned in the indictment and by then in custody, alphabetically or otherwise carried last on the list of defendants to the murder charge: Isidore Zimmerman, alias "Beany" or "Beansy"—to whom his lawyer will refer as "the forgotten man" in the Foley murder case.

CHAPTER 2

THE
TRIAL

HOWEVER ASTUTE, however conscientious, however impassioned the lawyers defending O'Loughlin, Guariglia, and Friedman, they are unlikely to prevail. For one thing, the defense will not contest—and the jury not forget—the presence of the three at the scene of the crime; the capture of Dominick and Hutch on the Dutchman's premises can no more be blinked than the police bullets lodged in Harvey's body. For another, there is no argument at law available to attenuate the responsibility of any defendant—that Dominick was unarmed; that Hutch, though armed, did not fire; or that Harvey's bullet was not the one which killed Foley—which Judge Nott does not demolish in his charge to the jury with a legal definition of the charge against the East Side boys: felony murder.

"... The law says that when a man or more than one man goes out to commit a felony, and, in the course of the commission of that felony, they kill a human being, the . . . design to commit the felony takes the place of the design to effect death, and that, therefore, the person who kills another in the commission of a felony is guilty of murder in the first degree . . .

"The law goes further and says that everybody who is committing a felony is responsible for the act of the person who commits the killing.

29

"Of course, that places a very heavy responsibility on people who go out in the commission of felonies, for each is responsible for the act of the other, if the other during the course of . . . a felony sees fit to kill. While that responsibility is very heavy . . . it is very easily avoided. To avoid it all a man has to do is refrain from committing robberies or burglaries and, if he refrains . . . then he is just as safe as you [the jury] are sitting in that box at this minute."

The prosecution's case against Joseph Harvey O'Loughlin is overwhelming, and the arguments invoked for the other defendants—poverty, ignorance, police coercion—carry no weight. There is no disputing that Harvey was at the Boulevard; Harvey was armed; Harvey fired a .38 Smith & Wesson at around 3:20 A.M. on the morning of Saturday, April 10; and by 10:30 A.M. on the morning of Sunday, April 11, Detective Michael Foley ("white adult male, five feet eight and a half inches in height; weight by scale 175 pounds . . . well nourished, well developed and well muscled . . . about 37 years of age") was waiting on a slab at the City Morgue, 400 East 29th Street, for identification and autopsy. Harvey's co-defendant, Friedman, has remarked to Detective Gallagher during an appearance at Felony Court: "We would have been all right if it wasn't for that Irish bastard losing his head." Just or unjust, the notion is hard for a jury to reject.

Of necessity, then, O'Loughlin's lawyer, Banton, adopts a blunt, no-nonsense attitude, disdainful of nuance. His defense hangs on two pegs: the police brutality allegedly inflicted on Harvey in his hospital bed, and the hypothesis that Little Benny —not Harvey—fired the shot that took Foley's life. Banton's summation before the jury is the shortest of any delivered for a defendant in the trial of the East Side boys, and in addition to brevity it has the merit of ingenuity. The prosecution can ignore as irrelevant the hypothesis that Harvey's bullet did not kill Foley. And by conservative count a dozen witnesses— doctors and nurses as well as police officers—will take the stand to deny the charges of brutality.

Guariglia's defense was handled by three lawyers: Maxwell

Lehrhaupt, Edward McDonald, and Louis Lefkowitz, later to
run unsuccessfully for mayor of the city of New York and
ultimately to serve as attorney general for the state. But three
lawyers can produce no more than two principal arguments,
which Judge Nott will qualify as "more or less academic":
Dominick's stupidity and, corollary to it, his susceptibility to
coercion. Characterized by his defenders as "a stupid boy, a
moron, a nitwit . . . who by circumstances and training, unfortunate surroundings, has not the mental ability . . . he
should have," Dominick bears out their contention by his
bearing in court. "You have seen him on the stand," Mc-
Donald reminds the jury, ". . . in this most serious moment of
his life giggling at times."

Supporting testimony is provided by a teacher from the
Metropolitan Vocational High School which Dominick began
to attend part time after obtaining his working papers. Having administered the Otis intermediate group test to Dominick
in May, 1936, in accordance with standard procedures for
rating students academically, she reports that of the test's
seventy-five questions he managed to answer only twenty-two
correctly, whereas for a rating of normal intelligence, fifty-
eight correct answers were required. By this criterion his I.Q.
is under 70. According to the witness, Guariglia is "in the
moronic group" and his mental age "is between nine and ten,
about nine years and four months."

But Judge Nott makes it abundantly clear that Dominick's
witlessness is irrelevant to his guilt; no plea of insanity has
been entered on Guariglia's behalf, and so the degree of his
intelligence is simply not germane to the proceedings at hand.
Counter by the defense: Dominick's lack of intelligence increased his susceptibility to coercion, first by Little Benny—
to obtain his participation in the robbery of the Boulevard
Restaurant—and then by the police—to confess. McDonald
quotes from the notebook of the doctor who examined Guariglia on his arrival at the Tombs Prison: " 'The scalp, two lacera-
tions, left ear lacerated, nose contused, abrased,' with a comma
followed by a question mark with the word 'fracture' after it

. . . 'Left eye, ecchymosis and contusion. Teeth: lower incisors broken. Upper incisors broken. Central missing . . . Buca mucosa lacerated,' and when . . . [the doctor] was asked what that was he said it meant that the lining of his mouth was all torn. Now, in plain ordinary English, Dominick had had his teeth kicked out . . . Is there a man in that [jury] box that does not know that defendants are beaten up in police stations . . . ? You can let your imagination run riot and you can't vision some of the things that happen to . . . defendants in the police station."

But the District Attorney is not disposed to let the jury's "imagination run riot." The beating administered to Guariglia was real enough, he is willing to concede, but it was administered by irate patrons of the Boulevard Restaurant after the abortive holdup. Cooperstein, the Dutchman, testifies that fifteen or twenty angry customers had kicked and beaten Guariglia—and Friedman as well—after their disarming and before the arrival of the uniformed police. Max Gevirtz, the waiter, recalls seeing Harry Gold strike the two men with a chair to shouts of "Kill them! Mob them!" and Leo Fink, the Dutchman's pinochle partner, says in corroboration: "The people in the place jump on them fellows and start beating them up . . . I was lucky that I didn't get my share of it." Max Rockower, the cabbie who drove the dying Foley to the hospital, and Patrolmen George Callahan and William Steffens of the Ninth Precinct provide further confirmation: "These two men were on the floor and there was a group of men kicking them. They were all around them."

For Arthur Friedman, too, there is the defense of police brutality, which, whatever its credibility in some contexts, is by now undergoing a sort of progressive devaluation for the members of the jury. The District Attorney can deal with the charge precisely as in the case of Guariglia. Counsel for Friedman is Vincent Impelliteri, who will serve as mayor of New York City from 1950 to 1953, and his defense of Hutch will be reminiscent of the defense of Dominick in another respect: the plea of irresponsibility by reason of mental impairment.

Friedman's mother testifies, without the corroboration of medical records, that her son, struck by a truck at the age of seven, suffered concussion of the brain. Impelliteri is therefore enabled to refer to his client as "this moronic boy," "a subnormal moron—that is what he is." "Look at that boy Arthur Friedman," says Impelliteri to the jury. "Look at that face of his. If there is any boy that I have ever seen in all my days who has the face of a moron, that is that boy Arthur Friedman—and it dates back to his early youth. It is not his fault . . . He is just a shell."

The demonstration clearly carries no weight with Judge Nott, nor does the jury seem overly impressed. Hutch Friedman was, after all, the first man through the door of the Boulevard Restaurant with a gun in his hand. From the mass of dismissible argument advanced by Impelliteri only one talking point emerges: on the night of the felony three or four whiskies, together with two or three marijuana cigarettes, had brought Friedman to a state of stupefaction equatable with irresponsibility. A pharmacologist-physiologist with a specialist's knowledge of the effects of marijuana states that all alcohol greatly increases the response to the drug, and that both alcohol and marijuana tend to depress the inhibitions and affect reasoning, memory, and the powers of association. "I can't conceive of an individual in normal mental faculties deliberately going into a restaurant containing this many people and attempt [sic] to hold up such a restaurant": thus the testimony of the pharmacologist-physiologist. Impelliteri puts it more simply: "He didn't know what he was doing."

The classical response in law to the production of an "expert" by one party is simply to produce another "expert" to contradict him, after which the jury can forget the testimony of both. The prosecutor knows his classics—when trial resumes on April 12 the People call Dr. Perry Lichtenstein, a practicing physician since 1910, medical assistant to the District Attorney of the County of New York since 1931, vice-president of the World Narcotics Defense Association, consultant to Second Avenue Hospital (then a center for the treatment of narcotic addiction), and author of a number of treatises on narcotics ("Narcotic Addiction and the Law," "Narcotic Addiction Disease," "Infant Addiction"). In Dr. Lichtenstein's opinion, Friedman was quite able to form a criminal intent and, demonstrably, able to carry it out.

For Hutch, for Harvey, and for Dominick—these three—the arguments advanced in extenuation of their act are, as Judge Nott qualifies them, in effect "academic." It is certain that the jury are less receptive to those arguments than they are impressed by the sight of five commonplace objects resting on a table in the courtroom, in plain sight, since the session of March 28: a topcoat containing a bullet hole, a jacket containing a bullet hole, a vest containing a bullet hole, a shirt containing two bullet holes, and a pair of trousers containing a bullet hole. They are the effects of the late Michael Foley, introduced in evidence by the prosecution and numbered in order as People's Exhibits 11 to 15.

=========

Sonny Chaleff, whose defense is handled by a trio of lawyers—Frederick Sullivan, Louis Gribetz, and William Harris—was not like the others. For one thing, there can be no attempt to present him as retarded like Guariglia, or moronic like Friedman, in extenuation of his role. His bearing as a witness, his manner of speech, his manifest awareness—as compared to the indifference of Dominick or the aggressiveness of Hutch—clearly rule out any such strategy. For another thing, Philip Chaleff is the only defendant on trial, with the exception of Isidore Zimmerman, to have gone of his own accord to the police in connection with the murder of Detective Foley. Finally, unlike Dominick, Hutch, and Harvey, he charges no violence on the part of the police. These three considerations lend weight to Chaleff's defense, the burden of which is that, except for the walk uptown in the company of the other defendants to the Boulevard Restaurant, he had "gone his own way," divorced from the commission of the felony as he had been divorced from the conspiracy to commit it.

Hanover's Candy Store, corner of East Broadway and Clinton: cigars, ice cream, stationery, soda, open for business from 7:00 A.M. to 1:00 A.M. It is Friday evening, May 9. The expeditionary force is laying its plans for the assault on the Boulevard in booth number one, according to the prosecution —the conspiracy to commit the felony. But Chaleff's appearance in the store, shortly before midnight and after the double-feature breaks at Loew's Canal, leaves him no time—or little time—to participate in the planning. He is, after all, accompanied by his friend Leah Lepson, who confirms his movements and their departure together for the bus stop at Madison and Clinton; and on his return Hanover is preparing to close, so again there is no time—or little time—for him to participate in the conspiracy. While he is installed in Boruch Dworkin's cab—along with Chester, Smitty, and Fat, in whom the prosecution shows no interest, and Popeye Cooperman, a major witness for the prosecution—there is no evidence that the conspiracy was furthered, argues the defense. But when Harvey crosses a dozen feet of sidewalk from Muskin's Restaurant to the cab and invites him to come for a stroll, Chaleff takes, knowingly or not, the first step on the slide down to oblivion.

"Yes," concedes Chaleff's counsel. "He took a walk. It is difficult—I admit—for me, for you, to understand why should [sic] this boy walk by night, at three o'clock, and with whom? It is difficult." But, he urges, "Don't judge his walk as you would mine or yours. Judge his walk alongside of his station in life, his special diet, his exercise, his—perhaps, in a sense— his wandering life, his illness, the fact that he is an incurable diabetic; incurable; insulin twice a day—he does not work; he rises late; he cannot sleep; he goes to bed late; he stays out; he stopped his hard physical exercise. That's how you are to judge it . . . Don't judge his walk as you would mine and yours. You will be mistaken . . ."

But on his walk up to 144 Second Avenue, Chaleff—even supposing his innocence total, up to this point—begins to

understand; the intelligence that has served him so far would
rule out any other hypothesis. Certain proposals are made to
him, which he cannot fail to comprehend. And, comprehending, he has become part of the conspiracy; comprehending, he
becomes a candidate for the electric chair. In the words of the
prosecutor, opening his case for the People: "The defendant
Sonny Chaleff, it was then agreed, would go up and look the
place [the Boulevard Restaurant] over to see whether or not
it was dead or whether there was a sufficiently good crowd
present to make their effort worth while. And he went up to
look the place over . . . brought the news to the boys it was
all right; let's go, boys."

In the legal sense neither the utterances of the prosecutor
nor those of counsel for defense are offered to the jury as
evidence; only the declarations under oath of the witness
on the stand carry that weight. So the prosecutor's charge
that Chaleff scouted the Dutchman's as a preliminary to the
holdup would be damning if established by the testimony of
a witness; but unsupported by such testimony it is not properly
receivable as evidence against him. Chaleff's counsel con-
siders the charge a weapon to be turned back against the
District Attorney. "Gentlemen, no one was produced to identify Chaleff as having gone up there. It was very important
for the District Attorney to do that. He did not. He could not.
Nobody could identify Chaleff because Chaleff wasn't there."
For a jurist, the point is well made: by the defense, at the
expense of the prosecution.

But the men in the jury box are less concerned with legal-
ism than with murder. For them the image subsists of
Chaleff, walking the pavements of the Lower East Side in
doubtful company at three o'clock of an April morning, listening to certain proposals which he cannot fail to understand—
it is enough for him to have listened to be freighted with guilt.
He listens; he is guilty. Even for Gribetz: "I believe . . . [this
boy] is guilty of indiscretions. He has much to atone for,
much sin to acknowledge. But . . . he did not participate in the

conspiracy. He was not the man who planned, not the man who participated in, the shooting of Foley."

If the jury will believe this—that Chaleff took no part in the conspiracy hatched in Hanover's Candy Store, in Muskin's Restaurant, and in Dworkin's taxi, and that Chaleff never set foot in his life in the Boulevard Restaurant, where, moreover, no witness for the prosecution can place him—then Chaleff's chances for survival are appreciably better than those of his co-defendants, prejudice notwithstanding. Though the prosecution charges that Chaleff first suggested the Boulevard as a likely place to rob, cited the precedent of its successful holdup some weeks earlier, and volunteered to scout the premises, the critical area for him, now, can be situated on the sidewalk of Second Avenue, a dozen steps from the Dutchman's doorway. Did he walk up the stairs to the Dutchman's? Was he—merely—willing to walk up the stairs? The law requires no more to take his life. No witness can establish that he walked up. But was he willing? For a second—for a minute—for a quarter of an hour? "I was supposed to do it," says Chaleff on the stand. "I was supposed to go upstairs, I was supposed to take property, I was told what I was supposed to do . . ." But, "I swear by God that I never, never went to commit this crime."

On the sidewalk in front of the Dutchman's, then, Chaleff's reason comes belatedly to his rescue. The "finger man" is not the first man up the stairs; that honor is reserved for Hutch Friedman. Five yards from the door—the prosecution will contend that he had five yards to walk to reach it, and had no time to walk up the stairs; the defense that he reached the door and passed it with no intention of walking up—Chaleff realizes, however imperfectly, what is being done and what he is being asked to do. His role has changed now: "Somebody asked me to go upstairs, and when I did come upstairs, if everybody had their hands up in the air to go through their pockets." Chaleff's response: "I don't do them things and I am not going upstairs." He takes Little Chemey—who has announced his intention to go upstairs with the others—by the arm, and walks away, turning his back on the felony. There is the sudden noise, as of an engine backfiring, or of shooting. A minute later O'Loughlin emerges from the building, two bullets in his body. "Take a walk," he says. "Turn around and take a walk."

Chaleff and Little Chemey walk. Back at the corner of East Broadway and Clinton, Chaleff orders coffee and bagels in Muskin's. Little Chemey has evaporated. What is Chaleff thinking? What does Chaleff know of what has happened? The morning papers, which he purchases on his way home, tell him nothing—it is too soon. What does he expect to find, reading them in the apartment on Canal Street, while he waits for his father to leave for synagogue? Chaleff goes to bed at daybreak. How does he sleep?

The news is in the afternoon papers. Chaleff has reason now to be alarmed, even though Foley's death is not yet a fact. The police are holding Dominick, Hutch, and Harvey, probably looking for Little Benny, Little Chemey, and . . . Sonny Chaleff. Sunday night he sleeps, as he has done frequently in the past, on the living-room couch in the Lepsons' three-room apartment. Where he sleeps Monday is not established with certainty. Tuesday and Wednesday, again, he passes the night in the Lepsons' apartment. The papers are full of the killing at the Boulevard Restaurant. Thursday morning Chaleff sees his mother. She tells him that the police are looking for him.

Thursday afternoon, April 15, at 4:00 P.M., Chaleff, accompanied by his lawyer Milton Lerner, presents himself at the office of the District Attorney. Lerner advises the clerk of the Homicide Bureau of their presence, and after a brief wait in the corridor he is admitted with his client to the office of Assistant District Attorney Delehanty. A call goes out over the police switchboard. Within ten minutes the Homicide Bureau of the District Attorney's office is occupied by Detectives Gallagher, Farese, Wandling, and Lieutenant of Detectives Kiernan. The police officers confer briefly with

Delehanty in his office. Thereafter Philip Chaleff, accompanied by Delehanty and Assistant District Attorney McGuire, is questioned in the room opposite Delehanty's office.

The questioning lasts nearly an hour. On three or four occasions Chaleff is escorted out of the room by a detective and permitted to consult with Lerner. At about 5:15 Chaleff makes a statement, which he later acknowledges to contain falsehoods. At around 6:00 P.M. he is confronted with Guariglia. Shortly thereafter, he recognizes the falsity of the first statement and makes a second. "The reason I made the first statement, knowing that I was absolutely innocent of any crime that did take place: I felt ashamed, worried about my family, and knowing that I was innocent, that is the reason I did give that story to the District Attorney."

There is enough material at the disposal of the prosecution in the two statements to damn Chaleff along with the rest: his acknowledgment that he had been promised a share of the "take" for participating; his acknowledgment that at one point he "was supposed to go upstairs and search the parties"; his acknowledgment, when asked how many people were involved in the expedition against the Boulevard, "As far as I know . . . there was only supposed to be five"; his acknowledgment—on Delehanty's question, "Do you know who had the guns?"— that "I knew three of them were carrying guns because they told me." These admissions, and others—many of which Chaleff will contest on grounds they were part of his first statement to the District Attorney, deliberately falsified by him (". . . I felt ashamed of myself . . . They tried to put me into something that I didn't know nothing about and I didn't want to disgrace the family. I knew I was absolutely innocent")—are grave enough to shatter the presumptions of innocence skillfully conveyed by Chaleff's counsel.

Twelve character witnesses are called by Gribetz on behalf of Sonny: a physician, a dentist, the president of the synagogue, social workers, lawyers, friends. More are available. But Gribetz, in his summation, makes his appeal more to the heart than to the mind, quoting Chaleff: " 'I swear to God . . .

that I never, never went to commit this crime.' Couple that," he continues, "with a clean life and I think you have the answer . . . The burden of proof is upon the prosecution to satisfy you beyond a reasonable doubt. The State must satisfy you beyond all doubt that this boy is guilty of the crime. He [Chaleff] is not called upon to establish his innocence . . . It is not certain that you have the right to say that this boy, who was created and destined to live—that his life should be forfeit . . . I know the infamy upon his family. I know the degradation, the sorrow, the empty chair. I know the meaning of that . . . There is more than a reasonable doubt that this boy did that. Take into consideration the clean life, with no incident. Illness—no guns. Yes, he walked. He should not have walked, but he said he was innocent. I thank you, and I hope I have not abused the privilege of addressing you."

═══════

It is not until March 23, after selection of the trial jury, that counsel for the defense of Isidore Zimmerman—James Murray, Philip Poger, and Samuel Feldman—are officially apprised of the charge against their client, when the District Attorney, Jacob Rosenblum, lays out the case the prosecution will undertake to prove against the men on trial. Zimmerman's role is indispensable to the commission of the felony; his responsibility as a matter of law is fully as great as that of his co-defendants; greater, in a sense, than that of the man who, pulling the trigger of the .38 Smith & Wesson, snuffed out the life of Michael Foley. Zimmerman, contends the prosecutor, is the armorer, the man who knowingly supplied the guns with which the expeditionary force tried to take the Dutchman's place.

To establish the movement of the guns, as they travel from hand to hand and from place to place, in such a way as to make them clearly traceable, by the jurors, to Isidore Zimmerman is a task which will require first hours, and then days, of testimony. There is contradiction, error, confusion, repetition; but the effort is necessary for the prosecution to link Isidore

Zimmerman—who never, like Sonny Chaleff, "took a walk"; who never, like Harvey, Hutch, and Dominick, set foot in the Boulevard Restaurant; who never, like Little Benny Ertel and Little Chemey Perlmutter, dropped out of sight after the felony—with the death of Michael Foley. And for the prosecutor Isidore Zimmerman is "this monster who started the thing, who practically made it possible . . . because if he did not provide the guns, for all I know we wouldn't have any widow or orphan child today. If he did not provide the guns, the very gun that took the life of Detective Foley . . ."

The very gun that took the life of Detective Foley is a brown-handled, black-barreled .38 long, manufactured by Smith & Wesson. It belongs to a butcher, Salvatore Scalogna, whose permit for it has lapsed. He keeps it in a bureau drawer in the bedroom of his two-room apartment on Oak Street. In the drawer of the night table there is a box of rusting cartridges for the pistol. Scalogna's fifteen-year-old son Ralph is, like a good many boys, interested in guns—interested enough to fire two rounds from it into the bedroom wall, interested enough to show it to an acquaintance, sixteen-year-old Danny Rose, after school. On April 7, Scalogna lends the gun, with ammunition, to Rose. On the same day Rose, having no place to hide it, turns the gun over to seventeen-year-old Buddy Boyles for safekeeping in his cellar at 277 East Broadway. Overnight Boyles has second thoughts about the advisability of holding the gun. He goes to the Scammel Street Boys' Club at Henry and Clinton streets to return it to Rose. Rose does not appear at the club. Boyles meantime displays the gun to Philip Savoy, a nineteen-year-old nicknamed "Footke." There is some talk of selling the gun to Footke, who is apparently collecting weapons, but nothing comes of it. Reluctant to carry the gun around further, Boyles returns it to his cellar; when, later that day, Rose finally puts in his appearance at the club, Boyles is unable to return it to him as planned. On the following evening—Friday, April 9—Boyles manages to return the pistol to Rose in the presence of Footke and of other club members. Rose and Footke leave the club together.

By Friday, Footke has acquired a weapon on his own: a
.32 short. Reluctant to carry it on his person, he has hidden
it under the stairs in the hallway of the tenement at 201 Henry
Street. Rose now transfers to Footke the .38 belonging to
Scalogna, the butcher, and the second gun is cached with the
first under the stairs in the hallway.

In the course of the same evening, contends the prosecution,
the conspiracy to hold up the Boulevard Restaurant is in the
planning stage—at a booth in a neighborhood candy store run
by a man named Hanover—Harvey, Hutch, Dominick, Chaleff,
Little Benny, Little Chemey, and Zimmerman are in conclave.
Plans are sufficiently advanced for Friedman to raise the
question of the weapons necessary for the holdup. States the
District Attorney: "The defendant . . . Zimmerman . . . at that
time said he would get some or all of the guns which would
be needed.

"It was then agreed . . . that Zimmerman said he would not
go along but would provide his gun for the cut he was to get
out of the take of the holdup . . .

"Zimmerman and Popeye [alias Harry Cooperman, a witness for the prosecution] then went to the Scammel Street
Club, and there they saw Rose, who took them to 201 Clinton
Street, where the two guns, the .32 caliber and the .38 caliber
gun, were hidden under the stairway.

"Beany (Zimmerman, also nicknamed 'Beansy') and Danny
Rose went into the place. Popeye stayed outside—that is,
Cooperman—and Beany came out and had the guns on his
person—that is, the defendant Zimmerman. And from there
the three of them went to [sic] across the street, to 206 Clinton
Street, and the defendant Zimmerman and Popeye went into
the hallway, and there Zimmerman gives the two guns to
Popeye . . . and told him to go to 219 Henry Street, that is,
the place where Dominick lives—and to wait there until Beany
. . . that is, Zimmerman, sent Hutch Friedman and Harvey . . .
to 219 Henry Street to get those guns.

"We will prove," declares the District Attorney, ". . . that
Hutch and Harvey came to 219 Henry Street and that Popeye

delivered the two guns to Hutch and Harvey." Somewhere along the line the expeditionary force picks up a third weapon: the "broken" gun which Little Benny removes from its hiding place behind the toilet bowl and entrusts to Guariglia, along with Footke's .32 and Scalogna's .38, for the thirty-block march to the Dutchman's.

In its case against Zimmerman the prosecution will call Ralph Scalogna, Raymond "Buddy" Boyles, Philip "Footke" Savoy, and—particularly—Daniel Rose and Harry "Popeye" Cooperman to establish the movement of the weapons he is charged with providing. The prosecution has a second task: to establish that Zimmerman met conspiratorially with the other defendants for the purpose of planning the holdup. For this the District Attorney will rely principally on evidence given by Rose, Cooperman, and Tobias Hanover, proprietor of the candy store at 201 East Broadway where the conspiracy was elaborated. If it fails to demonstrate these two points to the satisfaction of the jury—that Zimmerman purposefully provided guns, knowing they were to be used for the commission of a felony, and that he joined the others in conspiring to commit the felony—the prosecution has no case against this defendant.

The testimony of Rose, the testimony of Cooperman, the testimony of Hanover: three millstones around the neck of Isidore Zimmerman.

Walk into Hanover's Candy Store from East Broadway: to the right the marble-topped counter of the fountain runs halfway to the rear wall of the square box—twenty-five feet to a side—where Tobias Hanover, known to his customers as Tevyah—tiny, pallid, thin; silver-rimmed glasses; sparse gray hair balding from the forehead; the rapid, nervous gestures of a bird making the deep voice seem curiously out of place in so frail a frame; the hands moving this way and that to help you see the words he cannot find—has presided as proprietor for seven years, assisted only by his wife, who takes over the store from two to four while Hanover naps, and again from seven-thirty to eight while he dines. To the left of the entrance, aligned from front to rear, are five booths with tables, three against the left-hand wall and two toward the center of the store. Between the two rows of booths is a narrow aisle, and another aisle separates the short row from the fountain counter. Alongside the two booths slightly to the left of the center of the room is a pinball machine, and at the rear of the store are a telephone and a candy counter. It is about 11:00 P.M. on Friday, April 9: the radio is blaring; customers playing the pinball machine add to the din. For the past three hours Hanover has been on duty dispensing sodas. Before midnight, he knows, there will be the usual spill-over when the double feature breaks at Loew's Canal.

At booth number one—the first along the left-hand wall as you enter—are, seated or standing, Friedman (known to Hanover only as "Hutch"), Little Benny, Isidore Perlmutter (whom he knows as "Chemey"), Guariglia (whom he knows only as "Dominick"), and O'Loughlin. They are talking together, but Hanover, fifteen feet away behind the marble-topped counter, cannot hear what they are saying over the noise of the radio.

Zimmerman ("Beansy" to Hanover, who has known him for only a month or so because, unlike the other boys, "he wasn't in my neighborhood") enters, orders a soda at the counter, and "one of the . . . people sitting at the table" calls him over. He stands for a while talking to the occupants of booth one, returns the empty soda glass to Hanover at the counter, goes back to the table, where he sits briefly, squeezing in with the others—there is room comfortably for two on a side—and leaves the store with Popeye Cooperman.

Almost coincidentally with their departure, Chaleff enters—it is around half-past eleven—with the influx from Loew's, drinks a glass of water, then another, walks to booth one to speak with the others, brings the water glass back to the counter, leaves the store, returns, leaves again. "He is a very big drinker of water . . . no sodas," says Hanover. "I know

him, he never stays in; he always do the same thing, walk in
and out." There is, in fact, a continuous ebb and flow of cus-
tomer's in Hanover's little shop; over and above the group at
booth one, their number throughout the evening never falls
below six or eight. In the course of the evening Footke comes
and goes. Both before and after the conclave at booth one,
Popeye Cooperman is in and out of the store on three or four
occasions. Working as a racker in the poolroom nearby, he is
in the habit of dropping in at Tevyah's sporadically, for
change, for cigarettes, for a soda. Hanover is aware of him as
he talks to the group in booth one, as he converses with Zimmerman and leaves the store with him.

James Murray, Zimmerman's lawyer, questioning Hanover:
"You didn't expect that a robbery conspiracy was going to be
hatched in your store that night, did you?" "No." ". . . So
there was nothing particularly suspicious in the action of any
of these men, was there?" "No." "And there was nothing
particularly suspicious in their conduct to make you remember
where they sat or how they were grouped on that night, was
there?" "Well, they were not only that one night. They were
usually customers. They used to come in and out during the
week and any night . . ." "So they were probably there on the
night before, weren't they?" "That is what it is . . . They didn't
come in just special that one night . . ." "They were such
frequent patrons of your store that they came in in the afternoon and also at night, didn't they?" "Yes, sir."

Hanover, like the classical trio of monkeys, hears no evil,
sees no evil, speaks no evil. The matters under discussion at
booth one are unknown to him, and the group at booth one,
he concedes, might have been there on the seventh or the
eighth as well as the ninth, afternoon as well as evening. But
all the boys at booth one are, for the prosecution, involved
one way or another in the felony, and for Hanover, Zimmerman was at that booth with those boys at that time. Hearing
no evil, seeing no evil, speaking no evil, Hanover nonetheless
hangs the first millstone around Zimmerman's neck. And the
prosecution has at its disposal two witnesses who will speak

evil against Zimmerman: Daniel Rose and Popeye Cooperman.

———

Danny Rose: a face made up of sharp angles; fair-complexioned; dirty blond hair; voice pitched high; rapid of speech; aggressive in manner; hands moving continually as he talks; age, seventeen. Occupation: "Nothing; nothing right now. Just once in a while I work in the *Jewish Daily Forward* . . . helper on a truck." Before the night of Foley's shooting he has never had any dealings with Zimmerman, whom he has known for about a week. During that week, the degree of their acquaintance is that of "virtual strangers" by Counselor Murray's definition; by Rose's definition, "Hello and good-bye." "I knew Zimmerman by sight but not to speak to." Rose left school before his seventeenth birthday, and although he cannot remember his exact age at the time, was awarded a diploma. Was he classed as a moron, academically? "I wouldn't say moron, but I always had fights in school."

The time is Friday evening, April 9. Sometime between 7:30 and 8:00, Rose and Footke have hidden two pistols in the darkness under the stairs in the hall of 201 Clinton Street. Rose returns to the Scammel Street Boys' Club, then walks to a candy store at the corner of East Broadway and Clinton— Tevyah Hanover's—for a soda. There, says Rose, he meets Zimmerman. "Had a little conversation with him. I told him I had give [*sic*] Footke a gun . . . He didn't say anything and I just walked back to the club." Shortly thereafter Zimmerman turns up at Rose's club in the company of Harry Cooperman, also known as "Ellie," also known as Popeye. Rose: "Popeye didn't say anything . . . Beansy asked me to take him down where the guns were, and I asked him, 'What about Footke? What is Footke going to say?' He said, 'Never mind about Footke.' So I went downstairs with him, with Popeye and I went in the hall with Beansy and I gave him the guns [hidden under the stairs at 201 Clinton] . . . We walked over to 206 Clinton . . . Beansy and Popeye walked into the hall of 206.

I did not. [Now the guns have been transferred from Beansy to Popeye.] . . . Popeye walked around the corner of Henry Street and I walked back to the candy store [Hanover's] with Beansy . . . I repeated that question as I did up in the club. I asked him, 'What is Footke going to say about the gun?' And he says I should make up a story saying that they are not there."

The next day, Saturday, Rose encounters Zimmerman by chance at the Henry Street poolroom. It is about eleven in the morning. They talk. Says Rose: "Beansy asked me if I read the papers and I told him no, and he said that Harvey was shot and a cop was shot in a stickup, and I thought he was kidding; so he bought me a paper . . . I read the paper and I walked away." Before they separate, says Rose, "He said that in case I got picked up that I shouldn't say anything about him." Rose, then, has handled the guns—as have Footke, Boyles, and Scalogna—more or less at random; ignorant of the conspiracy to hold up the Boulevard, and ignorant therefore of the purpose they will serve ["I thought he was kidding"], he is a witness for the prosecution. Zimmerman, on the other hand, has taken the initiative in procuring the guns for a purpose—the holdup—and displays full awareness of what he has done by showing Rose the news in the paper and asking him not to mention his name in connection with it: he is on trial for his life.

Rose is not a savory witness, either for the prosecution or for the defense. Under interrogation he is aggressive, frequently inconsistent, and manifestly unintelligent. In his summation for Zimmerman, Murray will say: ". . . I can show you [with the trial record] that between fifty and one hundred questions that I asked this man Rose, that he answered he did not remember." The unsavory witness makes unsavory admissions, thus: although he has never been arrested or convicted, Rose acknowledges having been questioned, along with Footke, by a grand jury for violations of the Sullivan Act in connection with their arms traffic. He acknowledges having been picked up by the police as a suspect in the Foley killing.

He acknowledges having paid Scalogna the sum of two dollars for the rental of his .38, having been promised ten dollars in turn by Footke for rental of the same gun, and having been given to understand by Zimmerman that he would be compensated further for making weapons available to him. So his material interest in the movement of the weapons is clearly established. (Rose justifies renting the gun from Scalogna on grounds—uncorroborated—there were rumors Wednesday of a plot to hold up the Scammel Street Boys' Club. The .38, though unloaded according to Rose, is for defensive purposes; if, after the holdup fails to materialize, he does not return the gun, it is because in the interval Footke has offered him ten dollars for the use of it.) Murray, cross-examining Rose: "So you were going to make a sweet little profit, weren't you? You paid two for the gun and Footke was to give you ten, and you make eight, is that right?" "Well, I was a businessman." "You were a businessman? [No answer.] You thought it perfectly proper to hire out guns, did you?" "No, I didn't think so at that time, but I didn't have any money." "You didn't think there was anything wrong about it?" "I don't know what they were going to do with it." And on the afternoon of March 24, he acknowledges having lied on the stand—"That's right"—respecting the presence of certain persons in court on the morning of the same day.

Further, Rose admits his initiative in mentioning the guns to Zimmerman. Murray, in cross-examination: "How did he [Zimmerman] know that you had guns, did you tell him?" Rose: "I told him about it." "How did you come to tell him? Did he ask you?" "No, he didn't ask me. I just said. I wanted to see what he was going to say . . . I just told him I had given Footke a gun, that he had one of his own, and he put them away. I didn't tell him where." (Rose will declare on the stand that Footke never mentioned Zimmerman's name in connection with the guns; and Footke will declare on the stand that he never talked with Zimmerman about pistols, never heard anyone talk to Zimmerman about pistols, never saw Zimmerman in possession of pistols.)

Finally, Daniel Rose, under Murray's cross-examination, concedes that in the twelve months since Foley's killing he has been questioned repeatedly by the police. Murray: ". . . When is the first time that you made a statement with a stenographer present concerning this case?" Rose: "About three or four days ago [i.e., March 19 or 20]; about a week, I would say—approximately a week." This statement was given in the District Attorney's office, under questioning by Jacob Rosenblum. "Now," continues Murray, "when you talked in the Clinton Street station house to the police for the first time about this case [in the absence of any stenographer] . . . you didn't mention Zimmerman's name at all, did you?" "I didn't mention anybody's name." Perhaps it was three weeks, perhaps a month, before the beginning of the trial that Rose recalls first naming names in the case; as late as December of the previous year he has no memory of having been questioned by the District Attorney about the guns in connection with the name of Zimmerman. "I don't remember that," affirms Rose. "Do you mean to say you don't remember whether or not the District Attorney asked you if Zimmerman was in any way connected with this case?" "I don't remember."

Rose's bearing on the stand comes in for special attention from Counselor Murray in his summation. "You remember," he says, addressing the jury, "how he growled and spat at me as I cross-examined him, as I felt, fairly and respectfully. You saw the type of cur he was. That is the type of cur— without his testimony, gentlemen of the jury, this case would not even be submitted to you, I say, as a matter of law, unless he claimed to support this man Cooperman."

Who is this man Cooperman? The third millstone around Zimmerman's neck . . .

═══════════

Counsel for Arthur Friedman is categorical: "This boy Popeye is not the type of witness that you can believe." Popeye's very nickname is sinister. His pupils are dilated because, as Isidore Meichenbaum, a witness for Friedman, testifies, he is a marijuana smoker. Meichenbaum has purchased "reefers" from Popeye and smoked them in his company. Hanover testifies that Popeye suggested he sell marijuana cigarettes in his candy store, and quoted the going price for them—three for fifty cents, procurable in Harlem. Counsel for Friedman has a difficult case to plead, and to wax wroth on the subject of Popeye becomes as much a pleasure for him as a duty: ". . . This boy, this star witness for the prosecution, this witness who, by his own testimony, is guilty of murder in the first degree and is not here at the bar of justice [with the defendants] at all . . . a filthy, dirty creature, who just crawls along the ground—I don't even want to use the expression, because . . . in addition to everything else this boy Popeye is, he has made it possible [by providing him with marijuana cigarettes] for a young man like this boy Arthur Friedman to be here at the bar of justice, charged with murder in the first degree . . . The man who ought to be sitting there in the seat occupied by Arthur Friedman is not Arthur Friedman at all; it's the People's star witness, Mr. Popeye."

Guariglia's lawyer McDonald also has a few harsh words to say about Popeye, even though, "after all Popeye Cooperman said about that conspiracy when he related the conversation [between the defendants in booth one of Hanover's store], he does not remember a thing Dominick said." Or, as he rephrases it—in Cooperman's recollection, translated into testimony—"there is not a word spoken by Dominick in the furtherance or the making of this alleged conspiracy." Perhaps not, but Popeye has situated him in booth one with the other defendants at a time when the conspiracy was being elaborated, according to the prosecution; can it be reasonably supposed that Dominick was not involved? McDonald, therefore, measures out a ration of scorn for Cooperman: "Popeye . . . if he should be anywhere, should be at this defendants' table. He is an admitted conspirator who was going to get a cut and who was going to get money, and who helped carry the guns, and he knew there was going to be a stickup, according to his story. So why he is not sitting at that counsel table or at the defendants' table I don't understand."

Chaleff's lawyer puts it another way: "Would you trust this boy Popeye to carry from here to the Woolworth Building one hundred dollars? Would you trust him and take him into your employ? Would you trust this boy to count the pulse of life? Upon his words rest almost the issues of life. He says he overheard. He takes an oath. Is there the grasping of the principle of an oath in his character? Do you think that his head and his heart believe—go hand in hand with belief in the meaning of an oath? Gentlemen, I think that this foundation witness—he has been attacked by others—I believe that this foundation witness of the prosecution should be by you discarded one hundred per cent. So far as Chaleff is concerned he is perjurious. He was as perjurious, as black, as a pirate. It hurts me personally to stand here and rail against any human being, and rail against this witness. But . . . I am saying that this man, whom you and I would not trust in our employ . . . to carry a typewriter from here across the street—this boy who was interviewed a full day on Saturday [after the shooting of Foley]—you remember he was asked specifically: Did you mention the names of the defendants on Saturday? He said no, he did not give a statement. He was a full day in the police station. Is it conceivable that if this story [of the conspirators in collective conference in Hanover's] were true he would not on Saturday have given part of his story, the important part of his story, to the Fifth Street police station?"

Joab Banton, O'Loughlin's defender: "There are three little gunmen in the case—there is no doubt about it. That's Danny Rose, and Footke . . . and Popeye. They are nothing in the world but little gun-carriers, that's all they are; and you gentlemen can put all of the confidence in them that you wish, but I wouldn't believe one of them on a stack of Bibles as high as the Woolworth Building . . ."

Finally, Zimmerman's lawyer: ". . . If this man Zimmerman is guilty, is Cooperman guilty? You don't see any indictment hanging over Cooperman's head . . . Has Cooperman any motive in this case? Of course he has. His motive is to save his own dirty neck. Do you think that this man Cooperman is inspired by any motive or any thirst for justice, so that he wanted to come here and tell you the truth? . . . He is in exactly the same position as Zimmerman, only he is worse . . . a great deal worse . . . If his story is true, didn't he carry the guns himself, for a price that he was to get out of the robbery, to the men that are supposed to commit the robbery? . . . Isn't he worse than Zimmerman ever thought of being?"

Popeye Cooperman: twenty-three years old; wiry; blond; a pointed nose; sharp chin; eyes fixed on the floor. Married; childless; living apart from his wife. Domicile, 226 Henry Street. In April, 1937, he has eight months' employment behind him as a racker in the Henry Street poolroom. Wages: a cut of the house take. Money is hard to come by; money is always hard to come by; but since February 10 of this year he has been held in Manhattan's House of Detention on 37th Street as a material witness in the Foley case, drawing subsistence pay at the rate of three dollars a day. Never convicted of any crime.

Popeye's boss, Arthur, is in the habit of sending him from the poolroom to Tevyah's candy store for change. On the night of April 9, Popeye makes more than one appearance at Hanover's. Shortly after eleven he notices, at booth number one, Dominick (whom he has known for eighteen months), Harvey (whom he has known for eighteen months), Hutch (whom he has known for fourteen or fifteen months), Little Chemey (whom he has known for ten years or so), Little Benny (with whom he has gone to school). A little later they will be joined by Zimmerman (with whom he has gone to school) and then by Chaleff (whom he has known for three or four years). They are in conversation. Popeye takes up a position close to the booth, by a radiator one or two feet away.

"There was a conversation," affirms Popeye on the stand, clasped hands resting in his lap, "about a heist . . . a stickup . . . They were all talking; everybody was talking together, they were all talking about it . . . To take the joint; they were going to take a joint on Second Avenue . . . I don't remember who said it complete . . . Sonny [Chaleff] said there was a place [the Boulevard] taken about two or three weeks ago for $3,500, and he said, 'Well, we will . . . look over the place, maybe it will be good enough for today.' . . . Then Benny said, 'If it is for $3,500, like last time, it will be all right.' Then . . . Hutch said, 'We haven't got no guns.' So Beany said, 'I will go up and see if I see Danny [Rose], he might have some.' So he told us to go out to the clubroom and we went up to the clubroom, me and Beany."

At the Scammel Street Boys' Club, where a dance is under way (declares Popeye) "Beany asked Danny if he's got any guns. So Danny says, 'I loaned it to Footke.' So Danny says, 'I think I know where they are. I think I know where Footke put them.' So the three of us walked out to 201 Clinton Street . . . Beany and Danny went into the hallway." Cooperman stayed outside. "When they come out . . . the three of us walked to 206 [Clinton Street] and Beany and myself . . . walked into the hallway." Now it is Danny Rose who stayed outside. Inside the tenement door, continues Cooperman, "Beany give me the guns and told me to go around to 219 Henry Street . . . He just said he will go to the corner and tell Hutch and Harvey to come around and take them away from me."

Cooperman waits on the steps of 219 Henry. "Then Hutch and Harvey come over and . . . I gave the guns to them," he testifies. Then he goes back to Hanover's Candy Store, where he sees Little Chemey, Dominick, Little Benny, Harvey—returning now from 219 Henry Street—and Zimmerman. Popeye says he speaks only to Zimmerman. "I told him I gave them the guns." "All right," says Zimmerman. Popeye walks Zimmerman home. On the way they talk. "He said he is going to see me after they come back . . . He says he was going to get a cut out of it." Cooperman spends the following day—Saturday—answering questions put by the police concerning the holdup of the Dutchman's, but he is not arrested.

That evening he meets Zimmerman. "I told him I was picked up . . . They just asked me to identify them, if I knew them." Cooperman has identified Hutch and Dominick, he reveals. Then, he states, Zimmerman cautions him, "Don't mention my name."

Cooperman clinches the prosecution's charges against all the defendants and, where Zimmerman is concerned, serves to link Rose's testimony to Hanover's. On the stand Popeye denies involvement in any robberies before this one, denies having carried guns for robbers, denies having been in conflict with the law. Murray: "But you went into this enterprise willingly, did you?" Cooperman: "Yes." "You wanted to make money, is that right?" "I did it for a favor." ". . . You did it for a favor plus some money, is that it?" "Yes."

Presumably, the favor done is to Zimmerman. In point of fact, the term "disservice" seems more appropriate.

Hanover, Rose, and Cooperman: three millstones around Zimmerman's neck. Hanover situates him with the conspirators; Rose ties him to the guns; and Cooperman links him to the guns at one end and to the conspirators at the other.

All the same, the prosecution's case against Zimmerman suffers from at least two serious weaknesses. Hanover, to begin with, cannot affirm with certainty that the conclave at booth one was actually discussing the holdup of the Boulevard. Second, the roles of Rose and Cooperman are so equivocal that there is less reason to consider them as witnesses for the prosecution of those indicted for Foley's death than as co-defendants, charged with the same crime as Hutch and Harvey, Dominick, Sonny, and Little Benny. In effect, Judge Nott rules, when the case for the prosecution closes, that Popeye Cooperman is, as a matter of law, an accomplice of the accused; and by New York law the testimony of an accomplice to a crime is legally worthless unless supported by other evidence tending to corroborate it. The advantage to

Zimmerman is academic, however: the Court deems the testimony of Hanover and of Rose to be "other evidence tending to corroborate" Cooperman's testimony.

Zimmerman's lawyer protests the inequity of the situation. "If this man Zimmerman is guilty, is Cooperman guilty? You don't see any indictment hanging over Cooperman's head . . . Has Cooperman any motive in this case? Of course he has. His motive is to save his own dirty neck. Do you think this man Cooperman is inspired by any motive or any thirst for justice, so that he wanted to come here and tell you the truth? . . . If his testimony means a thing in this case, he is in exactly the same position as Zimmerman, only he is worse . . . a great deal worse . . . If his story is true, didn't he carry the guns himself, for a price that he was to get out of the robbery, to the men that are supposed to commit the robbery?

". . . Do you think Rose is lily-white in this case? . . . If there is a scintilla of truth in what he said—let us accept this for the sake of argument—don't you think that Rose is just as black as Cooperman? And . . . if the prosecution's contention is true, that this man Zimmerman is guilty, don't you think that Rose is guilty? Don't you think that Cooperman is guilty? But only guilty in a greater degree?

"Now, if they are part and parcel of a conspiracy—and . . . I don't accept the prosecution's theory [that Zimmerman is involved in the conspiracy] . . . aren't they just as guilty as Zimmerman? And . . . the law is that you can't let two such men fight their way out of the grip of the law at the expense of a third man."

Hanover's testimony regarding Zimmerman is inconclusive; and that of Cooperman and Rose, though conclusive, is dubious; but the prosecution will run no risk that Zimmerman may, in Murray's phrase, "fight his way out of the grip of the law" because of attacks by the defense on the probity of its two foundation witnesses. In his closing, the District Attorney will take precautions to justify before the jury the prosecution's right to use such witnesses. Rosenblum: ". . . Popeye gave you testimony. Danny Rose gave you testimony. Footke gave you testimony . . . I assure you, gentlemen, that if I were trying a contract case, if I were saying that some man . . . a broker or some substantial businessman had a deal with a bank, and they were in a boardroom, and they had five or six witnesses . . . officers of the bank, or the company, of course I would call those people. I would call those people, so that they could tell.

"But if I brought down every priest and every rabbi and every businessman, what would they know about what happened in Tobias' candy store? How can they help you? Do you think I like to bring witnesses like Popeye? Do I make witnesses? These defendants made the witnesses. They made the witnesses who testified against them. They created them; when they did things which could be testified to by witnesses, those witnesses were called. When they went into 144 Second Avenue, you heard the witnesses that were . . . there, whether they were businessmen or a man who was at sea, or a man who was a chef, or a man who played cards—because those are the people who could give you the testimony . . .

"It is my duty to bring you the witnesses that can help you decide the issue which is before you. You have the job of deciding whether or not these people were engaged in the commission of a felony. I got to [sic] bring you the witnesses . . . When Popeye can give you the information, I have got to call Popeye . . . I can only bring those witnesses who can be of help to you." As for arguments that the Grand Jury, indicting Guariglia, Friedman, O'Loughlin, Chaleff, and Zimmerman for the murder of Foley, ought to have indicted Rose and Cooperman as well, the District Attorney dismisses them as "side issues that are created" by the defense.

Notwithstanding Rosenblum's reminder that the defendants have the witnesses they deserve, the prosecution will offer one more witness against Zimmerman whose probity the defense will be hard put to attack: a police officer, Detective William Wandling, Shield No. 1628, Seventh Squad Detectives, twenty-one and a half years a member of the New York Police Department.

On April 12 of the previous year, Wandling, along with his colleague Detective Sullivan, is given special assignment with the Second Detective District under the direction of Captain Mitchell. His assignment: an investigation of the case arising from Foley's killing. Wandling is among the police officers present when O'Loughlin gives a statement—nicknames and physical descriptions—which orients the investigation in the direction of Little Benny, Chemey, and Sonny Chaleff, and leads to Chaleff's arrest. By 11:30 P.M. on June 2, Detective Wandling has brought Footke in for questioning, and statements made by him to Lieutenant Kiernan interest the police in Zimmerman.

Early morning, June 3: Detective Wandling, accompanied by two colleagues—Detectives Bambrick and Flynn—climb the stairs to a third-floor apartment at 64 Rutgers Street. The time is 2:30 or 3:00 A.M. Zimmerman's father Morris, convalescing from double pneumonia, admits them, his head in a whirl. "They ask me, 'Where is your son?' I told them he went down for coffee and as soon as he will be back he will be there. 'Well,' they said, 'Mr. Zimmerman, there is nothing to be scared for . . .' And I told them as soon as he will come I will send him there [to the police station]. Well, they told me . . . 'Don't be afraid, nothing is going to happen; we have to ask him some questions about the murder of Detective Foley who got killed on Second Avenue.'" The detectives leave.

Twenty-odd minutes later Zimmerman arrives home. In the company of his father and a brother he reports to the Clinton Street police station. There, for the moment, no one knows the reason for his being called. His father and brother wait with him for a quarter of an hour, then return home, leaving Zimmerman in the station.

Wandling testifies: "About 4:00 or 4:30 we [detectives] came back to the station house, and defendant Zimmerman was upstairs in the squad room. We kept him there until the next morning. He wasn't questioned at all." In the morning, says Wandling, the police "took him over to District Attorney

Delehanty's office and he questioned him—Zimmerman first, Savoy [that is, Footke, who had also spent the night in the Clinton Street station], and then Zimmerman; and they were questioned several times."

Zimmerman's recollection on the stand of the same events is somewhat different. Arriving at the Clinton Street police station, he seeks out one of the detectives on duty: "I told him that I am Isidore Zimmerman, and two detectives had been in my house and wanted to question me about the murder of Detective Foley. So I says, 'I am here, and what is it?' " Zimmerman is told to sit down and wait. An hour or so later, about 4:15 A.M., Detectives Wandling and Bambrick return to the station house. "They came in the [detectives'] room and they sat down toward me and I smelled whiskey on their breath, and one of them said to me, 'Why, you little c———, we have been looking all around for you and you are sitting here.' I said, 'Well, I am here; what can I do for you?' . . . They brought me downstairs to a tier of cells, and . . . I saw this fellow Footke there . . . And they says to . . . him . . . 'Is this the Beansy you meant?' He didn't answer. He went back in his cell and Wandling went in after him and he come out and he says, 'He said yes,' and they took me and they put me in a cell . . . about a quarter to five [in the morning] until two o'clock that afternoon." No charge is made, no one from the Police Department talks to him, and neither breakfast nor lunch is provided.

Toward two o'clock, testifies Zimmerman, "They brought me back up to the detectives' room. They says, 'We have a statement here; we are going to read it to you, and I want you to correct it.' So they started reading off the statement; it was something about guns, and I said, 'I don't know anything about it and I can't correct it.' [The statement, Zimmerman is told, originates with Footke.] . . . Detective Gallagher kicked me in the side and he knocked me over a chair and all, and he said, 'You dirty little bastard, we will fix you in a little while.' And then the Lieutenant [Kiernan] got up; he pushed him, he said, 'Why don't you leave him alone? This man is not under arrest.' "

June 3, 3:40 P.M., at the office of the District Attorney, Leonard and Lafayette streets: Present are Assistant District Attorney McGuire, Assistant District Attorney Delehanty, Detectives Wandling, Gallagher, and Acting Lieutenant Kiernan of the Ninth Squad, a police stenographer, and Zimmerman, who is questioned for some twenty minutes and released in the custody of Detective Bambrick. Bambrick escorts Zimmerman to the Canal Street subway station, instructing Zimmerman to get off at Delancey Street and return home. Testifies Zimmerman: "I asked him, 'I thought I was supposed to be in your custody, Mr. Bambrick.' He says, 'I know you had nothing to do with this case . . . so when we reach Delancey Street, you just leave and meet me tomorrow morning at ten o'clock at Lafayette and Canal Street.' I said, 'All right.' "

June 4, 10:00 A.M., at the office of the District Attorney: Present are McGuire and Delehanty, Lieutenant Kiernan, Detectives Bambrick, Wandling, and Gallagher, a police stenographer, and Zimmerman, who is questioned anew and placed under arrest about four in the afternoon.

──────────

Between Zimmerman's first interrogation at the District Attorney's office on June 3, which concludes with his release, and his second interrogation on June 4, which concludes with his arrest, there occurs a meeting between Beansy and Cooperman "by his [Cooperman's] house." Testifies Zimmerman: ". . . He told me . . . 'I heard you've been picked up.' [Cooperman too has been picked up by the police in connection with Foley's murder.] I said, 'Yes. Why?' He said, 'Well, I am a friend of yours; I just wanted to know . . . You want to come up to my house . . . for a while? I want to talk to you.' I said, 'All right.' I went up there. He said, 'Well, what happened down there?' I said, 'They were asking me questions and they know I had nothing to do with that case.' He said, 'That's good. What are you going to do now?' "

Zimmerman tells Popeye he plans to go home for the evening meal, then consult with a lawyer named Sandler, whom he expects to find at the Downtown Tammany Club around midnight. Later, leaving the Rutgers Street apartment around midnight, Zimmerman runs into Cooperman again. "And he says to me, 'You still going over to see that lawyer?' I said, 'Yes.' He said, 'Come on, I'll walk down with you.' And he walked down too to Downtown Tammany Club, and there I saw Mr. Sandler, and I told him I had been picked up."

Cooperman is present at the meeting with Sandler, testifies Zimmerman. "I told him [Sandler] I was brought down to the District Attorney's office. He says 'For what?' I says, 'In connection with the murder of Detective Foley.' I says, 'But I don't know nothing about it and I don't know anything about any guns.' Just then Cooperman said, 'He don't know anything about it and I can prove it.' I says, 'How can you do that?' He said, 'Never mind. I will meet you tomorrow morning . . . and go over with you.' " (Sandler, called as a witness in Zimmerman's behalf, will testify in corroboration, with the weight of fourteen years as a member of the bar behind his words: "During the course of conversation Cooperman was there and present, and said to me that he can prove that Beansy . . . had nothing to do with the investigation . . ." But Cooperman, though recalling the conversation at the Tammany Club, denies having told Sandler he knew of Zimmerman's innocence and states: "I didn't go to see no lawyer. Zimmerman went to see his lawyer. He was talking to him . . . I just told him [Sandler] that he [Zimmerman] wanted me to go to the D.A.'s office.")

At the end of the evening Zimmerman goes home to sleep in his own bed, with the intention of reporting in the morning, as Bambrick has requested, to the District Attorney's office. But before they separate, Popeye says: " 'You going down to the District Attorney's office tomorrow? I will go down with you. I will be up your house [sic] to wake you and

we will go from there.' " And on the morning of the fourth,
though Popeye does not keep his date to wake Zimmerman,
he will appear at the District Attorney's office, where Zimmerman sees him.
Zimmerman's arrest follows thereafter.

Detective Wandling testifies to a brief conversation with
Zimmerman in the hallway separating two offices at the District Attorney's office on June 3. Zimmerman has a half-hour
wait ahead before he will give his first statement. "I said to
him, 'Why don't you tell the truth about this thing?' He says,
'I don't have anything to do with this.' He says, 'I thought
you picked me up for that drugstore killing down on Monroe
and Scammel Street.' So I said, 'Well, you know something
about the guns in this case, and I know you do.' And he says,
'Well, the only thing we did,' he says, 'we took the guns out
of the hallway, and,' he says, 'we bunked [concealed] them,
sold them on Footke, and,' he says, 'we had him crazy, running around in circles, looking for the guns.' I said, 'What
hallway did you take them out of?' He said, 'Next to Golden's
on Clinton Street [that is, 201 Clinton].' So then I went in
and I informed Lieutenant Kiernan of this and he relayed
that to the District Attorney."
   After Zimmerman's arrest on June 4, he goes to the Eliza-
beth Street station house for booking, and then to the Ninth
Street station house to be fingerprinted. Testifies Wandling:
"I took him out to the men's room there to wash his hands,
and he said to me, 'A fine pickle I'm in, Bill.' I said, 'Well, I
told you to tell the truth over there in the D.A.'s office,' and
he said, 'Yeah, tell the truth and be marked lousy for the
rest of my life on the East Side.' I said, 'Well, it's up to you.'
He says, 'Ah, I'll beat this rap.' "
   Whatever the jury may think of Popeye Cooperman and
Danny Rose, the credentials of Wandling as a witness seem
unassailable. In one conversation reported by Wandling,
Zimmerman declines to "tell the truth" and talks of "beating

the rap"—hardly the language of an innocent man. And in the other exchange with Wandling, he mentions taking the guns out of 201 Clinton Street, tying himself to the chain of guilt along which the guns travel.

Zimmerman's lawyer attacks. Cross-examining Wandling, he asks, "Did this defendant tell you that he had taken any guns out of 201 Clinton Street?" Wandling: "Yes; he didn't say 201; he said the doorway next to Golden's [a store next door to 201]." "He told you that he took them out of the doorway next to Golden's?" "Right." "He told you that he had done it, is that correct?" "He said, 'we,' either 'we' or 'I.' " Murray, pressing: "Now, what did he say?" Wandling: "Either 'we'—" " 'I' or 'we'?" Wandling: "I just don't remember whether it was 'we' or 'I.' " Murray: "Well, you knew that was a crucial point in the case, didn't you? [No answer from Wandling.] Didn't you?" Wandling: "At that time, no."

If Zimmerman used the word "I," he admits to handling the guns at a crucial juncture and confirms the charges of the prosecution. If he used the word "we," he merely admits to the knowledge that Rose removed the guns at one point with the consequence that Footke was "crazy, running around in circles," in which case the prosecution still has to demonstrate his connection with the felony. "I": Zimmerman may be guilty; "we": Zimmerman may be innocent. The difference is all-important. Unless Wandling is positive of the pronoun, his testimony against Zimmerman is inaccurate, therefore, false; "peddling perjury" is the term used by Murray. Wandling is not positive of his pronoun: the term used by Zimmerman may have been "we."

The admission, in the mouth of a police officer, does no harm to the prosecution; if anything, it tends to establish objectivity on Wandling's part. For Zimmerman the damage is done, and it is irretrievable. The jury is not likely to overlook the honest testimony of a police officer with twenty-two years' service, because of a quibble about pronouns.

The two short statements made on June 3 and 4 are introduced as evidence for the prosecution. That they play a
decisive part in the jury's assessment of Zimmerman's responsibility may be deduced from the fact that, early in their
deliberation, the jurymen request that the text of both statements, previously read into the record, be repeated for them.

The gist of the first statement: Zimmerman, acknowledging
his nickname to be "Beansie," recalls seeing Danny Rose
around 11:00 P.M. on April 9 at the Scammel Street Boys'
Club, where a dance is under way. Rose mentions having
loaned his coat and hat, as well as a gun, to Footke. Zimmerman offers his assistance, solicited by Rose, in recovering the
hat and coat. In the street Rose mentions to Zimmerman his
opinion that Footke has concealed guns in a hallway on Clinton and East Broadway. Zimmerman: "Well, look and see
if they are there." Rose looks inside the hallway, which
Zimmerman knows to be catercorner across the intersection
from Muskin's Restaurant, and confirms their presence there.
Zimmerman: "Well, take them and keep them and don't say
nothing to him [Footke] . . . I will wait here on the corner
until he comes and I will get your hat and coat." Zimmerman
waits on the street corner for Footke, whom he instructs to
return Rose's hat and coat. On his way back to the club
Zimmerman is reaccosted by Footke, who asks him if he has
taken any "pieces"—by which he means guns—out of the
hallway. On Beansy's disclaimer, Footke goes to the club,
collects Rose, and returns. Rose indicates to Zimmerman
that he does not want Footke to be told he has taken the
guns. Zimmerman obliges: Footke "was walking around in
circles for a half-hour." Then Zimmerman tells Danny Rose
to return the guns to Footke. Rose, according to Zimmerman,
"got them out of the hallway and he went back up to the
club with them." Whether Rose returns the guns to Footke
is unclear to Zimmerman, but he is satisfied that Footke has
returned Rose's hat and coat "because Danny came down
wearing it."

In this, his first statement, Zimmerman acknowledges

knowing of the guns' existence, and knowing in what building Rose claims to have concealed them. He does not, however, acknowledge handling them, nor does he know of the felonious use for which they were ultimately intended.

The gist of the second statement: Rose, meeting with Zimmerman, tells him there are guns hidden at 201 Clinton Street without telling him what purpose they are to serve. He does mention, however, that Footke has knowledge of them. Zimmerman: " 'Take them and keep them; and do whatever you want with them.' . . . All I was interested in was getting back . . . the coat and hat." Danny, not Zimmerman, goes into the hallway of 201; what he does with the guns is unknown to Zimmerman, who does not tell him he is foolish to turn them over to Footke and who does not, himself, turn them over to Popeye. Zimmerman denies meeting with Popeye in connection with the guns, though he does admit to having seen him "quite a few times" at the poolroom where he works. Some fifteen or twenty minutes after Danny Rose removes the guns from their hiding place, Footke appears on the scene; on Zimmerman's instruction Danny denies having removed them; and half an hour later, on Zimmerman's instruction to return them, advises Footke he has removed the guns. Zimmerman does not see Rose return the guns; he goes to have a soda, leaving Footke and Rose together on the street corner. He does not see Rose again until Sunday night, at the poolroom. Saturday he spends lounging around at home. He sees Popeye Cooperman—with whom he has no conversation concerning a holdup—at the poolroom on Friday night, and then again the same night after the interlude with Footke and Rose. After the Friday night in question, he never discusses the guns or the holdup—about which he learns for the first time through the papers Saturday afternoon around four—or those who took part in the holdup.

In this, his second statement, Zimmerman acknowledges a conversation with Footke, but maintains it had to do with Rose's hat and coat, not with guns. (Footke, on the stand, agrees that his conversation with Zimmerman did not relate to guns, except for his question as to whether Zimmerman had removed any "pieces" from the hallway.) And, as in his first statement, Zimmerman acknowledges having known there were guns hidden, but continues to deny having handled them or having knowledge of the felony for which they were intended.

Two points are made by Zimmerman's counsel in connection with the two statements of June 3 and 4. The first concerns the manner in which they were recorded by police stenographers Herman Schmarion and James Sheridan. In the course of the question-and-answer sessions with Zimmerman there were a number of interruptions: telephones would ring and be answered; a police officer would be sent from the room on the instructions of McGuire or Delehanty to check on this or that, would return, leave again; there would be confidential consultations in plain view of Zimmerman on matters naturally not divulged to him, and, on occasion, asides to the stenographer of the variety, "This is off the record," "Don't put that down," and to Zimmerman injunctions to "Answer that question a different way." One consequence of this procedure is that the accuracy of the stenographic record adduced in evidence against Zimmerman is, in the eyes of Murray, open to question. For example, Zimmerman testifies during the trial: "Well, I wanted to say that when they asked me what happened with the guns [relating to Rose's concealment of them from Footke], I wanted to say then that I said, 'Take them and get rid of them.' Instead, Gallagher said to wait a minute. And Mr. Delehanty says, 'Keep that off the record.' And then he says, 'Well . . . now continue in a different vein.' . . . And then I said, 'Well, take them and do whatever you want with them.' " In the stenographic record the statement attributed to Zimmerman is, accordingly, "Take them and do whatever you want with them." No such discrepancy, however minor it may seem, is trivial when the life of the accused may depend on it.

The second point made by Zimmerman's counsel, Murray, in questioning his client on the stand concerns the circumstances under which the statements were taken. On June 3, before being questioned, Zimmerman recounts a conversation with McGuire, alone, in the corridor outside his office: " 'Well,' he says to me, 'what do you know about the case?' I says, 'Mr. McGuire, I don't know anything about the case.' He says, 'Well, you see them detectives in the room there? . . . A mate of theirs was shot and they are pretty mad. If you go in and say that, well, I shudder to think of what is going to happen to you.' I said, 'Well, Mr. McGuire, I can't —I don't know anything about it; and what can I say?' He says, 'Well, you better have some kind of a plausible story,' and just when he said that, he said, 'Listen, I don't care whether you are the man who fired the shot that killed Detective Foley, as long as you can help us and do what we want to find the missing link, I promise you complete immunity.' So I says, 'Well, what can I do?' He says, 'Well, go in there and give some kind of a plausible story.' I says, 'All right.' "

So Zimmerman, asked questions, gives answers as recorded —inaccurately, he contends—in the first statement, and is then dismissed by the District Attorney's office. But before leaving, he testifies, there is a second conversation. "Lieutenant Kiernan took me out and brought me to a different room. He says to me, 'Supposing we release you. Do you think you could find out about the missing link?' I says, 'Lieutenant . . . I don't know anything about it. How can I find out?' He says, 'I am going to release you in Detective Bambrick's custody, and I want you to go around the neighborhood and try to find out about the missing link.' I says, 'All right.' And then I went downstairs to Detective Bambrick."

Not so, says the prosecution; no such promise of immunity was made by McGuire to Zimmerman, and no such instructions given by Kiernan to Zimmerman. Both men so testify. But Kiernan's testimony—that he was absent at the time, and so could not have held any such conversation with Zimmerman—is pointed out by Murray to be elsewhere at variance with the account given by the police stenographer of the conditions under which the first statement was taken. And

McGuire's denial that he ever promised immunity to Zimmerman is the testimony of a man who is, literally, dying. Brought to court on a stretcher, in the grip of an incurable disease which has brought his weight from 218 to 111 pounds in a matter of months, McGuire is not—contends Murray— a fit subject for cross-examination. If Zimmerman's contention is to be soundly refuted, Detective Bambrick can do it by simply stating the conditions under which Zimmerman was discharged in his custody. The prosecution does not call him, however.

"Here," says Murray, "is a man charged with murder . . . And what do they do? 'Isidore, go home. Be easy. Go home. Go out with Detective Bambrick and try to find the missing link.' Where is Detective Bambrick? Was he produced here as a witness? Is that the conduct of a district attorney's office and a police department that believes Zimmerman is guilty? Isn't that the conduct of a district attorney that did just what Zimmerman says . . . McGuire did do—'try to help supply the missing link; nothing will happen to you.'

"Bambrick," continues Murray, "a member of the Police Department with a suspected murderer put into his custody . . . says, 'Go home, Isidore. Go home,' he says. 'You're all right. You didn't do anything. I know you didn't do anything. Go home,' he says. 'I did not sleep for two nights, and I will meet you in the morning.' So this man that is accused . . . of the murder of a police officer is turned loose in the streets of New York. Is this conduct consistent with the position and statement of Zimmerman that he was told he was not accused, and that if he helped supply the missing link that he was O.K.? So he is footloose, conscious of his own innocence.

". . . And he could have disappeared again around the corner; some place in New York where they will never see him again; where you may see your brother today and you may move to the Bronx and he never see you again or you him. What did he do? He is waiting down here at the District Attorney's office at ten o'clock the next morning . . . Is that the conduct of a guilty man?"

And at ten o'clock the next morning, testifies Zimmerman,

McGuire again speaks to him in private. "Mr. McGuire says to me [referring to his statement of June 3], 'Well, you're doing fine so far but you're not really helping us. Do you intend to help us?' I said, 'I will try to help as much as I can. I don't know anything about it. Everything I am saying is just imagination.' He says, 'Well, don't let that worry you. I told you I would promise you complete immunity, whatever you say won't bother you or won't hurt you.' I said, 'All right.' "

District Attorney Delehanty then begins to take a second statement from Zimmerman: "You didn't tell us the whole story yesterday. Did you want to start over again and tell the story from the time you met Footke and Danny Rose in Clinton Street on the night of April 9, before Detective Foley was shot Friday night?" Zimmerman answers: "I didn't say I didn't tell you the whole story. I said, I am going out and try to find out about the missing link, and so I went around the neighborhood and I couldn't find anything there." Then, again with interruptions, consultations, asides and comments of the nature of "That's off the record" and "Don't use those words," he gives a second statement, deemed grounds for his arrest.

In neither statement does Zimmerman acknowledge even having seen the guns he is charged with procuring.

======

There is one more troubling element in the dossier of Zimmerman's defense: three witnesses will testify to an incident presenting curious parallels with Popeye's declaration at the Downtown Tammany Club that he could prove Zimmerman had nothing to do with the Foley case. They are Mrs. Ann Goldstein, a social worker connected with the Madison House, a settlement house located on the corner of Jefferson and Madison streets; Mr. Harry Levy, a practicing member of the New York Bar, who donates his free time and professional skills as a legal adviser to Madison House; and Hyman Liebowitz, lawyer and alumnus of the settlement house, and currently a member of the city's Corporation Counsel. Like

Mrs. Goldstein and Mr. Levy, he is devoted to the program at Madison House. The six-story brick building is bound up with the needs of the East Side community; members—adults and children alike—can avail themselves of the club's facilities, which include a library, classrooms, sports equipment, and playing areas. For members requiring specialized guidance, the staff includes psychologists, sociologists, and others capable of competent counsel.

Now Zimmerman's mother, after her son's arrest, turns for advice to Mrs. Goldstein, a family friend. The two women discuss the problem, and shortly after their conversation Mrs. Goldstein is visited in her Madison House office by a young man named Miller, of whom she knows next to nothing— not even whether he is a friend of Zimmerman's. Miller states to Mrs. Goldstein that he knows a boy with some knowledge of the Foley case as it involves Zimmerman: Danny Rose. Mrs. Goldstein asks Miller to bring Rose to her office, and makes arrangements for him to meet Harry Levy, who in Madison House is regarded not as a lawyer but as a "boys' counselor."

Harry Levy has originally been acquainted with the case through the efforts of Mrs. Goldstein; as a member of the bar he has even been permitted to meet with Zimmerman, then awaiting trial, in Tombs Prison. Their meeting took place sometime in September, 1937, and on the basis of their conversation, in conjunction with the urging of Mrs. Goldstein, his colleague at Madison House, he agrees to a further exploratory meeting with Rose and also with Footke, who are to be contacted through Miller. Footke does not respond to Levy's overture; Rose does, sometime in late October or November of 1937.

Present at the meeting in Mrs. Goldstein's second-floor office are Rose, Levy, Hyman Liebowitz—a friend of Levy's— and, intermittently coming and going, Mrs. Goldstein. Levy is not acting on Zimmerman's instructions. There is no lawyer-client relationship between them, nor will there be— but he has been asked to help, and his help is voluntary. In

his words, "I couldn't in good conscience go ahead and help
Zimmerman unless I was sure in my own mind that Zimmerman was innocent." And in the course of their conversation,
testifies Levy, "Rose told me very definitely, very positively
and conclusively, that Zimmerman knew nothing at all about
the whole thing." Leibowitz, on the witness stand, provides
corroboration.

Levy, under oath: "I asked Rose what connection Zimmerman had with the crime. He told me positively that Zimmerman had no connection whatsoever with the crime. He
outlined for me the story of what had transpired on the night
of the murder. He told me how he had brought it [the .38]
down to the boys' club [Scammel Street] on Henry Street, a
little above Clinton Street; how he had turned the gun over
to a boy by the name of Footke; how, when he turned the
gun over, Footke had opened a coat that he was wearing
and had placed the gun in a shoulder holster, I believe, under
his arm and at the same time, he saw a tremendously big
gun that Footke had in his belt; that the two went together
to a place on Suffolk Street, a building I happen to know—
because I know the neighborhood—right opposite Seward
Park, with a high stoop; that they tried to hide the guns there
underneath some refuse; that a woman came out and scared
them away; that they then went to Clinton Street near East
Broadway, and that they left the guns underneath a stairway
in the hallway.

"I pressed him a number of times on the connection that
Zimmerman had with the case," testifies Levy. "He repeated
time and time again that Zimmerman had absolutely nothing
to do with it; that the only possible point of contact was
that sometime during the course of the evening Danny Rose
had told Zimmerman that Footke had borrowed his coat and
that Zimmerman and Danny had seen Footke in or outside
of a candy store on the corner of Clinton and East Broadway
[Hanover's], and that at that time Zimmerman had gone over
to Footke and had warned Footke to return Danny Rose's

coat, and that was the only connection he told me that Zimmerman had had with the entire transaction."

Levy is struck with Rose's declarations concerning Zimmerman, but he does not ask Rose for a written statement of the facts disclosed. His capacity is not an official one and he is not acting as Zimmerman's lawyer—in his own words, he is "making an independent investigation for my own conscience." Nevertheless, it is clear to him that Rose's declarations should be relayed to the District Attorney's office. Accordingly, sometime in December, 1937, he approaches a Mr. Mendelson as well as another individual from the office of District Attorney Dewey, possibly from the Homicide Bureau. Levy does not recall the name, but "I remember that gentleman very clearly. He was a very efficient gentleman." He goes to the office on more than one occasion. He telephones as well, and speaks to a Mr. Sarafite, Rosenblum's deputy for the prosecution of the Foley case, whom he may have seen on a visit to the District Attorney's office, though he is uncertain of the name. On one occasion, affirms Levy, he receives a white slip from the receptionist, giving him access to the building's offices. Received by a gentleman in an office, "I told the gentleman my conversation with Rose." There follows a discussion of administrative procedures governing admission to the offices of the District Attorney, but it is inconclusive. There is no record kept of such visits as Levy's. Undeterred, Levy affirms, "I can pick out the office where I was interviewed."

Murray, examining Levy, tries another tack. "Did he [the man responsible for the Foley case, whom Levy requested to see] call a stenographer [in the course of the interview]?" Levy: "No." "Did he take your statement down in writing?" "No." "Did you give your name and address?" "I did, and I gave my telephone number." "And that was to someone representing Mr. Dewey's office, is that right?" "That's so." Levy is no stronger on names than dates: "I asked for Mr. Rosenblum's assistant, a man who was handling this case . . . I

don't remember the name. 'Sarafite' stands out in my mind."
His last visit, he affirms, takes place at least a month before
the beginning of the present trial. He makes no further attempt
to get in touch with the prosecutor after March 24, when the
trial begins, but he is frequently present in court. Murray's
assistant, Poger, visits Levy in his office to apprise him of
Rose's trial testimony.

Levy, Liebowitz, and Mrs. Goldstein appear as witnesses
in Zimmerman's defense.

In many respects the trial is an unusual one. Its duration,
from March 18 to April 14—twenty days of testimony, often
irrelevant, sometimes contradictory, always complex, the
transcript of which covers over 2,400 pages—tries the
patience as well as the physical endurance of all concerned.
Adjourning at lunch hour on April 8, a Friday, Judge Nott
remarks: "I decided [on adjourning at this time] . . . primarily to oblige one of the jurors. I am [now] reinforced in
that decision by the fact that I do not think that you [the
jurors] or I could really stand another afternoon at this time."
Judge Nott has earlier received a letter from Juror Number
Five requesting, because of "the unexpected length of the
case," that he be discharged and replaced by one of the two
alternates. "Without going into detail," runs the letter, "I am
writing to say that my absence for the present period of three
weeks, with another week in prospect, has now become a very
serious matter for my own business life and future. Anything
you [Judge Nott] can do to further expedite the trial will be
greatly appreciated. I realize and appreciate you are doing
everything you can. Incidentally, the length of this trial is an
excellent example of why so many citizens are reluctant to
do jury duty." Counselors for the defense urge that the text
be read into the trial record. The divulgation of such senti-
ments on the part of even a single juror is grounds for Murray
to move for his discharge: ". . . He is impatient and . . . he has
not the dispassionate attitude of mind . . . that every juror

ought to have in any criminal case." For Friedman's lawyer, Impelliteri, it is grounds to move for a mistrial. The Court denies both motions.

To present their case, the People call sixty witnesses, of whom over half a dozen serve to refute O'Loughlin's charges of police brutality and coercion during his hospitalization. The five defendants on trial—Little Benny and Little Chemey are fugitives from justice—will all take the stand, and, exclusive of their own testimony, call twenty-four witnesses: three for Guariglia; four for Friedman, including the toxicologist Munch; two for Guariglia and Friedman jointly, to establish the extent of their injuries; two for O'Loughlin (his mother and a social worker); seven for Chaleff, at least four of whom are straight character witnesses with no knowledge of the felony murder; and six for Zimmerman (three lawyers—Levy, Liebowitz, and Sandler; Ann Goldstein; Ralph Scalogna; and Morris Zimmerman, the defendant's father). Almost every witness for the prosecution is subject to cross-examination by the defense lawyers, who total twelve. The consequence, declares Impelliteri, is that the average juryman "probably feels that defense counsel are prolonging this trial, and not the District Attorney." That five defendants arc simultaneously on trial perhaps makes this inevitable, but the chances of any defendant—already seriously impaired by the very nature of the crime—are certainly none the better for it.

On one lawyer in particular—Mr. Murray, counsel for Zimmerman—this judgment "en masse" weighs onerously. In the opening minutes of the first day of trial he moves for a severance—that is to say, a separate trial for his client. Murray fears that Zimmerman's case will suffer from "guilt by association": put an innocent in the dock with a dozen murderers, and the jury will be inclined quite naturally to credit him with their guilt. In the course of the trial, Murray points out, "Evidence will be offered in connection with . . . [Zimmerman] that will be prejudicial; it will be as far as he is concerned hearsay . . . and will be of such a character that it will be almost impossible for the jurors to differentiate as to the evidence concerning . . . [Zimmerman] . . . It will be unfair and improper for him to be tried with the others."

Every lawyer for the defense follows Murray's lead, contending that the character of the evidence to be presented in connection with the other defendants will deprive his particular client of the fair trial to which he is entitled. But the District Attorney, arguing that the People intend to prove the existence of a conspiracy in which Zimmerman participated, counters that in cases of felony murder such as this, "We feel he [Zimmerman] is as responsible as the others regardless of whether he was in the place [the Boulevard], outside of the place, or miles away from the place." Judge Nott's ruling brings small comfort to Zimmerman. The burden of proof—proof not only that he furnished the guns, but also that he knew the purpose for which they were intended—must be borne by the prosecution. Without that proof, there is no case against Zimmerman; with it, the testimony of the other defendants is admissible against him. In like fashion, Judge Nott denies identical motions for severance made by other lawyers for the defense.

Over and above protracted medical evidence relating to O'Loughlin, Guariglia, and Friedman, and the number of men on trial, another factor contributes to the inordinate length of the proceedings: the testimony—conflicting—of experts. The conclusions of two toxicologists—Dr. Lichtenstein, for the People, contending in essence that Friedman's responsibility in the felony was in no way attenuated by his use of marijuana; and Dr. Munch, for the defense, contending the opposite—may cancel each other out, but they consume time. Another battle of experts is narrowly averted when it is decided that the testimony of Sergeant Henry Butts, founder of the Ballistic Bureau of the New York Police Department—establishing that Scalogna's .38 was in fact fired in the Boulevard during the felony—will not be contested by other ballistic specialists, if only for motives of economy. (On this particular issue Banton, O'Loughlin's lawyer, makes an astonishing statement: "You can't fingerprint a revolver as you can a human being . . . No two human beings are alike, [but] . . . you can't fingerprint a gun as you can the human being's fingers." The proof of this, claims Banton, is simply that in the past Butts's findings have been challenged by other experts —touching testimony to the state of the science of ballistics in 1938!)

When, on the morning of April 5, the People rest their case against the East Side boys, Murray returns to a familiar point: ". . . The defendant Zimmerman asks your Honor to direct a verdict of acquittal on the ground that the People have failed to sustain the allegations in the indictment by legal evidence; on the ground that there is no evidence whatever connecting this defendant with the commission of the crime nor with the conspiracy to commit the crime.

"The only evidence that has been adduced against this defendant is the evidence of Cooperman and Rose, and I ask your Honor now to rule as a matter of law that the testimony of Cooperman, if it is of any value to connect this defendant Zimmerman with the commission of this crime, is testimony of an accomplice, as a matter of law."

Judge Nott: "That I shall hold, that Cooperman is an accomplice."

Murray's point of law is a major one. With Cooperman officially recognized by the Court as an accomplice in Foley's murder, his motives in testifying against Zimmerman become highly suspect; and his testimony is not, in fact, admissible without corroboration from another source.

If Hanover's testimony against Zimmerman is discounted because of its tenuous character, only Danny Rose has provided "corroboration from another source." Murray pushes on: ". . . I ask your Honor to . . . rule that the only other evidence in this case is evidence supplied by a witness named Rose . . . insufficient to supply any corroboration of the testimony of Cooperman . . . And I also ask your Honor to rule as a matter of law that if Rose's testimony be of any value at all, it is the testimony of an accomplice . . ." But having conceded the point where Cooperman is concerned, Judge

Nott declines to make a similar decision concerning Rose. "I do not think I am called upon to rule upon that question at the present time, because whether he [Rose] is an accomplice or not, in my judgment the other matters that the jury might find tended to corroborate Cooperman. The law does not say he must be absolutely corroborated in every way. It says there must be other evidence tending to connect the defendant with the crime." By other evidence, Nott explains, he means Zimmerman's own statements and his conversations with Footke, apart from Rose's testimony. ". . . When a statement is made by the defendant the jury does not have to believe it all or reject it all. They can believe what they like about it . . . The question is . . . whether it tends to connect him with the commission of the crime . . . The weight of the evidence is for the jury. I think there is evidence to submit to them." The motion is denied; the jury will decide. The millstones are still firmly around Zimmerman's neck.

Before his summing-up on behalf of Zimmerman, begun at twelve noon on April 12, Murray makes one last attempt: "The defendant Zimmerman moves that your Honor direct a verdict of acquittal on the ground that the People have failed to sustain by a creditable degree of legal proof the allegations in the indictment; and further on the ground that the testimony against the defendant Zimmerman is that of an accomplice, who is an accomplice as a matter of law, and that there has been no evidence tending to support or corroborate his testimony." The motion is denied. Time is running out.

The last word belongs to Rosenblum, Mr. Dewey's prosecutor for the Homicide Bureau. At half-past two in the afternoon of April 13, he begins his summing-up to the Court and the gentlemen of the jury with a tribute to the general fatigue: "I guess you must be pretty tired by now. I am, frankly, and I think that I owe it to each of you . . . to cut down on my summation with the trust that you will remember the three and a half weeks of evidence . . . produced here." But the

District Attorney will take no chances. Though it was agreed that the summation for each defendant should not exceed ninety minutes, the aggregate time actually spent exceeds ten hours; and Rosenblum, taking two and a half hours to state the case for the prosecution, more than makes up for the time difference with his display of energy, of indignation, of virulence.

For the prosecutor there is "one clean, cold issue": the murder of Foley. "But you [jurymen] found a number of other issues drawn in constantly. Frankly, when I heard the termination of the summation [by the defense] . . . I didn't know whether I should get up and say, 'Is it my time to plead guilty or not guilty to some charge?' I didn't know whether I should call on the police officers and tell them, 'Now, you have been on trial. Maybe you ought to enter some plea in this case.' "

Rosenblum is a professional: "I spent eight or nine years on the other side of the fence [as a defense lawyer] and close to eight years on this side of the fence [as prosecutor]. I know what my duty as an officer of this Court is, and what it means when I took the oath of office to present cases for the People of the State of New York. I owe the defendants a duty, but I don't owe you [the jury] the duty of muddling you up with side issues. I don't owe you the duty to put in a statement which I, in my opinion, let us say, feel does not help you; there is no reason for that."

There is a simple explanation for the raising of these "side issues," or "sideshows" as the prosecutor will call them elsewhere. "You develop sideshows only because the defendants see that they have been so clearly tied into this picture [of the felony]; they are so guilty. I don't think in the history of this old building [111 Centre Street, adjoining the Tombs] that there has ever been a case where the defendants' guilt has been established as fully as this has been. This case is pretty nearly perfect." Guariglia's defense of being retarded, of having been coerced by Little Benny: a sideshow; O'Loughlin's defense that the gun given him by Little Benny was broken and could not have fired, that the police forced confessions from him when he was delirious with pain in a hospital ward: a sideshow. Chaleff, unable to plead police brutality, is harder put to organize his sideshow. ". . . So what does he say? . . . If you recall . . . counsel spent . . . about 40 percent [of his time in summation on] a sympathy plea . . . Don't think for a moment that I haven't got the emotions of sympathy. . . . Any normal being has. I have them and I felt them, as those poor mothers took the stand, as we heard the three mothers and one father testify, I tell you I got a twinge . . . and I knew I could create the same feeling if I put Mrs. Foley on the stand, or his mother or his children . . . That could be played two ways. It is unfair to play it [sympathy]; it is a dangerous weapon, and it is one that sometimes reacts to the detriment of the one who tries it . . . [but] if I permit that to affect me in any way [as District Attorney] I must resign; there is no law giving sympathy as a defense. There is no law which permits me to be affected by sympathy so that I don't do my job, or which permits any juror to violate his oath by not bringing in a verdict which squares with the evidence." Chaleff's defense, says Rosenblum, is "I think the most emotional I ever heard in my life." And when Chaleff's lawyer concludes, with tears in his eyes, Rosenblum is willing to concede that the tears are sincere. But they too are part of the sideshow: ". . . One other thing . . . [Chaleff's lawyer] forgot to point out. There was another statement from Sonny Chaleff; when he was in the lineup, he was asked, 'Were you in this stickup?' And the answer was, 'I was.' "

Sideshows too, for the prosecutor, are the multiple requests by the multiple defense lawyers for the multiple statements taken from the defendants in the Foley case. "There is no rule, no law that can compel me to give up my statements, no more [sic] than I can turn around and look at their statements, and see whether or not the first story [told by a defendant to his lawyer] said anything about marijuana or anything else . . . see whether the defendants then developed some new ideas to tell to their lawyers. I could not call on them, and they could not call on me, and his Honor said, 'I know of

no rule of law which will permit me to direct the District
Attorney to turn over to you that statement,' and I said, 'If
your Honor pleases, in fairness I will do what we have done
. . . in other cases that I tried before your Honor, I am willing
to hand the statement to you.' " This procedure was followed,
for example, in the case of statements, possibly conflicting,
made by Cooperman: Judge Nott was given them by the
prosecution, and enabled to decide on their receivability.
"Other statements were called for by Mr. Murray and by
others," continues Rosenblum. "Every statement that was
called for, every one without a single exception was given
to his Honor, so that his Honor could see whether or not a
witness under oath would mislead you [the jury] and testify
as to an important thing and testify differently in his statement
[made before the trial]. Did they [the defense] want any
others? Why didn't they call for them?" The question is a
rhetorical one, but it will nevertheless be answered—unexpectedly—a quarter of a century later.

Sideshows, contends Rosenblum: the crossings-out and cor-
rections and interruptions in stenographic records of statements
taken by the prosecution. Testimony by the stenographers
and examination of the original transcripts demolish the
charge they do not reflect the absolute truth. Sideshows:
Friedman's defense of being incapable of forming a criminal
intent by reason of his double intoxication, by marijuana
and by alcohol, on the night of Foley's murder. Friedman's
lawyer "never heard of marijuana before you gentlemen [of
the jury] were selected in this case."

Sideshows: the question of whether O'Loughlin's gun was
in working order. Harvey's participation in the felony makes
him as guilty as Chaleff or Zimmerman, neither of whom is
charged with directly taking a life by pulling a trigger, but
with making it possible for a trigger to be pulled. The fire-
power of the task force—five bullets in Friedman's gun, six
bullets Little Benny could fire, six bullets O'Loughlin might
have fired—in concert with a common criminal purpose:
these are the real indices of guilt, and the jury cannot blink

them. Without the chance presence of Foley and Gallagher on the premises that April morning, the half-a-hundred clients in the Bouvelard were quite simply at the mercy of the task force. "Seventeen bullets were there. Every one of these bullets can take a life. Every one of these bullets, if it hit in the proper place, can take a life." That only one life is taken is immaterial; immaterial too the identity of the man who fired the shot that took Foley's life. ". . . It makes no difference. I wouldn't care if you people feel it was Little Benny who fired that shot. Every one of these men are [sic] guilty as though O'Loughlin or any one of them fired the shot. That is the law. That is why we have that law. We want to stop occasions when men with seventeen bullets can start out possibly to take seventeen lives."

Sideshows: the suggestions by counsel that some, at least, of the prosecution's witnesses were perjurers. Dr. Solomon, testifying to Guariglia's physical condition on the night of his arrest: "Why should he commit perjury . . . a young . . . house doctor at Bellevue should commit perjury for whom? For me? Why?" The taxi driver, Dworkin: "Why should he come in and make a story which is false? What interest has he got? . . . Why should [he] commit perjury? . . . Who is . . . forcing everybody to commit perjury? For what reason?" The police officers and the patrons of the Boulevard who testify that Hutch and Dominick were set upon and beaten in the coffeehouse by outraged customers, and not in the station house by outraged police officers: "I assure you I don't think that any District Attorney is putting himself into the hands of any witness and say [sic], 'Commit a little perjury, my brother, because when you commit perjury I am guilty of suborning perjury. You say, because it is important for the People, that it was the customers [who beat up Friedman and Guariglia].' "

Sideshows: the issue that Cooperman, Rose, and even Footke might more fittingly be considered defendants than witnesses for the prosecution. "I don't blame counsel for saying that . . . [but] if you [jurymen] wanted to say the Grand Jury were remiss in their duty when they didn't in their indict-

ment include Danny Rose and Popeye, you can't say it. That
is not the issue before you. That is one of the side issues . . .
You can't say that in your verdict; it is not before you."

Side issues too, the allegations and implications of police
misconduct, police coercion, police brutality. ". . . You heard
counsel time and time again refer to the fact that Gallagher
first shot O'Loughlin in the hand and then sent another one
into his body. I suppose we ought to try him for it; maybe
we ought to prefer charges against him . . . for pulling out
his gun at that time? Let me tell you something about cops.
They could be yellow-bellied if they want to be. Foley and
Gallagher could have left that table . . . and get [sic] out of the
place . . . Instead of that, what did these men do? . . . Foley,
brave officer that he was, started going for his gun . . .
Gallagher put his life in danger, didn't he? Foley . . . put
his life in danger . . . Those men tried to do their jobs . . . as
a cop should do his job. And what do you find? Vilification—
vilification. You hear nothing but attacks, attacks, attacks on
the police. On the police! Why? The defendants don't like the
job that they did."

O'Loughlin's lawyer has been at pains to justify his client's
refusal to "inform." Nonsense, says Rosenblum: O'Loughlin
was the first to give the police their leads—names, physical
descriptions—to Little Benny, Little Chemey, Sonny Chaleff.
". . . Detective Wandling and Detective Sullivan got the story
[given by O'Loughlin] . . . They pieced it together. They went
to this source, got the information, got the second name, located 33 Canal, found Chaleff had been a fugitive from his
home—because that is what he was for three or four days,
and that shows consciousness of guilt . . . The detectives in
this case went out and pieced this job together. So for that
what do we find? An attack on Wandling, the perjurer."
Where is the incentive for a police officer to be conscientious
in the execution of his duty? "I say, gentlemen, by your verdict
. . . you must . . . indicate quite clearly that such work [by the
police] should be commended." The arguments advanced by

the defense along these lines simply do not make sense to Rosenblum. "But what else can they do?"

Nor can the defendants' youth be offered in extenuation of their crime. "It is a fact that between the ages of eighteen and twenty-five . . . you find the greatest number of criminals. You don't find men with beards going out to make stickups. The law is designed to stop anybody from going out, regardless of their age, so long as they reach the age where the law holds them responsible." Nor can the defendants be presented as unfortunate victims of a callous society. "They had schooling . . . They went to the Educational Alliance . . . to the Madison Street House. Good institutions. I certainly would testify to that. I belonged to it [sic] too . . . They had religious guidance . . . When Guariglia wanted work, he worked, as he told you, one job after another. But when he wanted to participate in the commission of a felony, to rob and steal, he did that. They all had jobs when they wanted. O'Loughlin . . . had a job with the W.P.A. for a while. You and I and everybody else paid him money so that he could go out and pay forty cents a drink, when he has a wife and child he is supposed to take care of . . . when he had the money from his pay envelope." President Garfield, dying from an assassin's bullet, did not get the medical care that society gave to O'Loughlin—society saved Harvey's life. Society gave the defendents eighteen lawyers, "the best men of the Bar, pretty near," for their defense, claims Rosenblum; society pays for the testimony of ballistics experts, toxicologists, psychiatrists, spares no expense. "But it would seem that the defendants had taken the position that society had not treated them well. Therefore, they were given the right to rob and the right to kill."

Unacceptable, says Rosenblum, is any defense tied to a consideration of the milieu of which the "East Side boys" are a product. "They told you about the East Side. Some of the counsel right here come from the East Side. Some of them live within a few blocks. You have criminals on the East Side, on the West Side, on Upper Manhattan, and other places. Rich men have gone to jail within the last week when they violated the law. If you want to be decent you can live anywhere . . . Of the three men who work with me on this case—I am not ashamed to tell you—one was a conductor, and the other worked on hats, and one . . . shined shoes and sold papers on Mulberry Street . . . and I lived down there on the East Side, going to law school . . . If you want to go out and violate the law, you can do it. But you can't say 'East Side.' . . . With what right can they [the defendants] say that the law says because they lived on the East Side they may go out and take other people's money and commit robberies and if . . . people interfere with them they may kill . . . ? There is no such law."

Circumstances exist, says Rosenblum, under which the sentence of imprisonment for life may be recommended—rather than death in the electric chair—for parties guilty of a felony murder. But no such circumstances exist here, and no such recommendation is possible: seventeen bullets, recalls Rosenblum; perhaps seventeen lives. "All five had knowledge of the guns. They knew the guns were going to be used. For what? Why didn't they take the bullets out? Why have I got these bullets here [as evidence]? They knew they were going to be used to effect their purpose, and if there was interference those guns would be used, as they were used, to take life. And I say to you that where that is so clear, where people start out against the law, that they start out merely for the purpose of committing a felony, and life is taken by anyone, then . . . under those circumstances each and every one of them is as guilty as the man who fired the shot.

"And I don't care who fired it . . .

"I say they are not entitled to a recommendation."

It is nearly five-thirty in the afternoon. With the briefest of recesses, District Attorney Rosenblum has been talking since two thirty-five. Now, to conclude his summation, he will exorcise the final danger with which the prosecution must contend. "You have heard so much about this business of sympathy. You have seen, I think, the greatest exhibition of sympathy that could be exhibited: mothers brought here, fainting. I feel sorry for them. I do. I tell you I do. Sometimes

I could not get up to examine when I looked at one of the mothers out in the hall. I tell you frankly I would not look at any before I came in here, because sympathy might affect me. You mustn't. You mustn't. If you permit sympathy to affect you, then your verdict cannot be a fair one and a decent one, and it does not square with the evidence.

"... In many cases ... to identify the body of the deceased ... they call the wife or the orphan child or the mother. You did not see Foley's mother on the stand. You can't pick out Mrs. Foley, the widow, and she is in this courtroom." These are methods of gaining the jurors' sympathy, says Rosenblum, which are unfair to the accused. "I would not permit it ... You [jurors] might have had so much sympathy because of that widowed wife, the mother, and the orphan child, that you might have returned a verdict of guilty when the evidence did not warrant it ..." Alluding to the "great appeal for sympathy" made by Chaleff's lawyer, Rosenblum continues, "It plays no part; it does not. We must do our jobs. It is a tough thing to do; I know it is tough. I know it is hard.

"But, gentlemen, if the facts and circumstances warrant it, you have no choice, because you are being watched, in the sense hundreds and hundreds and thousands of other people ... are waiting to see [whether] you by your verdict are going to say, 'You may with impunity violate the law, you may concoct defenses, you may go out and commit crimes and commit felonies, you may kill; and then if you have the sympathy you may be acquitted.'"

This is the moment toward which everything, for three and a half weeks, has been leading. It comes as no surprise, but it is no less terrible for being expected. "I think I can rely on your observations that I have been very fair in this case. I owe it to myself, no one else. I am asking for a serious penalty ... I don't want my conscience to bother me at any time of my life. I am asking you to send five men to the electric chair."

Rosenblum asks the jury for a verdict of murder in the first degree, without a recommendation.

At 12:02 the jury retires to deliberate.

At 2:45 the jury returns to the courtroom, requesting that

Zimmerman's two statements, dated June 3 and June 4, be read to them. The reading takes ten minutes. At 2:57 the jury retires for a second time.

At 3:30 the jurors file back into the courtroom. The court clerk reads the roll call: "Reed, Nelson, Harris, Wilson . . ." The clerk requests the jurors to rise. "Jurors, look upon the defendants; defendants, look upon the jurors. Gentlemen of the jury, have you agreed upon a verdict as to the defendant Dominick Guariglia?"

Down the line: Guariglia, guilty; O'Loughlin, guilty; Friedman, guilty; Chaleff, guilty. To the forgotten man, the last man alphabetically, the last man to know his fate: Isidore Zimmerman.

The clerk: "How say you: do you find the defendant Isidore Zimmerman guilty or not guilty?"

The foreman: "Guilty."

The clerk: "Hearken unto your verdict as it stands recorded: you say that you find the defendant Isidore Zimmerman guilty of murder in the first degree, whereof he stands indicted, and so say you all."

The last word belongs to Judge Nott, eight days later, when sentence is pronounced. "The judgment of the Court is that you, and each of you, Dominick Guariglia, Joseph Harvey O'Loughlin, Arthur Friedman, Philip Chaleff, and Isidore Zimmerman, for the murder in the first degree of one Michael J. Foley, whereof you are convicted, be and you hereby are sentenced to the punishment of death; and it is ordered that within ten days after this day's session of the Court, the Sheriff of the County of New York deliver you, and each of you, together with the warrants of this Court to the Warden of the Sing Sing Prison, at Ossining, New York, where you shall be kept in solitary confinement until the week beginning Monday, the 30th day of May, 1938, and upon some day within the week so appointed the said Warden of the Sing Sing Prison at Ossining, New York, is commanded to do execution upon you, and each of you, Dominick Guariglia, Joseph Harvey O'Loughlin, Arthur Friedman, Philip Chaleff and Isidore Zimmerman . . ."

CHAPTER 3

THE
WAIT—part I

AFTER THREE AND A HALF HOURS I knew the worst. Twelve good men and true had decided I was just as guilty of Detective Michael Foley's death as if I'd pulled the trigger myself. Guilty right along with Harvey O'Loughlin, Hutch Friedman, Dominick Guariglia, and Sonny Chaleff. Judge Nott had explained the reasons in his charge to the jury, and my counsel, Mr. Murray, had explained it to me before the trial began: let a hundred men together entertain the idea of a felony that only one of them is foolish enough to commit, and in the eyes of the law all are equally guilty. I could see why there might be need for a law like that, but I could see even better why it shouldn't be applied to me. Despite the pretty package District Attorney Rosenblum had wrapped up for the prosecution, I'd neither had advance knowledge of the holdup at Willie the Dutchman's, nor had I taken any part in the holdup operations that cost Detective Foley's life. As far as that went, I'd never even set foot in the Boulevard Restaurant.

Still, "Guilty" was what the foreman of the jury had said. And I knew very well what that meant. The death sentence was mandatory. We were all headed for the electric chair; and when, in a week's time—Friday, April 22—we next appeared before Judge Nott, the news he'd have for us would be no surprise to anyone; it was just a matter of finding out what week they planned to electrocute us. That was something

I preferred not to think about. If I'd been guilty it would have been bad enough; knowing I was innocent made it intolerable.

When the verdict was announced I simply refused to believe it. Day after day I'd sat in court with the others, watching the hands of the clock creeping toward five; day after day for twenty days, hearing testimony by strangers, about strangers; day after day when my name was never even mentioned. Murray had been right when he referred to me as "the forgotten man" in the "trial of the East Side boys"—the label the press hung on us—but the jury, taking its cue from Prosecutor Rosenblum, didn't seem inclined to forget me. Others had been forgotten, though: Little Benny Ertel and Little Chemey were guilty, at least on paper, but nobody expected them to show up in time to be electrocuted at Sing Sing with the rest of us out of sheer loyalty. And Popeye Cooperman? And Danny Rose? If I was guilty, why weren't they? And if nobody in the D.A.'s office had even remembered to bring charges against them, why was I sitting there, waiting at the age of nineteen to be sentenced to death by an old man in a black robe for something I hadn't done? Something had gone wrong, and it seemed to be too late for correction at this point.

Mr. Murray had been right too in trying to get a separate trial for me. If his motion had succeeded, if a jury had been permitted to judge my case separately, to divorce it from the climate of outrage over Foley's murder, he was confident my acquittal would have been assured. But Murray's motion had been denied, and the implication left by the prosecution had been something like "guilt by association"; the jurors had to feel that if I was in the dock alongside O'Loughlin and Friedman, or even if I was there in place of Little Benny or Izzy Perlmutter, I must be just as guilty as the rest. Just after the verdict was announced, Murray made another motion in my favor—that the verdict as it applied to me be set aside as a travesty of justice. Motion denied: Murray was just going through the motions. One more setback for me—one of a series—in a fight I was losing on points.

They put the cuffs on to take us back to the Tombs. The papers said we "made a pretense of unconcern" when the verdict was announced. Poker faces in court, or smirks; and on the way back to our cells jokes, laughter; even singing. When the papers weren't calling us bloodthirsty killers they were calling us kids, but we were kids trying to act like men. Friday was a whole week away, we told ourselves; something good was bound to happen in the meantime. But if the others were like me, then deep down inside they were scared to death.

During the week we waited in the Tombs for sentencing nothing much happened to change the routine. After the verdict they decided to move us up Murderers' Row close to the office, where they could keep an eye on us now that it was official we were killers: Chaleff in a cell by himself because he was still going off to Bellevue, as he had been throughout the trial, to be treated for his diabetes; Friedman and Guariglia together; and O'Loughlin and I sharing a cell. Mornings at nine they opened the cell doors—that was the beginning of our day. We'd take turns mopping, making up the bunks, and by ten o'clock the breakfast—ordered from the commissary the night before—would be delivered, along with the morning papers—paid for in advance—and we'd read them from the first page to the last, even the ads. The Giants evened a series with the Indians, 6 to 6; Loew's State was advertising its big Easter show featuring what it called "the nation's leading vaudeville": Rudy Vallee and his Connecticut Yankees were on stage, and the film was something with Charlie McCarthy and Edgar Bergen called *Goldwyn Follies*. Chaliapin died; the Eighth Chinese Army was busy attacking Japanese troop concentrations in Shansi Province; and the city of New York had just completed erection of a four-and-a-half foot fence designed to discourage jaywalking in Times Square. Anything that had to do with our case I devoured, and I remember feeling special discouragement as I read a declaration by District Attorney Thomas Dewey when Rosenblum advised him of the verdict involving us: "Robbery with a gun and murder are at last becoming unsafe in New York County. There have been eight convictions for murder in the first degree in the county so far this year as compared with two convictions for murder in the first degree for the entire year of 1937." I could see how the District Attorney would want to bring murderers to justice, but I didn't care for his purely statistical view of the question: the more convictions, the better—apparently—his batting average. By his logic, a good year would be one in which lots of murders were committed, and a slack season in crime would make for long faces in Albany.

The others kept telling me, as they had from the beginning, that there was no reason why I should contribute to improving the D.A.'s batting average. "We're involved, sure," they'd say, "right up to the neck. But what are you doing here with us? You had nothing to do with it." When I was down, that kind of talk only made me feel more down. "They've got me this far, haven't they?" I'd say. "Then why shouldn't they take me all the way to the chair?" One black morning I remember saying to O'Loughlin: "If they want to electrocute me, they're welcome. I'm fed up. I just hope they get it over with soon." When I talked like that to O'Loughlin or Friedman or Chaleff as we walked around and around the tiers for exercise—two hours in the morning and two again in the afternoon, if we chose—they'd say, "Don't worry, Beansy, the Court of Appeals will reverse it. Don't worry, kid—we've all told our lawyers you had nothing to do with it." That kind of talk, if I concentrated on it hard enough, would get me feeling optimistic again—that plus the knowledge of my innocence, which was getting easier and easier to forget in that atmosphere. Optimistic enough, anyway, so that when a visit came I could keep smiling for the thirty minutes or so it lasted, and convince my visitor of what I didn't quite believe myself—the possibility, the certainty, of a happy ending.

Actually, it didn't make much difference how I looked during visiting hours. There were two thick wire-mesh screens separated by about six feet of air space, and visibility was so poor you could hardly make out your visitor's face. You sat in a little open booth partitioned on each side like a urinal and shouted across the air space and through the two thicknesses of mesh. You shouted because there were identical open booths on either side of you, and other prisoners shouting too, to make themselves heard over your voice. The tumult could be heard in the corridors all over the floor, long before you reached the visiting room. There was only one way to try to beat the noise: get a booth at the end of the room, against the wall. Most of the guards, knowing we were headed for the death house, tried to give us an end booth during visiting hours.

My first visitor after the verdict was my mother. She was crying, and trying not to. I wanted to reach out, to hug her, touch her, smooth her hair. All I could do was repeat the words the others kept telling me: "Don't worry, Mama, don't worry. There's a Court of Appeals—they'll reverse my conviction. It's just a matter of time before I'm home again. Be patient—please don't cry, Mama . . ." By the time the end of the visit rolled around, Mama had stopped crying and I was beginning to believe myself. But it was always the same: back to the tier, to my cell, listening to the others, and then my heart would sink again. "Who am I kidding with this talk about a reversal?" I'd ask myself. "You've got to have money; you've got to be somebody, know somebody. They've taken me this far, and they're going to take me all the way, to the death house."

Once a day the prison cashier would come by and give me two dollars, the official limit for expenses, and I'd sign a receipt for my allowance. Meals delivered to the cell cost around thirty-five cents. They were adequate, and so I didn't bother to go to the mess hall. In the morning I'd order lunch; dinner at lunchtime; and at dinner, breakfast for the day following. Around quarter to three there'd be the man from the commissary with a basket of sandwiches, orange juice and milk, candy bars, magazines—I got interested in *Flying Aces of the World War*—and the evening papers at two or three cents a copy. By three o'clock my day was over. They'd lock the door on us till the next morning, when it began all over again. Eighteen hours—3:00 P.M. to 9:00 A.M.—is a long stretch for a man in a cage.

Harvey and I would play cards, or checkers, and talk about the case. He'd read my paper and I'd read his. We could talk to people in the tiers above and below our cell, but reading was my salvation then; every magazine, every book, I got hold of was given the cover-to-cover treatment. There were no radios allowed, no loudspeaker system. From the second floor of Murderers' Row we could see a little of the street outside, the people passing, the street lights coming on. When finally I could fall asleep, I was happy—it meant that for a while at least I wouldn't be thinking.

Weekends, the timetable was just about the same. We got up at eight instead of nine on Sunday for the benefit of those attending services. But there were no visitors allowed on either Saturday or Sunday, so the weekend was the hardest period to get through. And on Sunday there was no commissary—just the papers, if you'd thought to order them the day before.

But if the hands of the clock never seemed to move, the date on the calendar kept changing. On April 22 at 10:00 A.M. we were lined up again in front of Judge Nott, and this time I think we looked the part: scared kids with drawn faces, pale, searching the faces in the crowd for a sight of our mothers. But there were no mothers in sight, or sisters either, when sentence was pronounced. The D.A.'s office had decided to avoid unpleasant scenes and excluded them from the court-room. The D.A.'s office was probably right. Later on, we heard about the weeping and shrieking and wailing that had gone on in the corridor just outside when the bad news was relayed to the women. From where I stood I could see my father and my brother Carl, and the look on their faces made me glad my mother wasn't there with them.

The spectacle was impressive. I think it was there that I felt for the first time what people mean when they talk about the "majesty of the law." It made me think of something heavy, huge, and irresistible, like a glacier moving down a mountainside. Each of us had been assigned a uniformed attendant by the court; he stood, generally a head taller than the man he was guarding, just behind us. Then there was a swarm of lawyers, more lawyers than defendants. The court assigned three for the defense of each one of the accused, and guaranteed them a fee of $1,000, to be split three ways. Looking at some of their faces that morning, seeing their fatigue after the long trial, I had the sudden feeling—the frightening feeling—that for some of them the ceremony of sentencing was just the welcome end of a tiresome job that had lasted much too long and involved too much work, but a job that, like any other, had to be gone through with. It also occurred to me that $333 might well be too little to pay a man for safeguarding another man's life—too little, or perhaps in some cases too much. The courtroom was jammed. One after another, in alphabetical order, the judge called on us to rise. I was the last, as usual, but not the least. By the time my turn came I'd given up hoping for surprises. The judge, a tiny little man with bushy gray hair, didn't seem to me any taller than five feet or so, even on his perch high above everyone else in the courtroom, but his piercing gray eyes, raking one defendant after another, were all he needed to throw a chill into my heart. "You have been found guilty of murder in the first degree," he would intone in a flat voice after reading the name of the accused. "Have you anything to say before sentence is pronounced on you?" Generally, counsel for the accused would answer for his client, moving to set aside the verdict on grounds of insufficient evidence or some such technicality, reserving the right to appeal. None of them showed too much conviction, partly because for a lawyer such motions are a professional reflex, and partly too because they knew—everyone in court knew—that Judge Nott was not going to be dissuaded from the day's business no matter what motions they made. "Motion denied," was all he had to say, and then the cold gray eyes would move up the line to the next man. Then it was me they were trained on, and

I realized the words he was saying applied to me. "Isidore Zimmerman, I sentence you to die in the electric chair the week beginning May thirtieth, 1938. You will be taken from this court to the state prison at Ossining, New York, for sentence to be carried out. And may God have mercy on your soul."

I was bewildered, stunned, struck dumb. My mind was in a whirl. I couldn't think, couldn't focus my thoughts or—so it seemed for a moment—even my eyes. I looked at people without really seeing them. I think my mind was far, far away from the courtroom. I'd been expecting it all along, but still, it came as a terrible surprise. No, not a surprise. A shock. Just a shock. When I try to recall what I felt at that moment, it seems to me I didn't really feel anything. Just numbness. I was a man under anaesthetic. The others may have felt the way I did, or at least looked that way, for the newspapers, which had given us a thorough going-over during the trial, were able to call us a "stony-faced" lot and report we'd showed no emotion at the sentencing.

Things moved fast after that. We were handcuffed together in pairs, and then, cuffed again to the deputy sheriffs who'd been sent to escort us up the river to Sing Sing, we left the courthouse walking four abreast. A big black Chrysler with jump seats was waiting to take us to Grand Central Station, and on the way two deputies rode outside, on the running boards. At Grand Central there was a mob of news photographers waiting to get pictures of us. No photographs had been allowed in court, and certainly none would be allowed in prison, so it was their first and probably their last opportunity, but we were in no mood to do any favors to the gentlemen of the press. We ducked and dodged and looked in the wrong direction all the way to the train, and they never did manage a clear shot of us. And before we reached the dusty day coach in which we were to make the hour run to Sing Sing, Hutch Friedman succeeded, to his delight, in kicking one of the photographers in the groin.

The deputies undid the outside cuffs for the trip and seated us two by two: O'Loughlin on the riverside, where he sat looking at the Hudson, and me with my left hand still chained to his right, and the other cuff dangling free in the aisle. There were other people in the coach who looked at us with curiosity, not unkindly. Some of them bought us ice cream, which we all accepted, not knowing when we'd have another chance for it. Next they tried to talk to us, and that was the end: the deputies broke it up. I killed some of the time watching a pretty girl a few seats ahead of us. It struck me that she was in the same category as the ice cream, probably in short supply in Sing Sing.

At the little Ossining station there was an outsize station wagon waiting to drop us on the big stone steps leading up to the prison entrance, where another horde of photographers suddenly materialized. The deputies told them pictures were prohibited, and we gave them our usual co-operation, so that all the papers ever managed to publish were some uninteresting shots of our backs as we climbed the stairs. Deputy Sheriff Larkin knocked on the warden's door to advise him of our official arrival in Sing Sing. At that point none of us were concerned with our official departure from Sing Sing, scheduled for some time after the date of May thirtieth: we were hot and tired from the trip, and, to tell the truth, frightened. So to cover up we denounced the police, the prosecution, the press, and the prison on general principles. Sing Sing took us in stride—the business of our processing wasn't delayed by so much as a minute. Cuffs off; clothes off; shower; prison-issue clothes: gray shirt, gray trousers, gray coat, gray cap with a stenciled number—97485. No more Isidore Zimmerman; no more Beansy; just 97485 until they unstrap me from the chair some spring evening. They don't care what color socks 97485 wears: here's my chance to get away from gray. They don't care whether 97485 keeps his shoes from "outside," just so they're black. Any color shoes I want, just so they're black. The guard asked me what I wanted to do with my clothes—send them home? give them to charity? I thought of Mama sewing for us all, mending for us, saving pennies so we

could be the smartest, best-turned-out kids on the block,
thought of my younger brother Carl. I thought too that charity
begins at home, and I addressed the brown-paper parcel
myself with a broken stub of a pencil.

Then they turned the interrogators on us. Name? Age?
Date of birth? Next of kin? It made me furious to be asked
questions they already had the answers to. One question particularly irritated me: "To what do you attribute the crime
you have committed?" That was standard. They asked everybody that one, but with me it was different—I was innocent.
I'd stated all along that I was innocent, and now they were
asking me to underwrite their mistake and accept their version
of what had happened. It was as though their conscience was
bad, and they wanted reassurance from me: "That's all right,
gentlemen. If I'm here in Sing Sing it stands to reason I must
be guilty, so you were quite right in ignoring my claims to be
innocent." I wouldn't buy it. "I have committed no crime," I
told them. "I am entirely innocent. So I can't answer your
question." "All right," said the quill-driver. "I'll put that down
on the record. Now about these other questions . . ." "I
won't cooperate in giving my history," I said. "You can get
it from the records. An injustice has been done, and I refuse
to go along with it." So they told me to sit and wait on a
wooden bench until the others had finished their interviews.
Guariglia, Friedman, O'Loughlin, and Chaleff were all very
cooperative, and for a reason—they thought it might help
them get a commutation. But I was innocent and outraged. I
couldn't see why I was there in the first place. Only one thing
was clear to me: the prison authorities were in the process of
digging me a grave, and I wasn't going to give them any help
with it.

Sing Sing didn't look very attractive to me, but then I didn't
see much of it. There are fifty-odd acres and a dozen big
buildings behind those gray walls, but the death house—our
destination—located in the lower yard is really a prison
within a prison, entirely separate and self-sufficient: kitchen,
three hospital cells, two wings of twelve cells each where you

wait until they're ready to move you to one of the six pre-execution cells on the morning of the day they plan to kill you. Thirty minutes after the personal history bit, we were standing at the desk where they assign you to a cell. The West Wing was where new prisoners were generally sent, but the West Wing was full just then. We drew cells side by side in the East Wing: ocean-green walls with everything we needed to be happy—a bed, a washbasin, a shower, a toilet, bars—nothing movable. From now on until the end, that was home, except for the time we were allowed to exercise—one hour in the morning, one hour in the afternoon—in a walled-in yard thirty-five feet by seventy. In case of rain, no exercise.

I could talk to the boys in the adjoining cells, but I couldn't see them. In the interest of avoiding trouble prisoners went to the exercise yard singly, and in the corridors outside the cells, where a yellow lamp burned day and night, only one prisoner was allowed at a time. We took our meals in the cells, served on rubberized trays in utensils of soft dur-aluminum that would bend double if you leaned them hard against a boiled potato. The guard watched me while I ate, but it didn't interfere with my appetite. Not that the food was delicious. Standard fare in the death house is the same they serve elsewhere in the prison—that is to say, just ade-quate to keep you healthy with a minimum outlay of the taxpaper's money. Lots of potatoes, lots of bread, second helpings of most everything but meat. Some people lose weight when they worry. Some gain because they eat to take their mind off the worries; that was my style. I ate as though tomorrow would never come, and aside from eating there was very little else for me to do.

Seventy-five cents a week was allotted to cover our ex-penses. I spent as much on magazines as on anything else—they were delivered to us after the staples had been removed. No pencils. When I wrote letters the guard would pass me a pen, watch me use it, and see that I returned it. In the closed world of prison a fountain pen, a spoon, a pair of shoelaces, can become a deadly weapon. The men in death row have nothing to lose except the hope of a commutation. In the mood of despair that gripped us all, tempers were short, nerves frayed. It was enough to put one prisoner within striking distance of another for murder to be done. It was enough to leave a prisoner alone for seconds, if he meant to take his own life. Neither of these possible occurrences was acceptable to the authorities, if only because they implied that a prisoner still held within himself certain liberties they couldn't touch. If you could kill yourself, or the man in the next cell, it meant that you didn't belong to them entirely. And from the moment the gates shut behind you, everything was calculated to give you the opposite impression: that you were their property.

So they took my shoes away and gave me felt slippers, without laces. And when I wanted a light—we were allowed to smoke—the guard supplied it, one match at a time. And even when I wanted pepper in my stew, the guard would supply it— to his taste. (A mean con with a pepper shaker can make a prison tremble to its very foundation.)

It struck me somehow as funny that they should take such good care of my body if all they had in mind was to apply 20,000 volts to it on the date of their choosing. There were three chaplains there—one for each faith—to look after our souls, but the primary concern was clearly to deliver us in good physical condition to the executioner. I don't remember when it happened—but it didn't require much of a stay in the death house to blunt the sensibilities—that I lost the capacity to do any more than shrug at the case of Charlie. He was bent on cheating the chair, and he had a plan. In the course of his daily walks in the yard he collected pebbles, small stones, twigs, and other debris and somehow managed to swallow them unknown to the guards. The week before his execution he had his wish: a first-rate intestinal blockage that would surely have resulted in his death if only he could have stayed away from the hospital. But Charlie just wasn't born lucky. There was a very capable surgeon in the death house by the name of Dr. Sweet, a good man by all accounts. His job was

curing, not killing. He performed an emergency operation on
Charlie, eliminated the blockage, sewed him up, and put him
in the prison hospital. On recovery he was sent right back to
the death house for his date—on schedule—with the electric
chair. There was energy wasted there by Charlie, and energy
wasted by Dr. Sweet; but at that point I hadn't yet realized that
prison was dedicated to waste: wasted minutes, hours, years,
lives. A case like Charlie's only helped to prove the point.

Chaleff proved, a little later, that he hadn't got the point.
He decided he was another who didn't want to die on "their"
terms, and stopped taking his insulin for a while. How long?
A day? A day and a half? Just until "they" realized what was
happening. Then they opened the cell door and forced the
needle on him; until they killed him they were going to take
good care of him. More waste: the insulin, the struggle, the
hope, all wasted.

The very first day they'd given me a rule book setting forth
what could be done and what couldn't. Visitors, for example,
could see us from eight to eleven in the morning, and then
again from one to five in the afternoon. No night visits allowed.
But only the immediate family was eligible to see me without
special permission from the Commissioner of Correction,
whose office would conduct an investigation of the visitor's
character. That had a funny side too. I was awaiting execution
along with a group of certified killers, but the Department of
Correction was going to see to it that I didn't consort with people of doubtful character . . . like my friends.

The rules governing visits by women not of the immediate
family were even stricter. Only a Supreme Court judge could
issue the necessary authorization, and if he refused, you had
no recourse. There was only one girl in my life, only one I
still desired to see as I had been able to when I was in the
Tombs. Like a character in a bad movie, she'd said ridiculous
things to me, things I found I couldn't forget—words like
"Always . . ." and "Forever . . ." But even before she changed
her mind and wrote me to say that she was sorry, and that
"always" and "forever" didn't have much sense any more

where we were concerned, I'd begun to think that a visit from
her would do us more harm than good. I didn't really want her
to see me there, shut in like an animal with other animals; I
didn't want to see her there, in that place, where all my memories of a pleasant past were daily finding it harder to survive.
I didn't want her to come, and yet . . . I wanted it more than
anything else.

The days my family made the trip up from New York were
agony enough. And worst of all were the days when the two
people I loved most in the world—my father and my mother—
came together: they were the blackest days of all. At first I'd
be glad to get out of my cell, glad for a break in the endless
routine. Then I'd see the pain reflected in their faces and feel
shame for being, even in spite of myself, the cause of it. Mama
would be crying to begin with, and then would cry again at the
end; Papa would try to comfort her; and I'd be trying to cheer
them both up, convince them with the same old tired argument: "It's just a matter of time before the Court of Appeals
throws the whole thing out. Murray told me so. Just a matter
of time before I'll be back home, before we're all together
again . . ." Then I'd go back to my cell and eat my heart out,
hating myself for lying to them and physically exhausted from
the effort of it, hating the walls around me, hating the face of
the guard, hating the remembered face of the judge when he
sentenced me, the jury that found me guilty, the memories of
Rose, of Cooperman, of the police that night in the Seventh
Precinct house when my particular nightmare began.

I suppose the one thing that might have convinced my
mother that I wasn't worried and that everything would, after
all, turn out all right was the way I was gaining weight. The
food wasn't anything like Mama's, but there was plenty of it.
Lots of the men in the death house had poor appetites—understandably. But I ate and ate like a big, fat, contented cow. It
took me just nine months in the shadow of the electric chair
to gain forty pounds.

The human animal is quite a creation. Despair may have
been the dominant emotion I felt throughout those months,

but in some remote corner of my being hope kept alive somehow. I felt interested enough in my surroundings and in the men around me to take notes, like a naturalist studying unusual specimens. I tried my hand at some short stories, even a little poetry. "Well, well," O'Loughlin or Chaleff would say, "we have a writer in our midst." I didn't mind their kidding. But why, I wonder, should I have found the courage, where did I find the optimism, knowing as I did that I had an appointment to die.

There was no friction between the boys—Guariglia, Friedman, Harvey, and Chaleff—and me. They kept telling me they knew I was innocent, and promising to give statements to their lawyers that would be sure to exonerate me; and there was just enough hope, and foolishness, in me to believe now and then that everything would work out all right in the end. Talking to them I learned more about the case than ever I could have learned in court, and I filed the information away in the back of my head. The plan to knock over the Boulevard was hatched in Muskin's Restaurant, they said—not in Hanover's Candy Store. Popeye Cooperman was the man who supplied the guns—good old Popeye, who never spent a day in prison, who was never even indicted for his role in the conspiracy, who drew money from the city of New York as a material witness, and whose place in the electric chair he had arranged for me to take. Harvey told me that one day, casually—that Popeye had been the "armorer"—and I hit the ceiling. "Why in the hell didn't you say so in court?" I asked. Harvey had denied getting the guns from me in his testimony, but if he'd gone just a little further and stated they came from Cooperman, I would't be in prison under sentence of death. "Well, Beansy," said Harvey after a little thought, "two wrongs don't make a right, you know." And I was just young enough, and foolish enough, with my East Side upbringing and mistaken belief in the "code"—whatever the rap, a man never squeals, or some such nonsense—to answer, "Well, yeah, I guess you're right, Harvey."

My optimism took other forms, less foolish. I wrote letters

galore: to assemblymen, to congressmen, to New York State senators, to the governor, and even to the President of the United States. I was innocent, after all; why shouldn't I be optimistic? How many of those letters reached wastebaskets unread I'll never know, but I suspect the figure is high. It's a truism that the prisons are full of innocent people, all writing letters in their spare time. The terrible thing about the truism is that some of them really are innocent.

There were three chaplains assigned to the death house: a Catholic priest, a Protestant pastor, a rabbi. I spoke to all three. There's been a terrible injustice done, I said. Ask Guariglia; ask Friedman; ask O'Loughlin; ask Chaleff: they'll tell you I'm innocent. But how did you get here, they'd ask. What could I tell them? I don't know, I'd repeat; I don't know how I got here, but I'm innocent. That was going around in circles. They were all good men, all generous with their sympathy, their time, their ministrations. For all I know it may be, in part, thanks to them that I'm alive today, but after a while I gave up telling them I was innocent.

We were all in the valley of the shadow of death: Jew, Protestant, Catholic. Some of us had managed to keep our faith. I was one. Some had lost that faith, along with everything else, before they were to lose their lives, and some had never had it to begin with; but they never mocked the others, never tried to shake that faith in those who had it. When Father Martin set up the portable altar for the mass he celebrated in the corridor between the cells, he inspired the same respect, the same feelings of repentance and humility, in the heart of every prisoner there, Catholic or not. When the Protestant pastor led the hymn-singing I found myself joining in "Rock of Ages" or "Onward, Christian Soldiers" along with the others, to whom they were as familiar as, to me, the "Eli, Eli." These men who had killed, and who, given the circumstances, might be ready to kill again, were as solemn and well-behaved then as children singing in a church choir. The real miracle of those moments was that we knew, however briefly, what we had almost forgotten: that we were all one family.

Rabbi Katz was a good man. My mother didn't know how good—for her, it was enough that he was a rabbi; for her, it followed automatically that he was good, as a matter of principle. "Pray with him," she told me on her first visit. "Pray with him whenever you can." It was her very first trip to the death house, and in some ways it was the worst of all those visits I had to get through somehow, smiling at her as though I couldn't see her tears.

A friend had driven them up from New York to save the train fare, knowing that any money we could scrimp would go to fight my case: my father, gentle, gray-faced, fatigue showing even in the slope of his shoulders, ready to reason Mama— for the hundredth time—out of the tears he knew were coming; my sister Celia—she was twenty-four and a woman, capable of understanding why we were there—and my sister Ida, a kid of fifteen who didn't know what was happening but who knew it was bad; my mother, looking small and drawn, her hair grayer than I'd remembered it. How many gray hairs have I put on your head, Mama? was what I thought; and then she said through the mesh, "So this is where they're going to kill you . . ." That did it. My sisters both began to cry, my mother joined in the chorus, my father tried to comfort them—what can you say to comfort three weeping women—and I stood there helpless, wishing I was already dead. "All the things you said couldn't happen," said Mama, "all the things you said not to worry about—they're all coming true." "Mama, don't . . . You just don't give up. Right now it looks bad, sure, but I'll get a reversal in a higher court." "I don't want to give up. God knows I won't give up," said Mama, reaching for a handkerchief, daubing at her eyes. When I saw an opening like that I'd move in fast and talk, talk, talk about anything and everything —anything to stop the tears. What a job I did of making them believe something I couldn't quite believe in myself: that I had a future beyond the thirtieth of May.

Mama wanted to send me packages, mainly food. I had to talk her out of it. The food was wonderful, I told her, and anyway it was against the rules. What news could I give them for

the other boys' families? Mrs. O'Loughlin? The Friedmans?
Because our families were close together now in misfortune.
Were there other Jewish boys in prison with whom I could
speak Yiddish? Mama felt that for a Jew not to speak Yiddish
marked some kind of break with the traditions of our people,
and Mama was a traditionalist. And Hebrew? Wasn't I in danger of forgetting all my Hebrew here in this place? I told her
about Rabbi Katz, the Jewish chaplain; no danger he'd let me
forget my Hebrew, I told Mama. That was when she told me
to pray with him whenever I could, and I promised her I
would. (On later visits the rabbi always managed to draw a
smile of contentment from her when he told her how regularly
I attended synagogue, and how much I'd helped him in the
discharge of his spiritual obligations toward the other Jews in
prison.) As the visit drew to its close I even managed to get
the word to Celia and Ida: "Be very good to Mama. Help her
every way you know how, because she's having a terrible time
with me locked up here." Nobody was crying any more; they
just nodded and promised.

Then it was over: a two-hour visit that seemed to have lasted
thirty minutes at most. When the guard came to tell us visiting
hours were ended it started again—Mama crying with the
girls, Papa trying to talk them out of it and close to tears himself, and me . . . In a way it was a relief to get back to my cell.

O'Loughlin and the others had had visitors too that day, and
in the hour left before the evening meal—served at five—we
exchanged information. The boys all claimed to have told their
families of my innocence, but I didn't consider that grounds
for optimism; the lawyers were the ones to tell. It was only
logical that each family would be looking out for its own before it took time out to worry about me. "And if we don't get
commutations," they added, "don't worry. We'll all make statements in your favor." I remember being somewhat grateful for
their assurances—I had precious little to be grateful for at that
point—but skeptical about how much weight their statements
would carry on execution day. Better not think about it; eat;
sleep; and wait out the Court of Appeals. If I'd been able to

convince Mama they'd throw out my conviction, why not convince myself? Eat; sleep; wait.

Sleep didn't often come easy. There were few nights when I was tired enough physically to sleep right after dinner. The main trouble was lack of exercise. My time in the yard varied —only so many minutes to a prisoner if everyone was to get his ration of sunshine and fresh air. Sometimes the officer who escorted me to the exercise yard would be willing to play a little handball with me against the gray stone wall; more often I'd play by myself in the spring sunshine or simply walk up and down, down and up, the narrow walled-in rectangle, alone except for the officer whose eyes were always on me, the two of us alone except for the guard on the wall above us. From ten feet up he could see things I knew I'd never see again, a universe from which I was forever excluded: the curve of the Hudson, the ribbon of highway, cars moving along it. I remember knocking the handball clear over that brick wall one day. The officer with me shouted up to the wall man, who did a little shouting on his own, and minutes later the ball came flying back into my court, mysteriously returned from the world outside the death house, probably thrown by a con, dressed like me in gray, shut up like me behind the walls. But with a difference. When he'd served his six months or six years, he'd turn in his gray suit and his number, and life would begin all over again for him. But for me life was over, now, forever . . . unless the Court of Appeals took a long, hard look at the case against me. I didn't feel much like playing ball after that.

There was a public address system in our wing, piping in music and news from the New York stations, normally until about 10:00 P.M. when lights were supposed to go out. Fight nights we listened, took sides, made bets. One night I discovered that Zimmerman, the "forgotten man," had been remembered by somebody. A news program called "Five Star Final" told the story of the East Side boys with more concern for melodrama than for the facts. At the end of our trial they had me shrieking at the top of my lungs, "I'm innocent! Innocent!"

while little old Judge Nott shrieked back, "You're just as guilty as the others!" Maybe, after all, I should have tried shouting at Judge Nott. It was a cinch I couldn't be worse off than I was.

Except for visiting days, and days when the weather was too bad for exercise in the yard, every day was the same for me, the same for all of us. So the day I knew I was going to die—knew for sure—began like every other day: up at seven; mop cells; breakfast of cereal, coffee, and toast. The calendar said December 9. That was the day the Court of Appeals in Albany had denied, by unanimous vote, the appeal entered on behalf of Isidore Zimmerman from his conviction for murder in the first degree. Guariglia, Friedman, O'Loughlin, Chaleff too—their appeals denied. May had come and gone, and we'd managed not to keep our date with the executioner pending appeal. Now the last appeal was exhausted. No more fooling ourselves. No more fooling our families. Nothing left to do but display a little patience while they scheduled the most convenient evening to kill us, all together.

I'd been in the death house since April. After eight months I knew, like the others, how men died there. Some things I saw, that didn't help my sleep; some things they told us; some things we managed to learn, with the cunning given to animals who know their life is in the balance; some things they just couldn't hide.

You knew your time was up when they moved you from your cell to the long corridor running off at right angles to the East and West wings. The head keeper knew first who was going to make the move, and you knew around eleven in the morning when they came to move you from your cell. Around ten that evening, you knew, you'd be moving out of the new cell, and moving out forever. Evening is the time when they pull the switch, because the demand on the available voltage is less by then.

Between the time they move you, in the morning, to that corridor—fifty-odd feet long, housing six cells—till the time they treat you to 20,000 volts in the evening, they're reasonably kind to you. The last meal, for instance: it's the first and the last occasion when you rate food any different from what's being served to the rest of the inmates. You can have anything "within reason." No use trying to order something unobtainable or out of season, like oysters in July—they had that one figured long before you were born. A priest? A rabbi? Someone to minister to your spiritual welfare? Right away, sir. The barber, too. Up to now you've been shaved twice a week in your cell, but today you rate a special shave and a haircut, with special attention to the spots where they'll fit the electrodes later on. A nice warm bath is relaxing, and while you're at it you won't mind a quick physical to make sure you're not carrying anything—like poison—concealed on your person. Or a deadly weapon. The state of New York has no sense of humor—your departure from this world must be on the terms it sets, or not at all. Would you like to be fitted for a new wardrobe? Prison gray gives you the blues? Certainly, sir: a plain white shirt and a pair of green trousers, with stylish slits in the sides for the electrodes. And perhaps, while you enjoy all these creature comforts, you'd like a little music? Officially, the corridor where you stay so briefly is known as the pre-execution chamber; unofficially, to the men who pass through it, it is known as the "dance hall." The authorities will play phonograph records for you on request that day; but please, no more than five records to a prisoner. Music hath charms, they say. I wondered if there would be disk jockeys waiting at the gates of hell.

Because just beyond the green door at the end of the dance hall was hell, or as close to hell as most men come. Push the door to: there's the chair, and looking almost as ugly empty as it will look a little later, when . . . To your left a row of witnesses: newspaper people, police, prison officials. Straight ahead, the chair. Behind it, the man who pulls the switch—for him it's a living, and somebody has to do it. To the right, the warden, who gives him the signal.

The chair was designed to produce a standard brand of death—standard as cans of soup coming off a conveyor belt—but I knew it didn't. The men who sat in the chair saw to that.

Some of them died like animals. Some of them died like men. And some of them, I was sure, died innocent. I was going to be one of those, but would I go like an animal or like a man? I remembered the prisoner I saw one morning walking slowly, painfully, up the corridor to the dance hall. Behind him on the concrete floor were one, two, three, four puddles. It took me a while to realize what they meant: the halting walk, like a dog with paralyzed hindquarters, the pools of liquid on the floor. Then there was a wave of nausea in my throat. The man, I knew, was in the grip of a fear so strong that he had lost control of his body functions, and yet—somewhere, somehow— he had found the reserves of courage and will to keep his feet moving, his body moving, forward.

There was the man named Forte we all had reason to remember. His nerves went long before the trip to the dance hall. Night after night after lights out I'd lie awake and wait for him to start his chant: "Please, God, don't let them kill me; God, God, God I want to live; I want to live; I don't want to die; please God, God, God, God." At first no one would say anything. We were all in the same boat, all going to the same end; we didn't want to die either; nobody in his right mind wanted to die. Then his moaning and his crying and his chanting the same thing over and over and over would become too much to bear. The same thing that had made us tolerate him in the beginning—our common fate, our common misfortune —made him intolerable. What manner of man was he that his despair should set him apart from the rest of us, make him exempt from the punishment that was coming to us all? So one of us would lose patience—the cell across the way, the cell next door—and all of us would follow suit: shout obscenities, abuse meant to silence him, curses that he never heard. Never heard because his ears were closed to everything but the rantings of his own fear at the thought of death. Night after night. Even the guards must have hated him. And when the time came for him to go, he fastened his fingers to the bars of his cell with a death grip it seemed nothing could break: that was the force of his fear. We heard it took six guards together to pry him loose. A bawling, sniveling, shrieking wreck; dead—in a sense—long before he reached the execution chamber, he went to the chair on schedule just the same. We who survived were grateful: that night—the first night for a long time—we could sleep.

It happened more than once that the man who was "leaving" would throw a party for the others "staying behind." No drinks, of course; alcohol was forbidden in the death house. But with what money he had left he'd buy us cigarettes, candy, odds and ends from the canteen. The survivors always got a few more creature comforts just before an execution—those were the economics of the death house. By eliminating a consumer or two every now and then, the authorities artificially increased the supply of goods available to the rest of us. The consumer whose elimination made it possible knew better than anyone the meaning of the phrase, "You can't take it with you." I remember one of the party-givers saying, with a crooked little smile: "It's all on me, fellows. I won't be needing anything else in this world."

None of us were likely to forget a couple of boys from Brooklyn—George Lewis and Felix Cummings—who were executed the same evening. Somehow they managed to sing songs in the dance hall. Everybody liked them. When the final moments came, even the warden's face must have let them see how hard it was, in their case, to carry out the sentence. The rest of us heard about it later: Don't look so glum, Warden, they said. Don't worry, we know this isn't your fault. Before they turn on the juice they ask you if you have anything to say —it's the last courtesy they extend you. Here again, I knew, the presence of the killing machine, empty, waiting there with its straps undone in the room with you, meant there was no such thing as a standard reaction. There were those who made long incoherent speeches, filibustering against death; there were those with nothing to say who just wanted to get on with it; there were those too anesthetized by fear to talk; there were those who tried to unload all the hate and resentment that filled their hearts at that moment and hurl them at the world like a bomb; and there were those who were simply reduced to blubbering. Cummings was smoking a cigarette when they asked him if he had anything to say. He flipped it, half-smoked, to the floor. "I figure," he said, "I'll be gone before that butt." That was all. He was right.

I gave a little thought to my own last words. What I said would have to be dignified and yet defiant at the same time, something like: "A terrible mistake has been made somewhere along the line. I'm going to my death as an innocent man. I know my conscience is clear; I hope others can say the same tonight." But all the speeches in the world wouldn't change a damn thing—I knew that. Would I remember my little speech? Would anybody? Would I find the strength to say the words, remember them even?

Two hours before execution was when they ended your last visit, separated you for all eternity from your loved ones. That was the only time in the death house you could take them in your arms and kiss them good-bye: the last time and the first time. In my cell I could hear the screams of the parents, of the wives, who could no longer put off the knowledge that this was the end, the end, the end. Around nine in the evening, right on schedule, they'd start to scream. On those nights sleep came hard to me if it came at all. Long after it was quiet in the block —quiet except for the sounds of breathing, snoring, sleeping men, men having nightmares in cells around me—I'd lie awake thinking black thoughts. One night soon, now, other men lying in their bunks like me would hear screams, tears, from my parents. And I'd have something like an hour left of life to live. On nights like those you could hear men sobbing in the cells. The tension was something visible, tangible, that hung in the air like a foul mist. On nights like that even the guards hugged the walls as they passed, to keep out of the reach of the men in the cells.

Most of the guards in the death house were good men. We were there to have our lives taken away from us, and they were there because it was their job to be. There was no bad feeling between us. We didn't blame them for being where we were, and most of them could manage a certain sympathy for us. The mangiest mongrel dog waiting to be gassed in the pound will arouse feelings of sympathy in most people; and with minor differences—"there but for the grace of God go I"—we were men just like them, which entitled us to more sympathy than the mongrel. So they were generally kind to us—anything the rules allowed. There were rules, though, that were strictly adhered to. No contraband, for instance. All the money in the world wouldn't bring you whiskey or dope in the death house. A message to the warden, a call for the chaplain, a chance to see the doctor, any official request, and—within reason—most personal needs would get prompt attention. There were guards who'd bring you extra food if you were hungry, and guards who'd take the can of chili you bought in the commissary to the prison kitchen and heat it for you themselves if the cook was off duty.

Inevitably, there was the other kind: the self-appointed representative of justice with a capital "J." In his book we were there to be punished, and he was there to help with the punishment, to set things right in the universe. It was a vicious circle: his behavior would draw abuse from us; and then, to punish us, he might curtail our yard privilege; which of course would only draw more abuse from us, inflame our resentment further. If he tried to up the ante, a guard like that was playing with fire. At that point few of us had anything to lose. Commutations were rare because they were bad business politically. The taxpayer had spent a lot of money to get us this close to the electric chair, and he was disinclined to vote for a man who brought his investment to nothing. Our strength, on the other hand, was that we could be executed only once, and there were those of us who, on the way to the death chamber, would cheerfully have torn the head off a guard who had tried to play God at our expense. Fortunately for all of us, not many tried.

As the days passed, my thoughts dwelt more and more on death. Christmas came, and New Year's. I imagined people jammed in Times Square, ringing in the New Year, ringing out the old, paper hats, confetti, noisemakers. We didn't go much for celebration in the death house, but we had our noisemakers —the worst in the world.

I remembered the sounds I heard the night Terry Roberts went. Terry was a prince—always cheerful, always ready with a smile, a joke, ready to share his things or even give them away to complete strangers. Terry was already an ex-convict on the outside when it happened: too much to drink one night and the next thing he knew, through the haze of a hangover, they were telling him how he'd killed a man. On his last night in the death house Terry sang, song after song in a fine tenor voice. Listening to the music, I felt a strange sense of relief. Roberts was going like a man, an example to us all. A girl named Rose was his last visitor: his sweetheart. They'd talk a little; then he'd sing to her, and sometimes she'd join him in a duet, her voice clear and high and pure. Then he sang "The One Rose That's Left in My Heart," and sang it alone—she must have been too wrought up by that time to join in. I knew the guards had told them it was over when Rose began to scream, again and again. At that moment every man in the wings must have felt like me. Suddenly we were all standing at the cell doors, shaking them, pitting all the strength of our muscles against the cold metal, all crying with one voice for it to stop, to stop, to stop. But the steel of those doors, even on that ghastly night, was stronger than all our anger and our terror combined. That night and forever, and it's probably just as well. But I know I'll never forget those sounds. Even in hell there can be nothing more terrible to hear.

The guards let Rose give one last kiss to her Terry, through the bars, hoping somehow to calm her, but she fastened on him with a grip Roberts couldn't break. The guards freed him, finally, and when Terry went through the door for the last time he knew there'd be at least one soul to mourn his passing. The last thing he said to us in the wing was, "Good-bye, boys —here's luck to you all. Maybe we'll meet again in the here-after."

I remembered others, too: the man that none of the killers

in death row would speak to, accept a cigarette from, or even nod his head to. For all of us he was "the man who wasn't there." His mother had had a little store. Needing money, he decided to burgle it, and in the course of the operation he killed his mother.

There was the Brooklyn barber who'd raped and murdered a little girl of six. She "enticed" him, he claimed, and besides he'd paid her good money for what he wanted from her. What happened afterward . . . Nobody ever came to visit him. Slovenly, dirty, unkempt, he acted like the animal he was. He was a whiner, a weeper. Like Forte, he'd lie awake at night and blubber out his fear to the universe. We complained he made it impossible for us to sleep; we shouted at him, insulted him, cursed him. He didn't give a damn. The night of his execution was, for all of us, the pleasantest we'd ever known in the death house.

I remembered Murphy, too frightened to eat or sleep: you could literally see him losing weight from one day to the next. Whatever strength he had was devoted to abusing the person he loved most in the world—his wife. She was the reason why he was in the death house. She was pretty, so pretty that Murphy decided one day she couldn't be faithful. Whatever she did was good enough for his jealousy to feed on: a smile he couldn't see the reason for; a friendly "Hello" at the grocer's; a wrong number on the telephone; a letter she mailed, or a walk she took. He took to shadowing her, settled on an acquaintance he felt had to be her lover, and shot him to death. In Murphy's book, his wife was to blame for everything. She was a good woman, full of patience, and she never missed a chance to visit him; but whenever she made the hour-long trip from New York, according to the guards, he'd spend their precious time together reproaching her, reviling her in spite of himself. She just sat and took it with her head bowed. And when he died, Murphy died jealous.

I don't remember when, exactly, the change began in me, but it was probably before the Court of Appeals threw out my last hope for a reversal. My mind had been over the same ground so many times: What am I doing here? You're here because of the Foley murder. But I had nothing to do with that, I'm innocent. Then what are you doing here in the death house? Everybody's guilty here. But if everybody's guilty, what am I doing here? Somehow, over the long days and endless nights, I grew tired of this circular monologue—like a squirrel in a cage I was running myself into exhaustion only to find myself back where I started—and little by little I grew to accept the idea of death in general, and my death in particular. Nobody lived forever. It was hard to die at my age—nineteen —but dying any time was hard. Hard unless a man had faith, for example, believed he was dying for a good cause, believed death to be a mere incident, a beginning rather than an end. I had no illusions that I was dying for a good cause, but my faith taught me there was a hereafter.

If there was another world to which death was only a door, dying might not be so dreadful after all. But what kind of world? It couldn't be any worse than this one; that seemed clear. I'd lie awake at night and try to imagine it. Maybe because I'm a city boy I imagined it looking like the country: great rolling pastures of green; no bricks, no concrete, no alleys. I thought about them so much I began to dream about them: trees and grass, grass and trees. Here and there, people. I didn't know them, but they were kind to me, smiling. Some of it, I think, must have got mixed up with my memories of a country day camp where I spent two weeks away from the city when I was eight. To a kid from the East Side even Mars couldn't have seemed stranger. Then an odd thing happened. In my dreams there'd be a familiar face—my brother Harry, who died of pneumonia when I was twelve. The family adored him; he was the best of all us kids. In the dreams Harry seemed to be speaking to me, telling me to be calm, without fear. "You'll be gaining by this, not losing," he said, and it seemed to me he must know. And now, finally, I wanted to die.

It seems strange to me now, and it seemed strange to me even then—so strange I kept it to myself. Telling the family could only add to their burdens. I didn't expect them to understand that their son wasn't tired of living, but only unafraid to die. So when they came to visit I kept on smiling, and talking about appeals and commutations. I could see they were amazed at my morale, and that it did them good. But in my own mind I was clearer and clearer. Prison had killed the hope in me. The horror of the death house is really that: you're left with nothing to hope for but your death. Somebody imagined a sign at the gates of Hell: "Abandon hope, all ye who enter here." Prison is surely as close to hell as anything a man can imagine, but when I accepted the idea of death, I discovered to my surprise that beyond it was an exit opening on hope. To get through that exit into the rolling pastureland all I had to do was sit down in the chair. Sure, I was afraid —deathly afraid of that moment. But in a way it was like being afraid of the dentist when you have a raging toothache: first the pain, and then through more pain to the release from pain. Let's get on with the dying, I told myself.

Albany was anxious to oblige and jolt me into the next world, but Albany was meeting with resistance. Our case had aroused a lot of interest and a good deal of controversy. For one thing, the night we went to the chair, one after the other— Guariglia, Friedman, Chaleff, O'Loughlin, and I—would mark the biggest mass execution Sing Sing had seen in eighteen years, and that made good copy for the press. For another thing, a lot of people had been struck as much by the comparative harshness of the sentences—seven death penalties handed out, if you counted Little Benny and Little Chemey, went a good deal further than the biblical "eye for an eye" principle—as by the condition of the defendants. We were all young—Dominick, nineteen; Friedman, twenty-two; O'Loughlin, twenty-four; Chaleff, twenty-eight; and I, nineteen—all from poor families, and all from New York's Lower East Side. Some people felt, I guess, that with that background we'd all been on a kind of waiting list for prison from the day we were born; some people were against capital punishment; and some people just went along with the movement that started. A group was formed called the Joint Committee to Aid the Five

East Side Boys; my lawyer had told me about it. My family seemed to think it could help, and before I'd reached the point of actually wanting to die it was just one more reason for me to keep hope alive. The Committee collected signatures—a good fifteen thousand of them—on a petition for clemency they planned to submit to the governor in Albany. They rang doorbells and buttonholed people on street corners for it; they took ads in some of the newspapers; they even found money somehow to pay for radio time to spread the word. I remember one of their main arguments: "This crime and others of a like character are really caused by the slums of the city and the hopelessness and despair brought about by the poverty of the people living in them." Of course any slum was preferable to any prison, and any poverty preferable to the three square meals a day I was eating in the death house, but it made me feel good for a while to think that the Committee could mean an outside chance for us, an outside chance for me.

On January 1, 1939, Herbert Lehman was sworn in for his fourth term as governor of the state of New York, and on the very same day Nathan A. Sobel, the governor's legal counsel, advised the Joint Committee that a representative of the group would be allowed to present arguments urging clemency at a hearing in Albany on January 11. Coming so soon after the rejection of my appeal—on December 9—by the Court of Appeals, the news might have perked me up, but as things were it didn't have much meaning for any of us. Albany was the place where they always said No. We knew our time was running out fast, and optimism was a luxury we couldn't afford. All but Guariglia, that is. Either he was a marvelous actor, or he just couldn't grasp the fact that the electric chair was just a few steps down the hall for all of us. "So what?" he'd say. "What's the matter with everybody? I'm eating good here. I get sunshine in my cell—nobody bothers me. This isn't such a bad place."

None of us paid much attention to the Albany hearing, but not for the same reasons as Guariglia. For our families, though, and the Joint Committee itself, it was the last big push to save our lives. I heard about what happened afterwards, from my father. A delegation of about seventy-five people representing the Committee made the trip to Albany to present the petition. The mothers of all us boys sat in a big, somber, high-ceilinged room of the Executive Mansion and managed somehow to keep quiet throughout the hearing; five attorneys representing us had stressed the fact that it wouldn't do any good, and might do us some harm, if they made a scene, so Mrs. O'Loughlin, Mrs. Guariglia, Mrs. Friedman, Mrs. Chaleff, and my mother sat there grim-faced, trying to follow the proceedings and keep their emotions under control at the same time. The five attorneys presented pleas for each of us, and five social workers who knew something about what it was to live on the Lower East Side backed them up with another set of arguments. Commutation of our sentences to life in prison was what they asked, and the petition was there to prove that a lot of people felt their request was a reasonable one.

The petition didn't sit well with Governor Lehman. He'd listened patiently to each plea, peering over his heavy horn-rimmed glasses, asking an occasional question, but once our side had had its innings, he made short work of the petition. Let nobody delude himself into thinking that document was going to carry any weight with him, he said, frowning. He was interested in the facts of the case, and the relevant facts had been in long before the Joint Committee's campaign in favor of the East Side boys. "Securing petitions of this kind by writing, print and the radio—even that has been resorted to in this case—has absolutely no effect and is a complete waste of effort." The words must have been hard for the mothers, sitting there, to grasp. The practice of petitioning, Lehman went on, was "a vicious habit which people have gotten into . . . Petitions have not the slightest effect on me . . . Not one in a thousand is familiar with the details of the case." I can see our mothers sitting there, recalling the lawyers' warning: no scenes. They were probably stunned to see their last hopes being demolished along with the petition.

Stanley Fuld, who was there to represent the District Attor-

ney's office of New York County, said he did not oppose
clemency but did not recommend it either. Governor Lehman
was probably glad to hear that. He had the reputation of being
a man who knew his own mind, and Fuld's declaration was an
acknowledgment that the final decision was up to him as governor. And Lehman made it clear that he was "one in a
thousand," that he had very decidedly studied the case. How
could it be, he asked Fuld, that Harry Cooperman and Daniel
Rose—two men charged by the trial judge with being co-
conspirators in the crime—were enjoying their liberty? Why
had neither been indicted for his part in the felony murder?
"They were accomplices, very definitely, in this crime," Lehman pointed out with indignation. Fuld was hard put to give
him an answer, but he felt sure that the District Attorney's
case was too solid, too massive, for a detail like that to budge
it at this late date. He explained that in criminal cases the
choice "frequently must be made to let those go who seem less
culpable to get those who seem more seriously involved." That
was it; the session was over. The Joint Committee, the lawyers,
the social workers, and the bewildered mothers went back
home to New York to wait for a statement from the governor.

My lawyer showed me a copy of the *New York Times* for
January 22. There was a piece in it about charges made by
City Councilman Joseph Clark Baldwin, who claimed there
was a murder a day committed in Harlem. Captain James
Pritchard, the police officer commanding the area, said it
wasn't so; according to his figures, there'd been only seventy-
one murders in his territory during the year just passed. Buried
a long way back in the same issue was a brief piece mentioning Governor Lehman's decision that the East Side boys "de-
served no executive clemency." So the way was clear for us to
die. It was my bad luck, I figured, to have to go to the chair
without having killed anybody, not to mention a person a day,
or even seventy-one a year. I was sorry, too, that the Joint
Committee to Save the East Side Boys hadn't saved its energy,
and spared Mama a lot of needless heartache by giving her—
and the other mothers, who were supposed to have offered to

go to the chair in the place of their sons—something hopeless to hope for.

January 26 was the day. Even my parents couldn't fool themselves any more. I knew I was never going to see another sunrise. I walked to the dance hall in a dream: eight o'clock in the morning. I was ready to go, as ready as you can be. But I didn't want to go—the pastureland could wait. Act like a man, I told myself, and tried to think of those who had gone before me, like men: Cummings, Lewis, Terry Roberts. After Terry I'd seen thirteen men go to their deaths—I was in practice. The guard asked me what I wanted for my last meal. Why make things worse than they were? I decided to enjoy it: a big steak, a salad, two desserts—ice cream and jello—a pack of Philip Morris, a few good cigars, and some cheese blintzes. Bad news on execution day: the death house kitchen couldn't cope with cheese blintzes. And there was no time left to send out for any. I knew what they meant by "anything within reason." I thought of a little hole-in-the-wall shop on the East Side near Henry Street where I used to go for blintzes. They were almost as good as Mama's. But why worry about blintzes on the day you're going to die? I settled for potato pancakes.

The barber took care of my hair: clippers on the spot where the head electrode rests. He was very discreet about it. The tailor took care of the slit in my trouser leg: the right side, at calf level, for the leg electrode. I talked with the rabbi in my cell. We discussed the hereafter. There was no reason for him to doubt the fervor of my belief in a good life, a better life after death. What concerned me far more, now, was the family. All my problems would be abolished in a few hours with the flick of a switch; things wouldn't be that easy for them. I asked the rabbi to give them all the comfort he could, and his promise made things a little easier.

They played my records on the wind-up phonograph in the dance hall: "Ah, Sweet Mystery of Life," "Who's Sorry Now?" "I Cried for You," and "I Wonder Who's Kissing Her Now." The last one was for the girl who decided not to wait, and who wrote me a letter in the death house to tell me so. Smart girl.

But she wouldn't have had long to wait. For Friedman they played "Daddy" and "My Wild Irish Rose." Guariglia chose "It's a Sin to Tell a Lie." O'Loughlin asked to have roses sent to his mother, and the guards played his request: "Did Your Mother Come from Ireland?" Most of them had ordered big meals like me—chicken, steak, potatoes, fancy desserts—but nobody seemed to be quite as hungry as he'd imagined.

My father and two of my brothers, Carl and Louis, came up to say their good-byes. Mama didn't come; it would have been too much for her. She was home, in the kitchen, praying for me before two candles. We had three hours together, Papa, my brothers, and I. It was more than enough to make arrangements for my funeral, to give them the last messages I'd thought out for the family. I'd written out some things I wanted them to read after I was gone, but it made me uncomfortable to think that someone in the prison would read them before they reached their destination (our mail was always censored). There were things I couldn't bring myself to put down on paper, and things I couldn't bear the thought of outsiders' reading: things I had to say to Mama, things my little sister Ida wouldn't understand until years and years after my death, and maybe not even then. Anyway, a man wants a little privacy in his death.

I think Papa believed me when I told him I'd lost my fear of dying. But I'm pretty sure that with all his love for me he didn't understand his son at that moment. "Tell them I died a good death with expectations of a better world," was what I said to sum it all up. It was one o'clock. How many minutes more together? A last embrace; tears; they'd go through one door and I'd go through another, and I knew I'd never see them again.

I was wrong. Suddenly the principal keeper was there, motioning me out of the "cage." "Zimmerman," he said, "I'm advising you officially that your sentence is commuted. Governor Lehman is granting you executive clemency."

I didn't believe it. What was more, I didn't care. For nine long months I'd been rehearsing my death, dying a little every day, dying a little more every night, while just up the hall from my cell they were killing men, thirteen of them. I knew my role as victim too well, knew it by heart, couldn't back down now. "I don't want clemency," I heard myself saying.

"You have nothing to say about it," the keeper came back. "You're being transferred out of the death house to B Block. Get yourself ready."

Finally the message filtered through. "All right," I said. "Good. Great."

———————

Governor Lehman had taken another long hard look at the record. Shortly before 11:00 A.M., the Executive Mansion in Albany was on the phone to Warden Lawes's office in Sing Sing with the commutation order. Chaleff's sentence was commuted along with mine. "That's fine," he said, when he got the word. "That's wonderful." That was all: no laughter, tears of relief, hysteria, not even something approaching enthusiasm. Like me, he'd lived too long in the shadow of death, grown too accustomed to the chill of it in his bones, to understand that it was over.

Chaleff's father Louis hadn't lost his capacity for enthusiasm, though. I found out later that when he got the news of the commutation he rushed out of the house to the Zion Memorial Chapel on Canal Street where there was an empty casket waiting for his son Philip. By the time he managed to buttonhole the proprietor, he was shouting, laughing, and crying all at the same time. "No business for you! You lose the order! Keep your casket—nobody wants it!" That was a day they must have remembered for a long time at the Zion Memorial Chapel.

At the time of the clemency hearing in Albany, Lehman had said, "Not one in a thousand is familiar with the details of the case." Reading over the official declaration issued by the governor's office, I thanked God over and over that Lehman, for one, had taken the trouble to familiarize himself with those details. "There is no doubt of the guilt of Friedman,

O'Loughlin and Guariglia," it began. "No facts were presented justifying executive clemency in the case of these three. The cases of the other defendants, Chaleff and Zimmerman, are by no means clear, particularly as they appear to have been convicted largely on the testimony of two accomplices in the crime. I am commuting . . . [their sentences] . . . to life in prison."

So Sing Sing didn't have its biggest one-night execution in eighteen years, and the executioner lost three hundred dollars —his fee then was one hundred fifty dollars a life—on Chaleff and me. But the forty-odd witnesses assembled by direction of Warden Lawes, waiting just opposite the chair, hadn't made the trip for nothing; three men were still available for a demonstration of the killing machine.

Arthur Friedman was the frailest of the three, so he was the first one to go—who knows why?—through the archway marked—who knows why?—SILENCE. It was one minute past eleven. Rabbi Jacob Katz walked at his side; Hutch's eyes were closed. He managed to say "Good-bye"—just "Good-bye"—before the first jolt of electricity. The first of three jolts: 20,000 volts. At 11:04 Dr. Charles Sweet and Dr. Ken McCracken placed their stethoscopes to his chest and Sweet pronounced him dead. Attendants unstrapped him, wheeled him away for the autopsy. Scratch one.

Guariglia went through the green door at 11:06, two minutes later. It took them thirty seconds to strap him in. At 11:09 he was dead. Three guards wheeled him away. Scratch two.

Eleven minutes past eleven: O'Loughlin's turn now. Walking at his side was Father Joseph McCaffrey, the Catholic chaplain. Only five minutes before, he had accompanied Dominick Guaraglia along the same route. O'Loughlin had something to say. Warden Lawes motioned him with his hand to go ahead. "I am glad the other boys got a break," said O'Loughlin, stressing "other," then adding words to the effect that he was disappointed, that as a Catholic his chances hadn't been as good as "theirs." He was looking straight at Lawes, and then suddenly he had no more to say. He was sitting in the chair; they were adjusting the electrode to his right leg. He said something to Robert Elliott, the executioner. Something like, "Make it strong, make it a strong one for me." They dropped the mask over his face—is it to spare the witnesses? Or is it to give you an illusion of privacy in your dying? Elliott made it strong. O'Loughlin's body strained forward against the straps, then slumped. The mouth sagged open; the mask doesn't hide your mouth. A little curl of smoke rose from his head. Scratch three.

By eleven-fifteen the witnesses had filed out and were entering the special van by which they left the prison. I was sitting in a dirty cell in B Block, smoking a cigarette, when a guard looked in and told me it was over. They had needed just fourteen minutes to take three lives, and clean up afterwards. By the books, neatly, with no confusion. By the books, now they had evened the score for the death of Detective Foley. Three men dead—no, four men, counting Foley. I thought of Little Benny and Little Chemey, and dismissed them from my mind. Four dead already, and two more as good as dead; the killing machine was waiting for them, would wait them out. Then I thought of Chaleff, up the hall, and then I thought of me. Nineteen years old. I looked at the walls, the steel bars on the door. Up the corridor somebody was having a nightmare—the same bad dream, or a new one?—the voice mumbling, rising, falling, rising again to a shout, then another, then another.

Then I realized. For Harvey, Hutch, and Dominick it was over. But for Chaleff and for me it was just beginning, and it would never end as long as I drew breath. The score for Foley's death hadn't been evened, hadn't even begun to be evened. Two or three cells away the nightmare started up again: mumble, wail, shriek, mumble. I was awake, and yet I was living a nightmare, someone else's nightmare that shouldn't have been mine. Because I remembered, after all my terror and my tears and saying good-bye to life, that it had all been for nothing: I was innocent. Harvey, Hutch, Dominick were dead. Maybe they were being buried at that very minute. I

wasn't dead, no. But every day from now on they'd bury me
a little more, and in the end it would be just the same for me.
Harvey, Hutch, Dominick would be buried dead. Me they
were burying alive. And I could live to be a hundred.

Just living in the death house is enough to throw a lot of
things out of kilter: appetite, sleep, nerves, bowels, even your
thinking processes. Normally, a man whose sentence has been
commuted is given a week in the prison hospital for "observa-
tion." I'd spent nine long months in the death house and
watched thirteen men walk their last walk to the dance hall,
but—maybe because of the forty pounds I'd gained in the
process—the Sing Sing officials figured me for the insensitive
type and decided to skip the hospital routine. They moved
me to a dismal cell in B Block, one of the oldest in the prison:
no running water—unless you counted what was running down
the walls; an ancient iron cot topped with a lumpy mattress,
and one tired electric bulb in the ceiling that gave just enough
light to count the roaches by. No exercise; no visits; no letters;
no packages. Somewhere up there they were deciding what
to do with 97485, who didn't know what to do with himself.
I lay back on the lumpy mattress and tried not to think. But
there was nothing else to do but think.

Of course I thought about the girl. I knew I'd never forget
her now. There was nothing left of my life but memories, and
so many of those memories were of her. First love, last love,
only love—for me, anyhow. I couldn't even hate her for that
letter she'd written at the end—or what we all thought was
the end. "Dear John" letters—that was what the soldiers would
call them later, during the war, when a lot of young men waiting to die—for different reasons than mine, but waiting to
die all the same—got the bad news through the mail from
The Only Girl in the World. I wasn't feeling much of anything
by the time she wrote it—just enough to know it hurt, and to
wonder when and why she changed her mind about us. Later,
when I got a chance to think, I realized why and decided

she'd done the sensible thing. There was nothing I could contribute to her happiness from the death house, and very little she could do for me. In a way, I had to admire her courage for facing the reality of the situation before I did.

So I tore up her photograph and her letters and tried to put her out of my mind. It didn't work, of course. Now, even without a picture, I could see her clearly, or I thought I could: pretty little Irish face framed with reddish-brown hair; blue-gray eyes; cute little turned-up nose with a saddle of freckles; and so tiny—just one hundred pounds on a frame five-two—that in high heels she looked more like an outsized doll than a small-scale woman. But she was a woman. She was seventeen when I was eighteen, and we had plans: get married and move to California. My brother Charles had gone out first and written back to me about job prospects. After that the plans included a family.

She was so pretty I was proud to walk down the street with her on my arm. People would come out of nowhere—fellows I barely knew to nod to in school or around the neighborhood—and hang around until I had to introduce them; that's how pretty she was. Lipstick and just a touch of powder were all the makeup she used. Nothing on her eyes—she was what you call a natural beauty. No jewelry, either, except for a ring set with her birthstone, a topaz, and on her left wrist a watch I'd given her: a Waltham, heart-shaped, with a little link chain. When I closed my eyes I could see us in the store together, picking it out.

Wherever we were she had a little habit of holding tight to my elbow. She said it was "to feel the current between us." I was young enough to be embarrassed by it when there were other people around and flattered by it when we were alone. Another thing about her that embarrassed me—her walk. She'd sort of swing along on her high heels, and I could feel every boy in the neighborhood watching her move. "Don't walk like that," I'd say to her. "It's too provocative." "What's provocative about it?" she'd ask me, and I wouldn't know how to tell her.

Along with the rest she had a real Irish temper, and sometimes we'd have one of those I-never-want-to-see-you-again-
as-long-as-I-live arguments. But making up was so nice. Now,
I knew, it had all come true—I'd never see her again as long
as I lived. That was all over. I remembered the time at the
neighborhood dance: we tangled because I didn't feel like
dancing, and she began to sulk and I offered to take her home,
and she refused to be taken home by a boy who didn't want
to dance, and I left without her. But then she kept calling me
at the candy store at 12 Rutgers Place where I used to hang
out. DRydock 4-8283 was the number; I could still remember
it. The owner would call me to the phone and say, "Beansy,
she wants to talk to you. Please, Beansy . . . what can I tell
her?" And I played the injured party for all it was worth: "I
have nothing to say to the party," in a voice I hoped would
carry all the way to the phone booth. As soon as I said it I was
sorry, but, I told myself, a man has his dignity. Ten minutes
later she walked into the store—she'd never looked more
beautiful to me than at that moment—headed straight for
me, threw her arms around my neck, and burst into tears. I
remembered it all: kissing and making up, with the store-
owner, Mr. Small, and half the customers looking on and
smiling from ear to ear, knowing they were in on a lovers'
quarrel with a happy ending.

She liked a simple skirt and blouse better than any dress,
and suits—especially white suits—best of all. I remembered
buying some bolts of cloth at a sale on Orchard Street where
the pushcarts were, taking them to a tailor, and having him
make up two suits for her. She was so happy she cried, with
her head on my shoulder, and I was too happy to do anything
but twist her ring around—the birthstone she wore on the
third finger of her left hand—so the stone didn't show, only
the gold band, and say, "Look: that's your wedding ring."

We had been together the night Detective Foley was shot.
Later, when I was questioned at the station house, the news
went through the neighborhood fast. We met at the bus stop
at Madison and Rutgers and I told her everything. She was

worried. "What's going to happen? What will they do to you?" she kept asking. "Nothing, nothing at all. I'm not involved. It's all a mistake," I told her. Still, like a woman, she worried. We stayed together till close to eleven that night, talking and kissing in a hallway near her apartment. (Her parents, like mine, weren't happy we were seeing each other, because of the difference in our religions. We weren't going to let that change our plans, but for their sake we tried to be discreet about our meetings.) "Don't worry, it'll all blow over," I said. "By this time next year we'll be in California and all this'll be forgotten." "I'm scared," she said. "I'm scared."

When I was arrested she'd come to see me every week. Every day she wrote me letters. We'd managed to put a little money aside for our marriage. Now that was postponed; just postponed till my acquittal, she said. Right after she finished business school—typing and stenography—she'd got a good job as secretary to an attorney, and she went right on saving for the day. While I was in the Tombs I had a cell on the street side of Murderers' Row, with a view of a little patch of sidewalk and a brick wall on the outside. During one of her visits I told her where to stand so I could see her. She'd come almost every night after work, generally around seven, sometimes with a girlfriend, sometimes with a brother who knew about us, often alone. When I saw her I'd trip the light switch in my cell off and on so she'd know I was there. She'd stand and wave, throw kisses, or just look up at my window until one of the police officers in the area noticed and made her move on. To see her, just to see her there, made me proud, gave me courage.

I told her I was innocent; I told her they'd acquit me; I told her I loved her. She told me she loved me. The day after the verdict she came to see me in place of my father. She told me she'd wait for my acquittal—it was just a matter of patience, of time, before the Court of Appeals would order my release. We could wait together.

She never came to the death house. It was just as well. Then one day she sat down and wrote me the letter. I know why she did it and I wish her well: happiness, a family, the things it would have been impossible for me to give her. But that letter hurt—one more break, running deep, deeper than my nerve ends, with jagged edges down the center of my life, splitting off the past from the hopeless present and the endless future. Back in that past—another world—was where I wanted to keep the little girl with the turned-up nose and the heart-shaped wristwatch, walking with me in the spring night, her fingers touching my elbow.

Next door to our tenement on Rutgers Place there was a public bath and swimming pool: boys admitted Monday, Wednesday, and Friday. I spent all the time I could there, learning to swim, but in the New York summer when the heat made the asphalt bubble, the big boys went down to Pier 36 to cool off in the East River. On my first trip, they threw me in as a matter of course. Nobody thought to ask if I could swim; that was the way you were supposed to learn. Swim or sink. Knowing how was only half of it. Diving, kids were always banging into submerged refuse of one kind or another, breaking a limb here or there, occasionally knocking themselves out and drowning. The scar I can feel on my right wrist reminds me of one of those days when I dove and fetched up against a water-logged boat rudder lurking just below the surface.

For us the line separating fun from danger was usually invisible—the city made it that way. When I played stickball or ring-a-levio it was manhole covers that served as bases, and the fastest base-runner in the crowd would have his career cut short this side of the big leagues if he met a car while trying to steal home. I was fast on my feet and proud of it. Later on, in school, they gave me medals to prove it. The hundred-yard dash on the straightaway was easy for a kid who'd trained on Mulberry Street with its pushcart obstacle-course. Sometimes running was simply the fastest way out of trouble: if there was one piece of fruit missing from any fruitstand, the nearest kids naturally got chased halfway up the block. The cops chased us too, sometimes in earnest, sometimes in fun. "Brass buttons, blue coat: you can't catch a nanny goat!" we'd tease one in chorus, and he'd finally charge up the block for the fun of seeing us scatter, waving his nightstick, vowing to run us all in to the station house. They were good men for the most part, those cops; big and tough, without being hard, they got to know everybody on their beat and they knew how to be friendly as well as they knew how to be tough. They kept order, and they were respected for it.

And keeping order was no picnic. From Water Street on the east to Madison Street on the west were the Irish: twelve solid blocks, ready to take on the universe if necessary. The Jewish neighborhood ran from Monroe and Rutgers across to Montgomery, up to Rivington, over to Allen, and down again to Cherry. The Italians clustered north from Rutgers to Mulberry Bend behind storefronts of sausage and tins of olive oil and cheeses; and the space bounded by Cherry, Montgomery, Clinton, Jefferson, and Rutgers streets belonged to the Russians and the Poles. Everybody fought with everybody else. For kids it's a law of nature; nobody questioned it. Blue eyes with black eyes; Irish versus Jews; Jews against Italians; Italians with the Poles; Poles against the Irish; ikons against crucifixes; crucifixes versus Star of David; blonds versus brunets. That was this week; next week we'd change around. You fought with your fists—you had to. Hard but clean. You had to be tough, but no knives, no guns. Rock fights sometimes; fistfights always. If you don't want trouble, stay on your own block. And if you do want trouble, you can always find it on your own block, without straying from home. Rock fights, fistfights. If you weren't a good fighter, you were in trouble. I was a good fighter. Still, I could always manage to get into trouble.

I respected the cops, but I respected the gangsters too. They were a fact of life on the Lower East Side. To lots of us—especially the kids—they looked like the only ones who'd managed the long hard climb out of the pit of poverty where the rest of us were wallowing. We knew you didn't have to be a gangster to make it out of the pit. There were people like

Eddie Cantor and Jimmy Durante, Al Smith and George
Sokolsky and Ruby Goldstein to prove it. We figured they
were lucky. The ones that ran with the gangs were bad—our
parents told us so in tones of sincerest outrage, remembering
the standards of another generation and another country—
but their badness seemed theoretical to most of us. You
couldn't help being impressed when you saw them—and we
saw them around the neighborhood oftener than we saw Al
Smith and Eddie Cantor.

It was just like the old movies: the long black car, the fine
clothes—custom-made—the spectacular platinum blonde with
the fur coat, the jewels, a general air of mystery, power, important unfinished business, made them romantic figures to
us: Ally Wagner, Moishe Berman, Kid Dropper. Their easy
way with money made our eyes pop. "Here's a half a dollar,
kid. Go tell Joey in the poolroom I want to see him." They
were always good to us kids. On the Fourth of July, I remembered, they'd buy tons of firecrackers for us, just for the fun
of seeing us have fun. Lots of kids worshiped them for their
kindness. Lots of kids got started wrong—and wound up behind bars, like me, or dead in a back alley or the trunk of an
automobile—because of wanting to be like them, or just out
of gratitude for kindnesses rendered. Some of the hoods, I
remembered, used the kids as scouts or spies when they
wanted to find something out; when it comes to spying, you
can't beat kids. But when my father passed them on the street,
hanging around the corner or sitting in their big black cars
while they waited for Joey to come from the poolroom, he'd
shrug his shoulders and say to me, "Forget about it, sonny.
They never wind up happy, those people."

Papa knew why I looked at them that way, and I knew
what he meant when he said that. Getting up one spring
morning, going out on the street, I saw a crowd around a
parked car. "Somebody hit him in the head," a voice was
saying. I elbowed my way into the mob around the car, and
saw one of the mob, behind the wheel of one of those black
limousines, his head tilted back, mouth open, a bullet hole

in his forehead. Mama sent me to the store one night, and on the way back, at the corner of Rutgers Place and Jefferson Street, I heard a shot, then another, then a fusillade that seemed endless. I flopped into the street, groceries and all. Two hoods were shooting it out from saloons on opposite sides of the street; they unloaded something like forty rounds before the police showed up and they evaporated. Nobody was hurt, but for a long time I stepped lively when Mama sent me after groceries. I remembered another night too. Some guy in the neighborhood threw his girl out of a fourth-story window, barricaded himself in his apartment, and shot it out —to the death—with the police. It was just like the old movies, growing up there.

A lot goes on, in a poor neighborhood, just below the surface. Rich neighborhood too, maybe, for all I know. Lots of times, if you wanted to eat, you had to be a little bit of a thief: fruit grabbed off the fruitstand, or selling stuff to the junkman that wasn't quite junk yet, or wasn't quite yours to sell. It was too bad, but that was the way it was—and everybody knew you had to eat. In spite of the poverty, people managed to be happy. The narrow little streets broke the big city up into dozens of little villages, where everybody knew you, smiled at you, said hello. And anybody who knew you well enough to say hello would lend you anything you wanted to borrow, including the shirt off the back. When I came home from school I was always finding strange children in the place, sitting at the linoleum-covered kitchen table where we all ate together, getting free meals and hugs and kisses from my parents. Sometimes I was jealous; always I was hungry; but it didn't do any good to protest. "Be quiet," Mama would say. "This boy has had nothing to eat all day." I knew there wasn't that much to eat in our house, but there was always enough, somehow. Mama used to say, "Just enough for the family and a little left over for strange boys."

The food we ate during the week was simple—black bread and potato soup, mostly—and meant to keep us going, not much more. What I looked forward to was the weekend.

Friday night almost always we had the same thing: gefilte
fish, chicken, a pudding. It meant the Saturday noon meal—
"dinner," we called it—the high point of the week for us
hungry ones, was that much closer. On Saturdays, the Sabbath
day, orthodox Jews were forbidden to burn fires, and that
included lighting the kitchen stove or even lighting lamps.
So the day before, Friday, Mama would make a wonderful
stew we called "chunt": potatoes and vegetables and a kind
of sausage called "kishka." Like the other women in the
neighborhood, she'd take the pot of stew to the baker—a Gen-
tile—and let it simmer all night and all of Saturday morning in
his oven. Then at noon the family would sit down and make
up in one meal for the hunger we'd felt all week before, and
the hunger we'd be feeling for the week to come. Nothing, real
or imagined, could be better than that Sabbath meal. I hadn't
had one like it since June of 1937, when I was arrested, I
recalled. And I wouldn't again, ever.

Saturday evening, cooking was still against the rules, so
we'd generally go out to a delicatessen: corned beef, hot
pastrami, "specials"—outsize franks—potato salad, beans.
Somewhere in the back of my mind I remembered the distant
Saturday night when my father put a plate of beans in front
of me on the kitchen table. I might have been seven. Some
vague cousins or friends of the family were there visiting,
watching open-mouthed at the energy I displayed wolfing
down the beans, and from that moment on—for the same
silly reasons other East Side kids had nicknames like "Shoey"
or "Fish" or "Jumper"—I was "Beansy."

Sunday's meals were as light as Saturday's were heavy:
borscht with sour cream and black bread at lunch; cold cuts
and soda in the evening. Then there was another week to get
through somehow, to next Friday night's chicken. How my
parents kept us eight children fed and clothed: I didn't think
about it too much then—children take those things for granted
—but I can hardly understand it now, looking back. Home
Relief kept a lot of people in groceries in those days. I remember Papa filling out the forms for people who didn't

know how, telling them how to apply, but it wasn't for him, Home Relief. An idealist, my father. Gentle, but a fighter in his gentle way. For instance, there were always people around who couldn't pay their rent, and in time they found themselves out on the sidewalk with their furniture, evicted. That didn't seem right to Papa. This was America, not Russia. So he was always among the first of the neighbors to move everything back upstairs. A matter of principle. The marshals who'd carried out the eviction didn't like that, or the landlords either; sometimes they roughed him up for his trouble. It made me proud to see he wasn't afraid, just as it made me proud he didn't want us accepting charity, no matter how bad things got.

And there were times when things got pretty bad. Eight kids—Harry, who was seventeen when he died in 1930; Louis; Charles, who was two years younger; Celia, four years younger than Charles; then me, two years older than Carl; Ida, a year younger than Carl, and Hilda, the baby, six years her junior —must have seemed more like sixteen mouths to feed, especially when we were too young to work. Papa worked on the West Side, in the garment district, between 37th and 38th streets, in a long loft building full of women sewing and cutters cutting out patterns. He and another man were the only pressers in the place, and some days they did as much as three or four hundred ladies' dresses. It was hard work. He'd leave early in the morning, spend the day sweltering in the steam of his irons, and get home, some nights, as late as eight or nine. The pay wasn't bad, but the work was seasonal— what he earned in a five-month peak period had to see us all through the other seven months of the year. Mama took the money Papa gave her and tried to make it stretch; we boys would take odd jobs after school or shine shoes to help; and Papa in the off-season even tried for a while to bring in a little extra with a pushcart, but it was physically more than he could handle.

So Mama, besides being a wife and a mother to eight children, took on another job. In the building where we lived at on Rutgers Place she was the janitor, in title and in fact. A little woman—no more than five-three—with hair that had begun to gray when she was thirty: I could see her carrying ashes in big galvanized cans, stoking the furnace so there was hot water enough for the whole building early in the morning, sweeping, mopping out the hallways. When she was younger, Mama loved to dance, I knew. But from the time I was big enough to have memories I was used to seeing her working, always working. The first one up in the morning to light the coal stove in the kitchen, and the last one to go to bed at night after the dishes. No time for dancing: only work. But any wrangling in the family was confined to us kids. When Papa bought us a hobbyhorse—how old was I? seven? nine?—he had to spend most of his time making peace among us and deciding whose turn it was to use it. But trouble between my parents? Never. They were made for each other. "It's a romance," my father used to say, and it was.

The two of them came here from Russia, early in the century—around 1902. They came separately, and met at a dance, an American dance. Neither of them knew English, and they suddenly found themselves speaking Russian together. Fifty years and eight children later they were celebrating their golden wedding anniversary, still very much in love. "A romance," my father would say, smiling.

Papa left Russia early to travel. Before he came to America he'd seen a good bit of Germany, of England and France. On the boat that brought him over he worked to pay his passage. He never went back to Russia, never saw his people again. Over the years he'd get an occasional letter from them, but that stopped in 1941 with the Nazi occupation. By that time, of course, he was an American citizen. He used to kid Mama because he got his papers before she did. The day she could recite the pledge of allegiance in English and sign her papers in front of the judge was the happiest and proudest of her life. Speaking English was never easy for her. She couldn't quite master it in spite of all her efforts, which included going to night school at the age of sixty-five to learn,

but she spoke it well enough to get along. At home we spoke
English and Yiddish, mostly English, because Mama wanted
her children to speak it perfectly. When Mama and Papa had
something to say that wasn't for our ears they'd go back to
Russian. When we wanted to show off, sometimes, we'd trot
out a few words of Russian, and Mama would say, smiling,
"Those kids are too smart for their own good . . ."

Most of Mama's family made the move to the States:
cousins, brothers, sisters, uncles. I remember her father, my
grandfather: a stately man with a long white beard, radiating
dignity. I remember thinking that God must look very much
like my grandfather. To walk down the street with my hand
in his—I couldn't have been more than four or five—was
one of my greatest pleasures. He always managed to slip
nickles or dimes to us kids, and when we visited him at home
he'd have candy hidden here and there, behind curtains,
in drawers, under vases. When I found a piece I'd bring it to
him in triumph; he'd put his hand on the crown of my head
as if he were blessing me and say, in Yiddish, one word:
"Joy." Grandfather hardly ever smiled, but Mama said he
had a laugh that rolled like thunder. He was a proud man who
would take no charity, and who worked almost till the day he
died. For people who saw him in the street he was a ragman
with a long white beard. But for me he was a fine, stately
gentleman.

Grandfather, when I was tiny, used to predict great things
for me, I remembered. I remembered . . .

Christmas wasn't really our holiday, because we didn't recognize Christ as the Messiah. The big holidays were Rosh
Hashanah and Yom Kippur in the fall, and Passover in the
spring. Everyone took the holiday meals at home, and the
entire neighborhood—stores and restaurants—would seem to
shut down. All the bustling activity normal to the street in
the Jewish section would suddenly cease. Holidays must be
that way, I imagined, in little villages in the country, but it
always seemed surprising in a city as big as New York. For
Passover, parents, no matter how poor, always managed to

scrape up enough for new outfits for the children. The clothes might be second-hand, hand-me-downs from people better off than we, but to us it didn't matter—they were new so far as we were concerned, and we were glad to get them. When Mama was through washing and darning and ironing, nobody could tell second-hand from brand-new. Then we'd all go down to promenade on the Williamsburg Bridge on Delancey Street —the "Lovers' Lane of the East Side," they called it—for something like the Easter Parade. Boys and girls together in their holiday finery, walking hand in hand: the girls with the prettiest hats their mothers could make for them, the boys with a fine shine on their shoes and a knife-sharp crease to their trousers. That was where, one evening on my way home to supper, I stole my first kiss . . . The big boys and girls had another lovers' lane where they'd go after dark when the weather was fine—down by Pier 36. Just to get their goat, the younger kids would go down in a gang; when we saw two pairs of feet sticking out of the weeds by the river we'd grab them and pull and then run as fast as we could.

Fourth of July was another fine holiday, but election eves were in a class all by themselves. For one thing the politicians would all be out in force, giving the kids nickels and dimes to get their parents to the polls. Sometimes they got them to vote more than once. I remember how indignant my father got when one of the crowd offered him two dollars for my vote. Papa was furious because it was obvious I hadn't reached voting age, and dishonesty always made Papa furious. There were other ways of getting votes that were inside the law: baskets of food were distributed where the machine thought they'd do the most good, so I was a little less hungry than usual in those periods. The most fun of all was the bonfires, which were traditional on election eves. We'd get together all the scrap lumber we could find, one group competing against the others; one block would even make a kind of game of trying to steal another block's wood. Some of the big boys would even steal wagons to burn. As fast as we lit the fires the Fire Department would come roaring up to put them out. And we hated them for it. When we saw them coming we'd head for the roofs, where we had pails of water waiting, and drench them. Knowing all the short cuts and hiding places as we did, and being able to make it from one roof to the next over the skyline, we hardly ever got caught. We kids were allowed to stay out later on election eves too, generally congregating someplace where there was a radio to follow the results, cheer for our side when it was winning and groan in chorus when it wasn't.

When I was a kid there was no radio in our place. Later on we got a battery set with earphones, and I remember the first description of a baseball game I ever heard over those earphones. What a thrill it was for me! I'd passed the stage of roller-skating in the streets and decided on a career: I'd be a professional baseball player, first a pitcher, then first baseman, and finally shortstop. Maybe I was nine years old; life can be very simple when you're nine years old. In summer, when the weather was fine, we'd go to Jackson Park by the river where there was a baseball diamond. Usually it would be a Sunday afternoon: the Jewish Sabbath was pretty strictly observed in that neighborhood. Except for the gloves, everybody's equipment was home-made. Mama made me sliding pads, and most of us wore sneakers; a man who had spikes was considered a semi-professional. I remember the day Eddie Hyman chased a fly ball and fell into the river. Older people would come and watch; the men would bet cigars or cigarettes on the game, and sometimes "pay off" the winners with ice cream. When that happened we were in our glory. No wonder I wanted to play as a pro.

Winters I played basketball at Madison House. There were half a dozen teams made up for the different age groups. I tried out for the team when I was ten and made it. I remember feeling proud: being a good athlete meant you were one of the neighborhood elite.

A game I always won at: Johnny on the Pump. The milk was delivered in big cans on the sidewalks outside the tene-

ments. Leapfrog over the can without upsetting it, moving it
farther from the curb every time

Kindergarten at six. Then to Public School 2 on Henry
Street between Rutgers and Pike: a big gloomy building built
around 1850. I was a good student, but they had to let me do
things my own way. If a given subject interested me I'd want
to stay with it, which didn't always suit the teacher or the
school program. I had a taste for doing one thing at a time
and doing it thoroughly. In the classroom we were all boys.
Forty of us to a class. I was anxious to learn; from 6B I went
to an RA (for Rapid Advancement) class, covering two
grades' work in one. Sometimes my attitude—trying to stick
with a subject until I was good and ready to go on—let me
in for disciplinary action, but my grades were good enough
to get me rated in some quarters as teacher's pet. Mr. Geb-
hart, German-born, teaching the RA French class; he taught
us French with a German accent. Old wooden desks near to
collapse in some of the classrooms; inkwells dried up.

Junior high school, grades 7A and 7B, 8A and 8B: the same
old building entered now not from Henry Street but from the
other side of the block, on Madison. First terms in high school:
Seward Park. Marks still good, and deportment good too by
now. Athletics—basketball in winter, baseball in spring. In
fall I began to play football. But I was changing. I'd abandoned
the ambition to become a pro ballplayer. Medicine or the law
was what appealed to me. If they remembered me at all at
Seward Park—and how could they, with all those faces changing every year, every time the buzzer sounded—if they remembered me at all it was as a boy sitting with a book in his
hand, reading.

Third floor rear at 19 Rutgers Place: home. Four apart-
ments on the dark landing: no numbers, no letters, no name-
plates. You just asked somebody, if you were looking for
Zimmerman, and hoped you were knocking on the right

door. One bathroom, in the hall, to be shared by four families. You entered our apartment through the kitchen: coal stove, icebox with a pan underneath—to be emptied—wooden table where we took our meals, folding bed in the corner where Carl slept. The other three rooms: living room connecting with the kitchen and in turn connecting with the rear bedroom, where my parents slept; bedroom off the kitchen where my sisters slept; all unheated. Bitter cold in winter. Lying in bed on dark mornings, hearing Mama move around in the kitchen getting breakfast ready for us all; waiting until the stove was going, to get up. In winter we all wanted to sleep in the kitchen, the warm room.

I remember, as a kid, taking glowing coals from the stove in a kind of asbestos tray to bed with me for warmth, heating stones on the stove as foot warmers. How did we manage not to burn the house down? We managed, somehow. There were fires enough, but never a disaster. The cold could kill too: Harry's pneumonia was there to remind us. Dying at seventeen. Why did he quit school to go to work? Paydays, I remembered, he'd give his check to Mama—the whole shooting match—in his pay envelope, unopened. He didn't seem to want anything for himself. Wiped my bloody noses after fights —how many fights? If I was right he'd stand up for me, but if I was wrong he'd tell me, and tell me why. Poor Harry, dying of the cold . . .

The rear windows in the living room—which was always a bedroom for two or three of us boys at night—and in my parents' room: through the black bars of the fire escape I looked down on the little paved yard, closed at either end by a wooden fence, separating us from the buildings on either side; a clothes reel; and facing us, the big blank red-brick wall.

Like everybody else, Beauty took orders from Mama and loved it. She looked like an ordinary dog, but she wasn't. For one thing she'd saved my life when I was a baby: my carriage starting to roll toward the open cellar door; Beauty grabbing a wheel with her teeth and waiting, waiting till my

mother came. So Beauty occupied a privileged place in the
Zimmerman family. She played follow-the-leader with us;
she went swimming in the East River with us; she howled
so loud, if you left her alone, she could be heard for blocks.
Mama was Beauty's special favorite: if she said, "Stay there,"
Beauty would stay. You couldn't move her with a dish of
liver. On hot summer nights she'd sit on the front stoop—
Mama's orders—while we took the fresh air, sit like a dog
made out of stone no matter what was going on in the street:
strange dogs, strange cats, fire hydrants that she'd never
dreamed of before. Whenever she could, she'd sleep in Mama's
room. Her dish was in the kitchen, under the sink. Mama'd
give her some of whatever we happened to be eating; she'd
finish it fast and come beg for more from us kids until Mama
saw and sent her back to her corner, head between her paws.
Two minutes later she'd be back again, and we'd be sneaking
her food. After they arrested me, I never saw Beauty again.

Foolish games I played, foolish games all kids play: I was
lucky to be alive. Games on the rooftops, six or seven stories
up, two or three yards between tenements. I'd jump the gap.
If I didn't, they'd say I was chicken. One day the kid who
jumped right after me fell five stories. We were a sad bunch
of kids for a while. But it didn't keep us away from the roofs
very long. I was nine years old.

Foolish games, foolish kids. I saw a Douglas Fairbanks
movie called *The Black Pirate*. Some of us, inspired, formed a
secret club, the Black Pirates, meeting in cellars. But there
was no secret club without an initiation ceremony. We knew
a building with an abandoned elevator shaft; to be admitted
to the Black Pirates you had to climb the shaft, holding on to
whatever was available—cables, concrete, brick—five stories
up and five stories down. I was eight or nine, but I figured
it had to be done. With a little bad luck I'd never have seen
the inside of the death house.

Papa was the head of the family. Mama was the power behind the throne. She was also secretary of the treasury; she had
to see to it, somehow, that the money lasted. But if she said

No when I asked for money, Papa would sneak me a quarter, wink, and say, "Don't tell Mama." I remember getting into fights—on the way to school, in school, on the way from school—and coming home with torn clothes. Mama, shaking her head, would say, "What, again?" If I really got a scolding I remember Papa, sometimes, taking me aside and saying: "Accept what your mother says. She's right, and she means it for your good. But she doesn't realize that sometimes a boy has to fight. Don't say anything back."

Mama's discipline was always verbal—never a slap, never a spanking. But she could give a tongue-lashing that was far worse, or even just look at me in a certain way, and I'd know I was in the doghouse. Sometimes a good beating from my brother Charles, the family disciplinarian, would have been easier for me to take than the simple knowledge that Mama was angry at me. Mama was great for nonviolence. I remember once the mother of a boy I'd whipped in a fight after school brought her son to see my mother just to show her the damage: black eyes, bloody nose, torn clothes. Mama, going from the real to the ideal without batting an eyelash, improvised a sermon on the evils of violence that should have been delivered to me, not to my victim, and she believed every word she said.

Beginning Hebrew school when I was eight: every afternoon from three-thirty—after school on Henry Street—to five. Twenty-five or so of us to a class, boys my age or a little older; a rabbi to teach us the alphabet, then to read and write the original texts in which our Jewish traditions are set down. Five years of study, learning at first by heart things I was too young to understand. At thirteen, the Bar Mitzvah ceremony, confirming me as a member of one of the twelve tribes of Israel, a descendant of one of the sons of Abraham. Technically, it meant I'd reached man's estate: I could marry, make my will, draw a contract, take my place beside my father in the community. In fact, though, it served to put us all on notice that I was more than a child now, if still something less than a man. So it was a solemn occasion and a joyous one at the same time.

I remember going to the synagogue on Henry Street with my father and brothers, early in the morning: three stories of gray brick behind an iron picket fence. Prayers. The rabbi called me to the pulpit, and I read aloud from the Torah, the Hebrew book of Mosaic Law. Later, at the Kiddush, by the fluency of my answers I had to demonstrate my knowledge of our traditions. Nervous and confident at the same time, I wanted to make my father and my brothers proud of me. For nearly an hour I answered the rabbi . . . before my father came forward, smiling, proud to assert his paternity, and my readiness to take my place as a member of the Jewish community. Solemn, the rabbi nodded his agreement: I was worthy of admission. It was over.

But the celebration was only beginning. How many guests at the banquet that evening in the little hall we'd rented for the occasion—fifty? a hundred? The little four-piece orchestra that played for dancing; the tables laid; the platters of chicken, corned beef, pastries. At the head of our table sat my father; I was at his left, and beside me, my mother. There were presents for me: a wristwatch, a ring, a pen and pencil set, gift certificates for the purchase of clothing. My father thanked the rabbi, sitting at the next table, for officiating and the rabbi, for his part, acknowledged his thanks and said I'd been a good student, eager to learn and easy to teach. Congratulations in general—to my parents, to me. I had to make a speech, in Hebrew if possible. For ten minutes I spoke, and the applause that greeted me when at last it was over made me as proud as my parents seemed to me to be.

It was one of the happiest days of my life: I knew it even then. We were the last to leave the banquet hall. Four hours later guests were still dancing, still eating and drinking, still stopping at our table to congratulate us. Back in our apartment on Rutgers Street the feeling of sudden quiet, of calm elation, relief, fatigue after effort. My parents told me again how proud they were of me, kissed me, sent me to bed. Two o'clock in the morning: too full of the events of the day to sleep, I lay awake thinking. No more Hebrew school from now on, but prayers each morning to commemorate events, tragic or triumphal, in the history of the Jews. And now that I was carried officially on the rolls of the congregation, attendance every Sabbath for a service lasting four or five hours. What it all meant I couldn't explain in words, but I was aware of the solemnity, the majesty of it. Dropping off to sleep, finally, to the murmurings of my parents that reached me from the next room. The words came faintly to me, intermittently: they were proud of me. I was proud too. Surely it was one of the happiest days of my life, remembered or foreseeable. Surely goodness and mercy would follow me . . . all the days of my life . . . I slept.

CHAPTER 4

THE
WAIT—part II

MY QUARTERS IN THE NEW CELL BLOCK should have been a welcome change after my seven-day quarantine in B Block. But it was still Sing Sing Prison, and I knew in advance I wasn't going to like it: a little room about eight feet by five; three immovable steel walls painted gray and a fourth—a sliding steel door set with bars—controlled by an electric switch from some central point in the prison's nervous system; a little metal table for letter-writing; a stool; beyond them a movable cot with dark gray cotton blankets bearing the monogram emblem of the New York Department of Correction, whose property—like the cot, the blankets, and the trays in the mess—I had become; a washbasin whose tap ran cold water only; a toilet; a broom. Anything else was up to me: pictures, an oilcloth cover for the table, linoleum for the floor. Walking in the corridors, I'd seen samples of the kind of pains some cons took with their cells, but I wasn't having any. They had me living in a cage for the rest of my life, and all the oilcloth in the world wasn't going to make it more livable, in my book.

But live there I had to: from five in the evening to six-thirty in the morning. In Sing Sing, I was told, they try to keep you out of your cell as much as they can during the day. At first that struck me as a pretty funny idea for a prison, but it didn't take me long to figure out why. When you're out of your cell—in the yard, on rec, or working in one of the shops—the routine is so maddening, so everlastingly dull, that you have just one thought: to get back to the cell, where you can write a letter, read a book, or just sleep. But when they do put you back in the cell and those steel doors clang shut, you know nothing will open them again until morning. And so you have just one thought again: skip the letters, never mind the book, forget sleep, and get out of the cell. Between your time in the cell and your time out you're ground down a little more each day, until finally you understand what they're trying to do to you—kill the hope in you. If you accept that, let them kill your hope and tell yourself you can live without it, why then, I suppose, it becomes endurable. I met men just as happy in prison as they would have been on the outside; they'd given up, the way a caged animal in the zoo finally gives up thinking about the forest where he'll never roam again, and the people staring through the bars at him, and just concentrates on when feeding time rolls around again. Then there were those inmates who, without actually giving up, simply accepted the prison universe with fatalism, the way they might have accepted military conscription or the amputation of a leg: not liking it, but learning to float with the tide, picking up what compensations they were smart enough to discover or to invent, and convinced that, even in the best of circumstances, life made you submit to an unpleasant set of rules. But they were the minority.

For the vast majority, there was only one reason to go on living—the hope of release. Release: there were those who got out when their term was up; those who got out before it was up, on parole; those who got out—the "prison lawyers" —by legal recourse; and those who got out by breaking out —the "escape artists." And there were the lifers, like me, hoping for God knows what. All of them were fooling themselves to some extent, particularly the escape artists, whose best efforts generally led to their prompt recapture and an increase in their term; but facing up, without illusions, to the reality of prison is beyond the capacity of most men. It was beyond me, I knew, so far beyond that I was hardly grateful for the commutation of my death sentence. The idea of my innocence still made me reject what most of the others had accepted: that there was a reason for my imprisonment.

I remember writing a letter to Governor Lehman. He was the man, of all men, to thank that I was still breathing, but I wasn't particularly gracious. A commutation wasn't what I wanted, I said: it was an investigation. An investigation, properly conducted, would clear me completely, open the doors to freedom for me. If they didn't want to clear me completely, they could damn well go ahead and send me to the chair. All-or-nothing Zimmerman.

The idea was so strongly rooted in my mind that there'd been a mistake, a foolish mistake in my arrest, conviction, and sentencing, that night after night for years—either before I could fall asleep, or waking after several hours on my cot—I'd get up, push my chair close to the cell door, sit down and wait, my eyes on the corridor, my ears straining to hear a footfall. Whose footfall? Why? Because, finally, the mistake would have been discovered; they'd have opened their files to check and recheck, notified Albany, phoned the warden's office in the middle of the night—"Notify Isidore Zimmerman that we're releasing him immediately"—and the officer of the guard would be coming down the hall any minute now—those footfalls—a smile on his face, to give me the good news. So I'd sit, night after night, until I fell asleep in my chair and woke up stiff and cold, telling myself it was probably too late for them to phone now, but tomorrow morning, first thing, tomorrow, tomorrow . . .

My tomorrows in Sing Sing began at six-thirty every morning when a bell blasted us out of sleep: get up; police the cell; sweep, make the bed, and be ready to move out when the big steel doors slid open about seven-fifteen. Breakfast in staggered shifts in the mess hall—an orange, hot cereal with milk, toast, and coffee; the meal took twenty minutes. We ate off metal trays; no second helpings; one spoon per man, returnable—the guard checked us as we left, because for one inmate the spoon could be a deadly weapon, for another the work tool that, properly utilized, meant a breakout.

After breakfast we walked without escort to the yard. Everything within the prison area—three high walls and, behind an iron-spiked fence, the Hudson River—and outside the cluster of buildings which they enclose (the shops, a gymnasium, the recreation rooms, the red brick cell blocks, the death house set in its clutch of flowerbeds) was the yard. Within those walls and between those buildings were grass, gravel, athletic fields and asphalt, and areas where on "yard time" you could walk, talk with the others, stretch your legs, sit in the sun.

Later, not now: I'd be on my way to a shop. Half the inmates worked at maintenance of the prison grounds and buildings—and Sing Sing, like most American prisons, was put up in the nineteenth century, so that was a losing battle. One third of the prisoners worked in the shops—shoe shop, dye shop, mattress shop, broom shop, sheet metal shop—turning out a total of 185 articles. The first two weeks an average prisoner spent in Sing Sing—which really amounted to a kind of medical quarantine—were passed in a reception company being interviewed by the superintendent of education, the correspondence censor, psychologists and MD's, and somebody in the office of the deputy warden whose idea was to fit your "outside" skills into the prison routine: a typist might get a clerical job in the chief clerk's office, a carpenter be set to making furniture, and so forth. My work on the outside as a truckman was of no use to them, so they sent me, like others with no classified skill, to one of the shops: the knit shop, where I reported for work at eight every morning.

Imagine a small factory installed in a long, low-ceilinged loft room: weaving machines—clattering, shuttling, clattering, shuttling—producing underwear or blankets or uniforms for prison use, and men wearing those uniforms serving those machines. For weeks I took blankets off a belt, folded blankets, packed blankets into boxes, stacked boxes of blankets, moved the boxes to a platform for loading and shipping. There was a production norm to be satisfied; slacking on the job would get me reported by the shop foreman, and that could lead to nothing but trouble, depending on how far up the complaint traveled: suspension of this or that privilege to begin with, and the isolation block for a month or so if they decided it might do you some good. The work wasn't hard, or even physically tiring: just monotonous, like everything else in prison. After a month, when I knew the routine forwards and backwards, they put me on a machine, a kind of giant knitting needle that helped turn out the blankets I'd been packing. It didn't require me to operate it so much as to watch it and head off breakdowns and accidents, but the equipment was pretty ancient, and stoppages were frequent.

At twelve o'clock I'd fall into one of the lines heading back to the mess hall—unless I'd made arrangements to mess in one of the rec rooms—and then report back to the knit shop to ride herd on the machine—shuttle and clack, clack and shuttle—until three-thirty when the workday was over. It may not seem so bad; lots of factory workers do essentially the same thing their whole lives through. But when the whistle blows at five they have somewhere to go, something to look forward to. We'd go—weather permitting—to the prison yard, or else back to the cell. Believe it or not, there's a difference.

In the yard there'd be an hour and a half of griping and gossip with our friends, fighting with our enemies, and generally trying to "score" for things we needed. Sing Sing then was full of contraband: whiskey, narcotics, and "special treatment" were all available—if you had the money. In theory none of us were supposed to have money on our persons; in practice almost everybody did. It goes without saying that when contraband was involved, all business was done on a cash basis: C.O.D. For lots of items, though, cigarettes were another acceptable medium of exchange: if I wanted a cushion for the stool in my cell more than I wanted a carton or two of cigarettes, yard time was the time to spread the word, to find the man who could put me on to the man who was looking for cigarettes, and, finding him, to agree on terms.

Some of the boys on yard time would want to play hand-ball or softball, or kick a football around, but in the early days at Sing Sing I wasn't having any of it. For one thing, I was still feeling bitter about the letter *she* had sent me in the death house. For another, I was still so incredulous about my predicament that I didn't quite feel I belonged with the others: what was I doing in prison in the first place? My case had attracted a lot of attention; there were people in the yard who seemed to know as much about it as I did; but I didn't even want to discuss it with them. I wasn't in prison for the reasons they were; I felt like a loner, and I acted like a loner. Not completely, of course: there were half a dozen people I was willing to classify as friends, not just acquaint-ances.

But when the talk did get around to my case, I found myself reliving the same set of frustrations I'd known in the Tombs and then in the death house. "You shouldn't be doing time at all," they'd say. "How could you have been convicted on the testimony of accomplices? I never heard of anything like it. Talk about a bum rap . . ." All the "prison lawyers"—in-mates with some knowledge, real or fancied, of the law—would tell me it was just a matter of time and a few well-placed legal actions before I got out. I suppose it should have encouraged me to hear these things, but actually it had the opposite effect: I'd heard them all before, and I wasn't any better off for them. Just a matter of time, they said! That's all any man's life is: just a matter of time. I'd shrug my shoulders and turn my back on them, walk away, try to walk off the bitterness I felt before the whistle that would send us all back to our cells again.

It was a good bet I wasn't missing much in the way of conversation by keeping to myself. If a con wasn't talking about his case—why he was doing time and why (dis-charge, parole, appeal, or breakout) he wouldn't be doing it much longer—he was likely to be talking about sex. So far, so good: that kind of talk isn't confined to prisons. If his sexual impulses were normal, he'd either tell you everything he could remember from his life before prison, or everything he planned to do when he got out, and generally let his imagination run riot. But to talk of "normal" sexual impulses where prison is concerned is a little foolish unless you can think of sexual starvation as a healthy, normal condition. And if the con wasn't "normal"—well, it doesn't take you very long in prison to become aware of a roiling, tumbling tidal wave of homosexuality all around you. If I say that it's not just beneath the surface, I think I'll be understood. So if he wasn't "normal" sexually, your possibilities of getting along with him—or even just talking to him—were pretty much reduced right from the start: he couldn't come to you, so you were expected to go to him. Every other con seemed to have a sweetheart—and I mean sweetheart: the language they used, the lovers' quarrels, the scenes, the coquetry, the jealousy, the whole psychology and conduct of the relationship was just the same as it would have been for a regular couple—one man, one woman. Just the same, that is, but for one important difference; and that involved some pretty revolting manifestations.

The homosexuals—"queens" or "queers," as they were called by those outside their circle—struck me at first as just one more disgusting element in a disgusting system. I didn't begrudge their existence in prison any more than I'd begrudge finding maggots in a rotten log: there isn't a prison in the world without them. But I gave them as wide a berth as possible. In time, though, I came to realize that a couple of "queens" conducting a love affair were fortunate at least in having something to think about other than the deadening prison routine. Furthermore, to the extent that they were wrapped up in each other, they had that much less time for other kinds of mischief. And finally I began to wonder if the prison authorities—who officially frown on homosexuality, but are unable to eliminate it—might not find a certain amount of it helpful in maintaining order in prison society, just as the police tolerate a certain number of minor criminals—bookies,

petty thieves, and so forth—to help keep tabs on what the
big boys are up to.

After sex, the other major concern of yard conversation
was putting labels on people, separating the sheep from the
goats, the possible friend—or ally, or contact—from the world
of enemies around you. X—the heavy-set con leaning against
the wall there, with his cap over his eyes—was a queen looking for a new boyfriend, but not a "rat." A rat was an informer, a stool pigeon; anything you told him would reach
the warden's office in a matter of minutes. Y and Z—those
two standing with their backs to you—were rats: watch out
for them. Sometimes a rat would do his work undercover, dis-
creetly: that made him really dangerous; whereas an ordinary
rat—like Y or Z—was just a nuisance, easy to handle once
you knew what he was up to. Q—the tall, thin con lighting a
cigarette—was a "peddler": anything for money was his
motto. Not a man you liked, but a man you might need; not
a man to inform on you, but not a man to trust beyond the
point where his material interest coincided with your own.
He'd get you a comfortable mattress—for a price; get you a
quart of whiskey—for a price; get you a law book—contraband—a box of cigars, extra writing paper, a uniform made
to your measure. But: handle with care. The two young
ones playing catch in the sun were "mickies": newcomers.
They'd been shipped in over the weekend, and nobody knew
them well enough yet to pin a label on them; but there was
a chance they might turn out to be "men," that is to say,
members of the elite among the cons. The prisoner who
proved himself to be of sound character, who had principles
he refused to sacrifice—loyalty to his fellows, disdain for the
finks and the rats, the "sharpies" and the "wolves" who ex-
ploited fellow prisoners—who would share whatever he had
with his friends, who tried to live up to the "code," that is,
refused to act like an animal in spite of the grinding horror
of prison life: that prisoner won the respect of his fellows
whose respect was worth having, and along with it the title
of "man." Among the prisoners there was no higher title to

be had. And there was none less flattering than that of "hack lover." The hacks were the screws, the turnkeys, the men whose job it was to lock us in our cages. The hack lover was at pains to ingratiate himself with the hack, often at the expense of the rest of us, to get special favors. Like the others who made no attempt to live up to the "code," he was often referred to simply as "scum." Then there were the "tony ones," the intellectuals who imagined themselves to be a cut above the rest of us, and who flaunted their knowledge, with the result that they were loathed. There were classifications by profession—criminal profession, that is: a "schlep man" was a petty thief; a "heister" was a holdup man, and a "short heister" was a sex offender, particularly the type that preyed on children; a "pete man" was a safecracker. The vocabulary employed was as limited as were the topics of conversation: sex, the rap—the reason why they were doing time—and the classification game—"Look out for X: he's a 'daddy'; don't talk to Y: he's a hack lover; keep your mouth shut: Z's trying to hear what you say." One session a day of that kind of talk was enough to make me long for my cell. The only time we could enjoy a little change of conversation was when a "big shot" arrived in prison. For a week or two everybody'd talk about him, and his rap, and his lawyer, and his appeal, and his reputation; and then our interest would decline. Like the rest of us, the big shot had become just another number in a gray uniform.

The five o'clock whistle was our signal to go to mess and thereafter back to the cell block. By that time it often happened that the thought of going on to mess hall with the finks and the hack lovers and the queens and the short heisters and the peddlers was too much for me. I'd go from the yard straight back to my cell where I could stretch out for a nap, read, or write letters. But even reading no longer held the same charm for me; my mind was too much on my own problems. I'd draw books from the prison library—two a day was the maximum permitted—and find when I reached the bottom of the page or the end of the chapter that I couldn't remember what I'd just read. Nobody cared how you spent your cell time: that was good. But even in your cell you had to live without privacy: and that was bad. The constant hubbub made letter-writing difficult: prisoners in the tier shouting, laughing, screaming from cell to cell—like the monkey house in the zoo—and that in competition with the blare coming over the PA system, which was used more often for piping in commercial radio programs than for announcements. So until ten o'clock in the evening, "taps" in prison jargon—cell lights off, talking prohibited—I'd listen to the radio: Amos and Andy, Eddie Cantor, Bob Hope, Charlie McCarthy. I'd listen, that is, to the extent my fellow inmates made it possible for me to hear.

But long before taps I'd be back under the prison whipsaw: longing for the yard when I was in the cell, longing for the cell when I was in the yard. Now I could hardly wait for the morning, to get out from the confining walls, away from the sensation of being slowly crushed, suffocating in this ridiculously tiny room; I longed for the vibration and the clatter of the machines in the knit shop, where at least a man could stretch his legs. I'd pace up and down, down and up my cell: you can't pace very far in an enclosure eight feet by five. Visiting the zoo as a child, I'd been struck by the way a lion —pacing then as I was pacing now—would progressively shorten the distance covered each time, anticipating the presence of the bars before he reached them, anticipating the need to turn and turning a step sooner, then two steps, then three, until finally he was no longer pacing but turning on himself, revolving on his own axis. After a while I'd find myself turning the same way, and, close to exhaustion, lie down on my cot to think and think: It doesn't matter a damn that you're innocent; you're here now with all the rest of them and you'll stay here until the day they move you in a box to the "end of the line," the prison cemetery. Then I'd tell myself that couldn't be so: any minute now the message would come through from the governor's mansion in Albany; telephone the warden's office; there's been a mistake; send the guard down to tell Zimmerman he'll be going home to his family, his girl, his neighborhood, the apartment on Rutgers Street, the steaming pot of chunt for Saturday dinner. And I'd get up and push my chair over to the bars and sit and wait for the guard to come with the news.

Not that I missed much in the way of sleep. Three or four hours at a stretch was the most I could manage at this point, and apparently it was all I needed. But the weirdest sounds in the world come out of a prison at night, and they're enough to make sleep incidental for a prisoner: the snores, the nightmares, the groaning and the sighs, the talkers in their sleep who could be arguing their case in court, fighting with their wives, selling door to door. So turning off the PA system and snapping off the lights at taps is an empty gesture: the hubbub continues pretty much as before. Then the bell jangles again at six-thirty, and you're set to throw away another twenty-four hours of your life.

The con who wasn't assigned work in a shop was likely to wind up in one of the rec blocks, to which he'd be restricted until three-thirty, when the yard was open to everybody. Imagine a rectangular room—maybe a hundred feet long—full of tables like cubes—maybe four feet square—with wooden lockers built into their sides for the cons to store their things: checkerboards and cheese, magazines and meat. In the middle of the room a long line of cooking ranges: rows of gas jets in line. The cons who didn't care to go to mess and who could afford to buy their own provisions did their cooking there at noon and then again at five. Some of the men had built iceboxes out of scrap lumber to store perishables, getting their ice from the prison ice plant. Perched on a central platform, perhaps a yard above floor level, an officer—usually unarmed except for a billy club—maintained order, handed out passes to men who had visitors, appointments with the priest, or in the prison hospital. You stayed put in the rec block till half-past three; leaving the area meant a "pinch"— that is, being arrested within the prison and forfeiting privileges. So you tried to kill time: cards, checkers, chitchat. It doesn't sound so bad; and some days, if I was with friends, it was even pleasant enough for a short stretch; but in the long run it was punishment too. Boredom would set in. When there was nothing more to talk about, nothing to look for in a hand of cards, nothing to do but wait and look at the clock and wonder how you could stand the wait till they let you into the yard. It's a terrible thing to be in prison, period. Innocent or guilty, it's terrible. Nobody who hasn't suffered it can know what the simple deprivation of liberty does to a man. But to be in prison, deprived of liberty, and have idle hands as well is even worse: nothing can stop you then from dwelling on your own misfortune. Do that long enough and you're a good bet for a mental breakdown. Anything is welcome that breaks the boredom. If you're a queen, it's a love affair; if you're not, in nine cases out of ten, it's a fight: a tooth-breaking, lip-splitting, rib-crushing, head-cracking fight. The funny thing is that it's welcome: a blessed relief. And the worse you get hurt, the more aware you are that you're still capable of feeling, even if it's only pain.

We fought as much from depression as from any other cause, regardless of the fondness of the sociologists and penologists and psychologists and members of the parole board for calling us "antisocial" or "misfits." We fought among ourselves if only because that was the one liberty the prison system couldn't deprive us of. Five days a week, the routine in the shop or the rec block; Saturdays, half a day's work; Sundays, off; and holidays you have your choice: the yard or the rec block. But every day in prison is the same, or as nearly the same as they can make it.

A letter from home could buck me up to Cloud Nine for a week: news from Mama about Ida, the "baby of the family," Beauty's run-in with a stray cat, Papa's plans to see another lawyer about my appeal. Or the very same news could plunge me into a pit of depression. The knowledge that they were there and I was here—that it would always be that way, as long as I lived—would be unbearable; I could even work myself into feeling that the very fact they'd sent me a letter, instead of coming to visit, proved they didn't care any more, that they'd written me off: the black sheep, Beansy, the one in prison. I remembered what an old gray-haired con told me one day: "The main thing, kid, is to feel the family's still with you. If they still care, you know you're still wanted somewhere. Then you're all right. You won't crack."

Why more men don't crack is a mystery to me. I came close to it myself, and the black days when I got to thinking my family didn't care were few and far between. Thank God for the family! The old con was right. The man with no family, or the man who feels cut off from all human sympathy outside the prison universe, who believes his wife, his parents, his children are beyond caring, is as dangerous to the others as to himself. He has nothing to lose. So, literally over nothing —"Pass the salt" or "What time is it?"—he smashes the nearest face. I know. I've done it.

Getting into a fight would win me a quick trip back to my cell, where I'd be confined until the deputy warden had a chance to "hold court" on the incident. I'd be hauled into his office between a couple of guards; he'd ask questions and I'd give answers about what had happened until he knew enough to come up with a decision. Sometimes I'd get off with a warning; sometimes with a loss of privileges; sometimes there'd be a term in the "box," the isolation block. If it seemed likely that one or the other of us was out for blood, the box might very well be the safest place to store us for a month or two, till tempers cooled or one of us was transferred. It was important for him to establish just how serious, how deep-rooted the quarrel was: during their confinement prisoners are wards of the state, and the prison authorities are technically responsible if one prisoner kills another. There are plenty of men with scores to settle who will go as far as murder in prison; you might even say that the conditioning of prison life makes it more likely than it would be outside. And whenever you're transferred from one prison to another, one of the first questions asked you during the reception period is whether, to your knowledge, you have any "serious" enemies among the inmates.

More often than not, though, the deputy warden would feel that a suspension of privileges was punishment enough. What area was covered by the term "privilege"? Simple: everything or anything. The first thing they tell you on your arrival in prison is that everything you do is a privilege, revocable at any time without explanation. That knowledge alone is enough to keep a lot of people—the hack lovers, for instance—in line for the duration. What's a privilege? Working in a prison shop. Going to the yard for fresh air or to the mess hall for a meal. Food is a privilege. Getting a package from home. Buying candy or cigarettes in the prison commissary. Writing a letter to your family. Being allowed to see your people on a visit. Anything, everything: just so you understand that you belong to them, and that they can do whatever they please with you.

In practice they usually avoid depriving you of privileges that have to do with the world outside: writing letters, for example, or receiving visits. Not out of humanitarian considerations, but because they prefer not to have to give explanations to your family that may backfire someday all the way to Albany. While you're in prison you don't vote, but your family does. Commissary privileges are good to revoke; yard time is easy to take away; and if you had a good job in the mess hall before you got into trouble, you might have a bad job hauling garbage after it.

Unless you happen to be a lifer, they have still another effective means of hurting you. It's called taking time away. Get yourself in the doghouse and they can decide that the last month—or six months or even the last year—just doesn't count toward the sentence you're serving. In other words, they simply increase your original sentence by anywhere up to twelve months per major infraction. Without a trial, unless you consider being called on the carpet in the deputy warden's office the equivalent of a trial.

When you reach the isolation block, you know your reputation is made: as far as the authorities are concerned you're an "incorrigible" from here on. The box is used for people who reach the point of not giving a damn about privileges. I reached the point early and often.

In my first nine years of prison I must have averaged four trips a year to the box—in round figures probably forty-odd visits. They threw you in the box when you made it clear that deprivation of this or that privilege didn't matter a damn. Thirty days was your minimum stay unless the circumstances were special—sometimes prisoners were put there for their own safety—and only the warden or deputy warden could order your release. The purpose of the box was isolation: the cell block itself was set apart from the others; the area was "off limits" to the general population; you spoke to no one; and for twenty-three out of twenty-four hours you stayed in your cell and counted the walls. They'd let you out to stretch your legs one hour in twenty-four, but keep you separate from the others—no one to walk with, no one to talk with—and then back to your box for another thirteen hundred and eighty minutes. If they were particularly down on you for something, they might do away with that one-hour stretch period or put you on "bread and water," with one solid meal every third day just to keep your stomach from drying up and blowing away. Loss of all privileges: no smoking, no reading, no lights, no furniture, even; just bed, mattress, blankets. Not even a cup to drink from. I remember a principal keeper at Dannemora who should have been awarded the Iron Cross for sadism: he was fond of getting two guards to hold a prisoner while he worked him over with his fists. It was something to see, something to remember. He'd give you a year in the box for looking sideways: it was quick, easy, effortless, and didn't require the services of two guards. But he didn't know, I'm sure, that the beatings hurt less than the box.

———————

You heard a lot about suicides in prison—not that the people in charge publicized them, but because they couldn't always cover them up. One man I knew of managed to drown by keeping his head in a pail of water; don't ask me how. Another managed to decapitate himself—not completely, but it did the job—with nothing more complicated than a single-edged razor blade. The easiest way to end it all is probably to provoke a lifer with a nasty disposition. In twenty-five years I gave a lot of thought to dying by my own hand, but it was only on five or six occasions that I got around to making concrete arrangements for it. One reason for my indolence was, of course, the knowledge of my own innocence, and the conviction I held to over the years that the wrong done me would be righted. Another reason is that the authorities don't make suicide easy: just desirable. Suicide requires privacy, as a general thing, and privacy is hard to come by in prison.

During one of my stretches in the isolation block at Auburn I had a curious conversation with the man in the adjoining cell. He wanted to know what day we had canteen privileges, that is, what day of the week we'd be allowed to renew our stocks of candy, cigarettes, shaving soap, and the other odds and ends to which all but the baddest boys in the box were entitled. "What for?" I asked. "I've got me a plan," said the man next door. "I'm going to buy up all I can eat, and eat it, and then hang myself." His tone was too matter-of-fact: like an announcement it was raining, or that he had bedbugs in his cell. And I was going through one of my mad-at-the-world periods: they hadn't slapped me in isolation for being a model prisoner. So I said, "Yeah, sure—funny man," or something on that order. "You'll scc," he said. "You'll see."

There was a tiny window in each cell, set high up the wall close to the ceiling, well beyond a man's reach. It occurred to me that if you could get to the window and fasten a rope to it, somehow, and then jump off your bed with the other end around your neck, you stood a fair chance of hanging yourself. But the odds were all against you: no rope; no way really to reach the window; and no way to fasten it. It was possible, I thought; but just about as possible as tunneling your way out of the block with a plastic spoon.

We went to the commissary and did our shopping for the week. On our way back to the lock-up I said to my neighbor, with the spirit of philanthropy prison does so much to develop in a man, "Lots of luck to you, friend." For a while I could hear him crumpling wrappers, moving around in the cell next door. I could imagine him feeding his face with candy bars. Twenty minutes or so passed, and I realized, with a little shock, that there was nothing now but silence. I called his name: silence. I began to think he might have killed himself after all, but it seemed incredible. First there was the problem of how, and then of why. No matter how odd a prison cell might make a man, no matter how much he might long for death, I couldn't see him having the patience to wait till he could go on a candy binge first. Still, I told myself, in the universe of deprivation inhabited by a prisoner, little things— a pack of cigarettes, a candy bar, a letter—can take on importance out of all proportion to their value. I called his name again: no answer. The hell with him, I thought. He's sleeping.

Half an hour later I heard the footsteps of the guard on his round in the cement-lined corridor beyond the bars: left, right, left, stop, right, left, stop again. He halted outside the door of the cell next door while I counted the seconds. Then the steps began again, but with a difference—he was running now. When he came back he wasn't alone; the sound of his footsteps—more rapid now than on his round—was indistinct, inseparable from other sounds: low buzz of voices, the noise of the cell door opening. Judging by the sound, there were at least three or four of them. What they did, I couldn't see, but I could imagine. It wasn't announced over the PA system, but I knew now I'd never see my neighbor again. I felt a twinge of conscience. A fellow human had told me he was going to fill up on candy bars and then kill himself, and the childishness of the first step made me overlook the awfulness of the second. Instead of trying to talk him out of his despair I'd turned his confidence into a joke, wished him luck. Prison had made us both that way: him crazy, and me cold. What the hell, I thought, maybe he was lucky. Prison made me think like that.

Once in isolation I tried to kill myself by running, head down, into the wall with all my might, but the system left a lot to be desired. It was good enough to knock me out, and when I came around it was with such a terrific headache I decided to live: dying that way was just too painful. On another occasion I fashioned a hangman's noose in a contraband piece of cord, looped one end around the bars on my cell door, and tried to strangle myself by letting my weight go dead against it. There wasn't enough room for the kind of drop a professional hangman gives to snap the neck, and there wasn't much cord either. I couldn't go cleanly from consciousness to unconsciousness; and while I was hovering uncomfortably in-between, the part of me that wanted to live in spite of it all would push me back to consciousness in spite of myself. It takes more than an effort of will to make your nervous system forget about self-preservation. So, after a few unpleasant tries that abraded my neck and produced a ringing in my ears, I decided to go along with the instinct for self-preservation at least for the time being. And, just in case I had a change of heart, I got rid of the cord.

Another time I considered doing myself in with a razor blade, but just considering was as far as I could get. The idea of dying didn't bother me; but the idea of dying that way did— for the same reasons, I suppose, that not just everybody can become a surgeon. Once, too, a friend working in the prison hospital promised to get me enough pills to do the job. It would have been quick and neat, and no turning back once I managed to swallow. Swallowing was an easy, familiar action, I told myself, unlike opening my throat with a razor; and I felt sure I could find the courage to go through with it. And then the friend couldn't—or wouldn't—deliver, and my mood changed. But the despair with which most men live in prison, taken in daily doses over a long period, can very easily reach the danger point where death is much to be preferred to life. Then, I am sure, if there was a "convenient" remedy at hand

—like an overdose of barbiturates, which most people wanting to die would prefer, for reasons of temperament, to a straight razor—then most men in prison would reach the point of making that choice and taking the step. I know I reached the point.

Again, in Auburn: I say a casual good-night to a friend in the adjoining cell. His nickname is "Jimmy Cabbage." He answers: "Don't say 'good-night,' Beany. Say 'good-bye.' This is my last night in prison." I know Jimmy isn't up for parole, but I don't think of suicide. I've known Jimmy since my early days in prison, and I think a lot of him: a good man, with both feet firmly on the ground. Maybe, I tell myself, he's half asleep already; maybe he's talking in his sleep, dreaming this is his last night in prison. But he'll be there in the morning with the rest of us. "Sure, Jimmy," I say, "Take it easy, boy." Jimmy had been a sailor. He made a sailor's knot and hanged himself.

Time was when the guards patrolled once a night. But after Jimmy and a couple others like him, they took to coming around every hour. Further, they instituted what was called the "early morning count." Nobody really counted; but when they came by your cell around 5:00 A.M. you were supposed to move to let them know you were alive. And if by chance you were in a deep sleep—too sound to hear them on the early morning round—they'd reach in through the bars and grab a leg to see if you were still warm.

———————

One Sunday afternoon in December: I am walking in the yard with three friends. It is bitter cold, and I am wearing a long brown woolen overcoat, my hands buried deep in the pockets. Indoors most of the population is listening to a broadcast of a football game. Outside in the yard the broadcast is coming over the public address system, but we are too far away to hear; the wind carries away most of the sounds. A con runs toward us, visibly excited. "There's a flash on the radio: Pearl Harbor's been bombed!" I turn to my friends. "Where's Pearl Harbor?" Nobody seems to know for sure, but there is general agreement it's nowhere in the United States. We walk to the loudspeaker, where a knot of men is gathering. There are more bulletins. Pearl Harbor is in Hawaii, we learn. There is talk now of the Seventh Fleet, of damage, casualties. The realization is dawning that something tremendous is under way, something that may affect us, even in the strange private world we inhabit. Our excitement mounts.

Up to now the war in Europe has been a mere topic of conversation for us. We have been rooting for the Allies, hopeful that Hitler will be getting his come-uppance shortly; but all that is far away and of no immediate concern to us. What is happening today at Pearl Harbor is another matter altogether. Our excitement turns to anger. Fortunately there are no Japanese available on whom to vent it: feeling is running high enough, it seems to me, for them to pay with their lives. The phenomenon is astonishment, as I realize when I have time to think about it. The bitterness, the resentment that all of us feel against society—we are, after all, "paying our debt to society," and for most of us society is simply the instrument of our being caged up in prison—these feelings fall away, forgotten, at least for the moment. Our country is in danger, and we are as anxious to defend it—along with the "society" that has imprisoned us—as any bank president, any congressman, any "respectable citizen." Have the penologists given any thought to war as a method of criminal rehabilitation?

As the news breaks, most of the men are in the prison theatre watching a movie. Prisoners are as fond of gossip as old ladies in a sewing circle; it is an integral part of their universe. We take up positions by the open doors to inform the men streaming out after the show. "Hey, you hear the news? Pearl Harbor's been bombed by the Japs." The inevitable question they ask is "Where's Pearl Harbor?" There is talk of volunteering, of writing letters to Washington, confidence expressed that, for many of us, the war will change something in the killing routine of our existence: khaki is a more appealing color to us than our prison gray.

In time these hopes were disappointed. In the first feverish days Army officers descended on the prison, waving endless draft questionnaires. Like the others I was interviewed. I told them I was willing and able to serve my country. I told them too that I was innocent of the crime for which I was serving time, and that I was ready "to die with honor" anywhere but in prison. But I was a lifer, and nothing came of it. Men up for parole were given a choice in those days: volunteer for military service and you can walk out the front door; don't volunteer and you can go back to your cell. But, of course, not everybody was eligible for parole in the first place. They put me in a nice, safe category: 4F. No dying with honor for Zimmerman.

Back in 1941 the family had spent all its money on lawyers; what cash I had went for war bonds. Most of all, I gave blood—whenever the Red Cross came by. During the war years I must have given a good five gallons. They used to give us a cup of coffee and two doughnuts afterward, and somewhere or other I still have a card they issued, certifying that I was a member of the "Gallon Club" of blood donors. We didn't often have the occasion to be proud in jail, but I was proud of that. And if it's permissible to speak of morale in prison, ours was incredible during the war years. The men were so anxious to give blood—probably for the coffee and doughnuts—that they'd turn downright surly on occasions when the Red Cross people told them the quota was filled and they'd have to take their turn next time around. And even in prison there were campaigns to get us to buy war bonds, and we bought. It didn't stop there, either: every day in the yard you could see guys making speeches to other guys about the war, pushing them to buy bonds. All but the meanest of us realized he had a stake in the country; and never, while the war was on, did I hear a con say he hoped we lost. I know that we couldn't be rated as model citizens by any stretch of the imagination, but as far as our patriotism was concerned, we didn't need coaching from anybody.

Right after Pearl Harbor the FBI got busy, and the prisons found themselves playing host to a lot of German-American bundsmen. Fritz Kuhn, the national leader of the Bund, shared accommodations with us for a while, and we made it as clear to him as to most of his followers that they were anything but welcome. Some of the boys used to go out of their way to start fights with the "supermen," and it was often surprising how the guards managed not to notice what was going on until after a suitable period had elapsed. It wasn't only the Jewish inmates who got a special satisfaction out of cutting them down to size; plenty of Protestants and Catholics—and for all I know even atheists—enjoyed it too. In the main they were as nasty a bunch as any I met inside the walls. I remember banging one of the bundsmen around for close to an hour— he'd sat down next to me in the sun and opened the conversation with some standard gambit about "the Jews"—while a bunch of people who felt the same way I did about the Bund stood around screening our exercise from the view of the guards. Fighting was, of course, forbidden, even with bundsmen, so there were times when the guards were duty bound to punish us, at least for form's sake. But we'd generally enjoyed ourselves so much that the punishment didn't matter. In time the bundsmen got tired of taking a beating: they stayed out of the yard altogether, and made a beeline from their cells to their shops—where they had the protection of the guards while they worked—and then straight back to their cells again, where nobody could get at them.

War or no war, blood banks and bond drives notwithstanding, time passed as slowly as ever for us in prison—so slowly that by the time the Germans surrendered, it came as something of an anticlimax. There was a celebration, of course, that lasted most of the night: the lights were left on until morning by way of marking the occasion. Most of us had a brother or a father in service, and V-E Day brought relief from the anxiety of worrying about them. But most of us were satisfied just to cheer a few times and go to sleep as on any other night. When news came of the atomic bombs on Japan we were impressed, at least to the extent our ignorance allowed. Everybody had the same question to ask: "What's an atomic bomb?" And nobody but Einstein had a satisfactory answer to that one. I do remember a discussion with a number of cons who, when they were told a weapon existed capable of wiping out a city, simply refused to believe it. After V-J Day the big excitement was over; nobody had the option of volunteering before the parole board, and those of us with long terms to serve kissed their illusions good-bye: nothing was going to change, and the long gray tunnel of days ahead would have to be walked to the very end. Nothing was ever going to change.

Prejudice in prison: it is everywhere, from prisoner to prisoner, white to black, religion to religion, national origin to national origin, from the men in gray, serving time, to the men in blue watching over them. I remember guards who were at pains during the early days of the war to tell Jewish inmates what Hitler was doing to the Jews in Europe. I remember a mess-hall keeper at Auburn for whom I could do nothing right: the silver was dirty; the table was badly set; the floor had not been scrubbed—if need be, he'd spill something himself and call me down for it. It had gone on for weeks when one day I asked him, "Why? Why? What have you got against me?" He was of German stock, with cold fishy blue eyes. In a low voice he said, "You're a Jew, and I hate all Jews." When I told him to go to hell he was happy: he had me called before the principal keeper's court and I got sixty days in the box for the breach of discipline.

Walking in the yard at Auburn, I am hailed by a guard: "Hey, kike, Jewish services today!" I turn my head and say, "You anti-Semite bastard!" and walk on to join a friend. Seconds later I am struck on the head from behind with a club; it is the guard with two colleagues. I fight back; my friend fights with me. For the PK's court the case is clear: we have committed assault on two prison officers. We pay for it with almost twelve months in the box.

In the kitchen there is a simple-minded Italian prisoner,

doing a short stretch, one to two years. The kitchen keeper is Irish—call him Reilly—and he hates Italians. Day after day, month after month, he rides him, torments him, humiliates him. "I hate all you guinea bastards," said Reilly. "I hate you all and I always make a point of telling you." For as long as he can, the Italian shrugs it off, swallows his pride; but he is a man, despite the color of his uniform, and a deep resentment burns inside him. At long last he applies for a transfer and obtains it. Packing up his personal effects to leave the kitchen for the last time, he is approached by Reilly for a final blast. Reilly is beside himself at the prospect of losing his victim. In addition to his routine verbal abuse of the prisoner, he slaps him hard across the face. The Italian, half in terror, half in anger, picks up a rolling pin to fend off Reilly, now further enraged by his action: another slap, a blow from the rolling pin, and Reilly is lying dead, his skull split open, on the floor of the kitchen. No one has witnessed the incident. The Italian returns to his cell as if nothing has occurred, then, in a random conversation with another prisoner, blurts out the news. His fellow prisoner is a stool pigeon. The realization reaches him at the same time as a squad of guards, who beat him literally to within an inch of his life. In the box he is beaten regularly, allowed to recover, and then beaten again until, somehow, word reaches his lawyer, and a court order puts a stop to it. Tried for the killing of the kitchen keeper, he draws a sentence of twenty years to life. Yet, to have put an end to Reilly's torments, he may not have felt the price too high to pay: he was, after all, a simple man.

Theoretically, of course, nobody is ever beaten—that's what it says on paper somewhere—with one exception: a "man in blue" has the right to "lay hands on" a "man in gray" if he's coming to the defense of a fellow officer. But beating, even though a clear violation of the law, is pretty much a constant in the prisons I know. A recent case in Florida where a sergeant of the guard and nine officers were given prison terms for brutality is the exception, not the rule. I know cases where inmates have been killed in prison; the coroner's report called them accidental. I suppose they were accidental: if a scandal was really outrageous the authorities could expect an investigation. There was a case I recall where an inmate was paralyzed after a bad beating—not dead, just hopelessly paralyzed. They couldn't write a death certificate and they couldn't remedy the paralysis, so the news finally got to the District Attorney's office. After an investigation the guard lost his job and his pension rights.

A con they called "Nick the Fighter" swung at a guard trying to break up a fight. Nick was wild; to calm him down they put him in a restraining sheet. The coroner's report said he strangled to death. An accident? An accident.

Sometimes the coroner's report lists "an accidental fall"—like down a flight of steps—as cause of death; sometimes it's "heart failure." I've heard of a good dozen such cases via the prison grapevine, but how can you prove what's happening? Write a letter? It'll never leave the chief clerk's office. Tell your people on a visit? No. Never have I heard of a case in New York where prison officials were held responsible for an inmate's death. Better keep your nose clean—it's the best way to keep off the coroner's report.

Told me by an officer at Dannemora: at Woodburn, New York, there is an institution for mentally retarded prisoners. One day some inmates refuse food. You can lead a con to food, but you can't make him eat, especially if he's retarded. For the guards, that spells "hunger strike" and strike spells trouble from Albany, investigations, reprimands. Their solution is to club the boys to bring back their appetites. Result: a small-scale riot in which one guard suffers a fractured skull; and the transfer of fourteen of the "ringleaders" to Dannemora. There, with the prison doctor looking on, fourteen mentally retarded prisoners are forced to run the gauntlet between two lines of guards. The blows that rain down, the shrieks, the sheer senseless terror, are still part of the nightmares of one man who recalls them.

Another hazard in prison is the mad. All around you: there are too many of them behind the walls for special facilities to be considered, no one to give them the treatment that might help them. You never know, then, when they will bother you, maim you, kill you. A friend of mine works in the mess hall with a con just released from Block A, where the demonstrably insane are lodged. Feeling real pity for him, my friend helps him in every way possible: extra rations, extra cigarettes, advice. One day in the washroom my friend—call him Smith— is set upon from behind by the man from Block A: he has a razor in each hand. Until he sees the blood streaming down his chest, Smith thinks it is a joke; then, in self-defense, he administers a beating to his attacker. They are hospitalized together, and Smith, still vulnerable to pity, continues to give the other cigarettes and candy. "Why?" he asks. "Why did you do it to me?" "Because," answers the man from Block A, "when I write letters home, you make the water drip in my washbasin."

I am in conversation with a friend in the yard. It is a private conversation; when Jones attempts to join us, we freeze him out. The next day Jones seeks us out with an iron pipe concealed in his sleeve. It takes a dozen of us to subdue him. "Why?" we ask. His explanation is lame, but credible: he was angry at us for slighting him. That night in his cell he begins to scream and curse God. The following morning he is in Section A with the criminally insane. When will he be out?

━━━━━━━

The "Fagin fallacy": young men, imprisoned for a first offense, learn all sorts of criminal dodges they would never have dreamed of without the corrupting influence of older, hardened offenders. This is true only in gangster movies. With any kind of luck at all, the young con will be told time and time again by the older inmates to take the lesson to heart and stay out of future trouble. It is an impressive thing to see a three- or four-time loser, hair turning gray, face seamed and pinched from having spent the best years of his life in a prison cell, telling a youngster: "Look at the mess I made of my life. Don't be a damn fool; don't be like me."

The penal authorities founded Comstock Prison and reserved it for youthful offenders. I remember making the remark to a guard in Dannemora: "That's one of the worst mistakes they ever made." And the guard agreed, knowing that the young ones will swagger and strut among themselves, raise the ante, try to prove how tough they are as a matter of principle. The history of Comstock has been one long history of gangs and trouble enough for two ordinary prisons: the kids come out far worse than they go in. The only way to get a young punk in line is with an old con—old enough for him to respect—who'll boss him into good sense. Most of the old cons—and some of them are pretty bad boys—see themselves in that kid who's started off on the wrong foot, and they'll try their best to give him the right steer: the one they never got.

———

Letters—writing them, getting them—were absolutely necessary to my survival: proof to me that the real world was still there, outside the walls. If I had to, I could do without visits, packages; but letters, never. My kid brother Carl—in the Army forty-four months, serving with the First Armored Division in Europe—talked more in his letters about my release than about World War II. He was convinced the day was coming: "It's just a matter of time, now," he'd write. The phrase had a familiar ring to it: I'd got a lot of mileage out of it myself, but I didn't much believe it any more. Still, who was I to break down the morale of Sergeant Carl Zimmerman? My letters to him and to the family reflected an optimism I was almost beyond—almost, not quite.

Just before he shipped overseas, Carl wrote to say he'd run into Rose on the street, quite by chance. They talked, and Danny said, "I didn't say anything damaging to your brother on the stand. Why should they be keeping him in prison? If there's anything I can do to help, I'll be happy to do it." It was flabbergasting, Carl said. Rose seemed quite sincere, but if he didn't realize why I was in prison, there was no reason to suppose anybody would: it was depressing as hell. It happened again, around 1947. Rose had moved uptown somewhere, away from the old neighborhood; but Carl turned the corner at East Broadway and Clinton and found himself face to face with Danny, who gave him the same routine. "It's a shame Beansy's still in prison. He really had nothing to do with the guns. I'll be glad to help him if I can. Give him my regards." It was flabbergasting.

Carl gave me news of Rosenblum, too, around the same time; it was no more encouraging. He was in private practice now, a little older, a little heavier, but otherwise unchanged. Carl talked to him for ten minutes or so one day as he was leaving the synagogue, and the pat refrain was as familiar to me as an old phonograph record: he had nothing against Zimmerman; he was just doing his job; the D.A.'s office had assigned the case to him; he was just doing his job and so on. I wouldn't have expected anything else, but Carl—who took time to visit me at Greenhaven when he should have been on his honeymoon—seemed to think he could move mountains. "I know," he'd write, "if we can just get one of the witnesses against you to tell the truth—just one of them—you have every chance of making a successful appeal."

Just one of them: Rose still didn't realize—judging by his remarks to Carl—what the truth was; Cooperman had dropped out of sight—somebody told Carl he was living in Brooklyn now, and Brooklyn is as big as Texas; and Hanover —poor, frightened Hanover—was just as frightened as ever. Tevyah was still in the old neighborhood, but he'd lost the store. Carl might see him—just see him from across the street —twice a week; and all he had to do was look at Hanover, without saying a word, to make him feel uncomfortable. He'd gone all the way to Albany, once, I knew, with the idea of modifying his testimony on some points; but he hadn't been talking very long when they began to frown over their glasses at him and start to talk about "perjury." Tevyah got the point, and promptly forgot about modifying his testimony and took the first train back to New York, wondering why it was so easy for an honest shopkeeper to get into trouble. For him, the mere sight of Carl meant trouble: it was his signal to disappear. Two or three times, though, Carl managed to speak to him. "If just one of the witnesses against my brother will tell the truth, now, after all these years . . ." Hanover's answer didn't hold out much hope: he was sick; the Foley case had caused him nothing but trouble; he was sick, under a doctor's care from worrying about the case, the appearances in court; there was nothing he could do; he was under a doctor's care. Just one witness willing to tell the truth, Carl would write: "Just one, and it'll only be a matter of time."

The chief clerk: in his hands is concentrated such power that, for practical purposes—and for the prisoners—he often becomes an "unofficial warden." The warden is, on paper, top man, answerable only to the Commissioner of Correction and the state governor: he lays down the policies by which the prison is run, but keeps pretty much to himself, like the supreme commander in a theatre of military operations, studying maps, reading reports, and talking on the telephone. But even if the warden is a hard man, with hard policies, the chief clerk can, by judicious use of his powers, soften the harshest measures ordered from the top. His primary functions are administrative, but they cover a lot of ground. He supervises the prison steward, who buys everything the prison requires from food to electrical fixtures: if the chef seems to have lost his touch, it may very well be that the chief clerk is concerned with balancing the budget. He notarizes documents—and a surprising lot of the letters coming out of prison require notarizing; decides who can be added to your mailing list—because prisoners are authorized to write only those persons whose names are on file with the chief clerk; advises you of your legal rights as a prisoner; allows you to phone home when there's an emergency—like illness—in the family; handles the necessary paperwork if your wife decides to divorce you while you're doing time; recommends—although the final order must be signed by the warden—that you be allowed to attend the funeral in the case of a death in the family, or visit the sickbed of someone gravely ill. (In the state of New York all prisoners are entitled to such visits "at the discretion of the warden"—which in practice means at the discretion of the chief clerk. A sickbed visit lasts a matter of hours, after which they lock you back in your cell. If death occurs you can re-apply, provided you can pay for the traveling and living ex-penses and the salary of the guard—or guards—they send along with you. There's one more "if": if the chief clerk is willing.) A good chief clerk can make life in prison a little more endurable; a bad one can make things even rougher than they seem. Practically, the prisoner's redress is nil. I re-call a period when the cons were drawing up "cease and de-sist" writs almost daily to curb the powers of a chief clerk; few, if any, of them got beyond the clerk's office, where they were filed in the waste basket.

One all-important hold the chief clerk has over the prisoner is computing his time. There is the time of the original sen-tence served, less so much "time off"—except in the case of lifers, like me—for good behavior, figured at the rate of five days for each month served, plus time added on for breaches of discipline. It doesn't sound complicated, but the chief clerk has a thousand other things on his mind: like banks, he can make mistakes in simple arithmetic. But for the prisoner those mistakes—columns of black figures on white paper, added, subtracted—are translated into an extension of the misery he feels in his bones: another day, another month, another year of living as a caged animal.

Judge Nott had sent me to prison for life, and as a lifer I got no time off for good behavior; as good or as bad as I chose to be, the only way out was in a pine box. But there was another law on the books: as a lifer, I was eligible to meet the parole board after serving twenty-six years and eight months of a life sentence. I asked the chief clerk for a computation of my time, and by his figuring it was a good eighteen months longer than what I had been told was the "official" figure. Why, I asked, are you adding a year and a half to the period required for a lifer to be eligible for parole? Because, said the chief clerk, as a lifer you're not entitled to five days a month "good time" like the others. I know my rights, I said; I'll go to court. Go, said the chief clerk. I wrote my lawyer; I wrote to the legislature in Albany; I wrote to the Department of Correction: everybody told me it was up to the chief clerk to compute the time as he saw fit. I'm a loser.

Later, I found there exists a difference of opinion even among judges on the subject of good time. Some hold that reducing a prisoner's sentence for his good behavior is mandatory: a kind of contract concluded between the parties. One judge, acting on this assumption, ordered a prisoner's release; a higher court reversed the release order and brought the man back to prison to serve the "balance" of his sentence; after which the Court of Appeals—the highest in the state— supported the reversal on grounds that the "contract"—which, if it existed, derived from a law passed around 1918—had been superseded by later legislation.

Time was when the chief clerk was generally the man who inherited the warden's job, but the Department of Correction now requires that he come up through the ranks. That means, in practice, that it's generally the principal keeper—the PK— who takes over. It means too that the new warden will bring to his job every prejudice he's acquired in dealing with prisoners in the process of working his way up from the ranks. Most of the prison staff are born and bred to their duties: a closed family where the profession of hack passes, almost like a hereditary title, from father to son. Paradoxically, the only way to let a little air and light into the system is to appoint, at the very top of the pyramid, somebody who's a complete stranger to the prison system: a doctor, a sociologist, an educator who can look at the problems without bias. The good warden can leave the day-to-day business of running a prison to his staff, and devote his time to finding solutions. But in most prisons the solutions have remained pretty much unchanged over the last few thousand years: the club and the box.

The primary concern of the PK in a prison is discipline, so the club and the box loom pretty large in his thinking. If the chief clerk wears civvies, and thinks pretty much like a civilian, the PK looks like a soldier—blue uniform, gold eagles on his shoulders, visored cap with gold insignia—and all the white-shirted "brass" under him, beginning with the captain of the guard—two bars on the shoulders—and working down through the sergeants—stripes on sleeve—to the blue-shirted, club-carrying "officers"—really the equivalent of enlisted men —are closer to the military than the civilian in their functions. The PK sees that the warden's policies are carried out, signs the bulk of official notices appearing on the bulletin board, maintains order, suppresses and punishes any sort of illegal traffic or activity prejudicial to order, judging the accused in a kind of summary court held in his office. Any violator of any rule is likely to find himself accounting for his action in the PK's court, and punishment can be anything from a simple reprimand or the deprivation of a week's yard time to a year in solitary. The PK, invoking discipline, can abolish any privilege he chooses, individual or collective. Only the warden can overrule him, and the warden never does.

The years pass; and in the drab gray world I inhabit nothing changes but the dates on the calendar. I sit in my cell and try one night, after lights out, to establish the chronology of all my wasted years: nine months in the Sing Sing death house; eight years in Auburn; three years in Attica; one year in Greenhaven; eleven years in Dannemora. Nothing changes: only the names.

I remember fighting with an inmate—why we fought I can't recall—fighting with the guard who tried to break it up, then being worked over by half a dozen guards, and being dragged off to the box, where they threw a bucket of cold water on me. While I was drying off I totted up the damage: a kick in the mouth cost me four teeth—the empty spaces were there to prove it—and I'd have laid odds I had at least four cracked ribs. But nobody sent for a doctor, so I'll probably never know.

1940: I am put in the box at Auburn. Why? Probably I deserve it—my rage at being imprisoned is new, and I have not yet learned to live with it. The box is a tiny dungeon, the bottom cell of the old block, without toilet facilities, without drinking water, without lights. I am in irons for a month or more. No bath, no change of clothes; my hair grows long and straggly; an unkempt beard reaches to my chest; I smell like a goat and look like the village idiot; I know neither the day of the week or the time of day: is it morning? is it night? Under guard I am taken to the office of the prison psychiatrist, whom I have met previously and whom I respect. "Look at this man," says the sergeant, pointing at me. "He's out of his mind. Can you certify him?" The doctor orders a bath and a shave for me, after which I look less like Rasputin, and requests an interview with the warden, recommending I be released from the box. The warden has no use for me: "There are so many charges against this man that the reasons for putting him in isolation are academic." But he promises to return me to my regular cell. Satisfied, the doctor withdraws and I am put back in solitary on the warden's order. It is a full week before the doctor manages to find me: I have been salted away in an out-of-the-way corner. He is angry that his advice has been disregarded. "What does it matter?" I say. "In the cell or in the box—it's still prison."

Another psychiatrist whose advice is disregarded: at Greenhaven. Interviewing me on my arrival, he suggests informal, group discussions, a kind of grievance committee to act as a buffer between the men in blue and the men in gray. No stool pigeons; no reprisals for speaking your mind: an honest attempt to reduce needless frictions in the prison community. Men like me, serving long terms and knowing the system, could be helpful. Would I come to such a discussion? Would I bring friends with something to contribute? At one o'clock on the following day I appear at the doctor's office with six or eight friends; chairs are placed in a circle and the doctor takes his place in the middle; discussion begins. Complaints are legitimate, not petty: visits are impaired because of the physical deficiencies of the visiting room—the poor visibility, the need to shout; prisoners in the four different "yards" are never allowed to mingle, even on Sundays, though many men have friends in other yards from whom they are isolated for no apparent reason; the composition of meals in the mess hall is predictable six months in advance down to the last split pea, the last diced carrot. We got along fine; the doctor was pleased with us and we with him, and it showed in the discussion. He'd see what he could do; we'd meet again: he favored weekly meetings and the formation of a regular committee to represent the inmates. That was the first meeting and the last. The PK got wind of it and told the doc it "wasn't his province" to set up a grievance committee inside the prison. And a few weeks later the good doctor resigned his post.

Louis Lefkowitz was one of Guariglia's lawyers at the trial. Dominick promised me he'd tell him I had nothing to do with the case. When Lefkowitz became Attorney General for the state of New York, the family got in touch with him. Did he remember the East Side boys? Did he remember Zimmerman? Yes, very well. But the trial was handled by the city of New York, and he was an official of the state. There was nothing he could do. Sorry. Sorry.

Carl's letters are growing increasingly optimistic. Hanover no longer heads for the hills when they meet on the street; he seems less nervous. He's not anxious to talk about the case, understandably enough, but he no longer seems afraid to discuss it. Carl is waiting for a chance to explain what the lawyers told him: that unless new evidence turned up, I'd be buried here in prison forever. Rose doesn't seem to understand what his testimony did to me; maybe Hanover doesn't understand either.

News from Carl: Detective Wandling is dead. Since around 1954. Not in my mind's eye, where I'll always see him as he was, a kind of caricature of the old-time, classical iron-hatted detective: the big brogans, the ruddy pink complexion—he was not the man to refuse a drink or two—the thin, sandy hair, shoulders back, stance erect, hands like hams. Six feet easy, and two hundred and ten pounds; when he put one of those hands on your shoulder you had the impression it was covered completely. A little brogue still. All he needed was a derby— which he never wore—and a handlebar mustache to be per- fectly in character, the All-Time Detective Stereotype. I wouldn't miss him.

And Hanover: he'd signed an affidavit and sworn to it, Carl wrote; this was new evidence. "You've got nothing to be afraid of," he told Hanover. And Hanover said, "All right, I'll see your lawyer now." I had a lawyer too, he told me: a con- scientious and energetic young attorney named Burlakoff who was really digging into the case, laying the groundwork for an appeal. And it didn't stop with that. When Carl told Danny Rose about Hanover's affidavit, Danny said he'd see Burlakoff too and make a statement of his own. Somehow, too, Carl got hold of a phone number for Cooperman and told him what was happening. Cooperman just said he didn't want to be involved, and that ended that. Carl says it doesn't matter about Cooperman; with the new lawyer and the statements by Rose and Hanover, it's only a matter of time before I'm home again.

It's only a matter of time. I am beginning to believe it.

CHAPTER 5

THE
APPEAL

TIME 3:00 P.M., June 11, 1956. Place: the Criminal Courts Building at 100 Centre Street, New York City. In Part VII of the Court of General Sessions of the County of New York, Judge John A. Mullen is presiding at the hearing of a *coram nobis* petition brought by Isidore Zimmerman, #31063 at Dannemora Prison. The purpose of such a petition or writ of error is to permit the examination by the Court of new evidence that may affect a legal decision arrived at earlier. The purpose of the present hearing—which will last ten days, to June 22—is to consider whether the petitioner Zimmerman's 1938 conviction for murder in the first degree should be set aside as improper. Counsel for Zimmerman is Bernard Burlakoff. Representing the People of the State of New York is Assistant District Attorney Alexander Herman.

The first witness to take the stand on behalf of Zimmerman is Daniel Rose.

=====

The witness has previously testified against Zimmerman at his trial in April, 1938; against Footke (for violation of the Sullivan Act in connection with the Foley murder) in April, 1940, before a Grand Jury; and again against Little Benny Ertel, apprehended in Washington, D.C., tried in New York

178

in February, 1940, and thereafter executed for his part in the felony murder of Foley. It was a teen-ager whose testimony helped send Zimmerman to the death house; today it is a man of forty-two who sits in the witness stand: older, heavier, with a wife, children, responsibilities. He has long since moved from the Lower East Side uptown to a ground-floor apartment in the East Sixties. He works as a welder-mechanic now, and for each day's absence from work he is compensated at the rate of $16.60. So far, thanks to procedural matters occupying the court, he is $33.20 richer. He has never served a day in prison in his life.

On October 24 of the previous year—1955—Rose, in a drugstore on First Avenue and 66th Street, swore before a notary public to the veracity of an affidavit he had dictated earlier that afternoon in the presence of Carl Zimmerman, Isidore's brother, and of Bernard Burlakoff, Zimmerman's lawyer. This affidavit, together with another of similar content executed by Tobias Hanover, justifies the present *coram nobis* hearing to the extent that it constitutes new evidence bearing on Zimmerman's conviction.

The last paragraph on the first page of Rose's affidavit begins: "In April of 1937, I was sixteen years of age. I lived on the Lower East Side with my parents. Two detectives came to my home and took me to the police station. These two detectives, Wandling and Gallagher, told me that a detective had been shot in a restaurant during a hold-up and that a fellow by the name of Footke Savoy told them he got the guns from me. I told Detective Wandling I had nothing to do with it. Wandling came to my house several times and took me to the police station and to the District Attorney's office for questioning. A couple of weeks later I admitted that I had given a gun to Footke, but I never knew what he did or intended to do with it.

"I was taken before the Grand Jury [there is as yet no indictment of O'Loughlin, Guariglia, and the others] and I testified, but I did not say anything about Zimmerman and I was not asked about Zimmerman . . . Nothing much happened in so far as I was concerned until about the middle of February, 1938, when Detective Wandling again came to my house to take me to the District Attorney's office."

Between the first visit by Wandling—in April, 1937, within a day or two of Foley's shooting—and the beginning of the trial of the East Side boys—in March, 1938—Rose receives between ten and fifteen subpoenas to appear for police questioning—"I remember . . . they give you fifty cents for each subpoena"—sometimes at the Clinton Street precinct house, sometimes at the District Attorney's office, sometimes in the presence of stenographers, sometimes not. Since, as Rose points out on the stand, nearly nineteen years have elapsed since the events under discussion, he is often uncertain of names and dates. On one of his appearances for questioning, which Rose fixes as "maybe the third visit . . . maybe second or third visit to the District Attorney's office up until before the trial" (i.e., by his testimony around mid-February), Rose mentions Zimmerman's name for the first time he can recollect to Detective Wandling. "Detective Wandling turned around and said, 'You are sure that you didn't give it [the gun] to Beansy?' I says, 'No.' I said, 'I did not give it to Beansy. I had given the gun to Footke and Footke had put it away in a hall.' And he [Wandling] asked me what time that I had seen . . . Beansy. And I told him that . . . it was after twelve, the first time I had seen him was about 11:30, a quarter to twelve, somewhere around that . . . and the last time . . . was a little bit after . . . around 12:30 or quarter to one when I walked home with him. I told that to Detective Wandling. He didn't believe me. He called me a liar . . . He said, 'Are you sure that is the truth?' and all that . . . and he says, 'You better find out something else to tell me . . . or you are going to get into trouble.' But I didn't know what else I could tell him. I mean . . . I didn't want to make up; but then later on . . . from one visit to another, he kept coaching me on what to say . . . He told me that . . . I should say that I had given the gun to Beansy and not to Footke . . . He told me that I was going to go up before the jury at the trial and that he wanted

me to say that I had given the gun to Beansy, and that Beansy
was the brain . . . as you would call it, that he planned the
whole thing; and he says to me that, if I wanted to stay out of
jail, that I should just do what he said."

He made a number of statements, declares Rose, "each the
same until . . . the last heavy amount of pressure that was put
on me, which was in the early part of January, 1938 . . . That
is when I started to change . . . I wasn't touched or beaten
up . . . What I mean by pressure was that I was told that I
could go to jail . . . I was told by Detective Wandling that I
could go to jail for maybe three to six years because of the
Sullivan Law, which states that I am not supposed to have a
firearm."

In the early part of 1938 Detective Wandling brings Rose
to the office of Assistant District Attorney Jacob Rosenblum,
who is to prosecute the case. Rosenblum confronts Rose on
three occasions, and on all three Wandling is present. At the
first meeting Rose does not incriminate Zimmerman. As he
testifies at the *coram nobis* hearing: "I understood that he
[Rosenblum] didn't believe the statement that I made . . . I
was called a liar . . . I think I was told to go home and I was
handed another subpoena . . . for a later date." On his second
visit to Rosenblum's office, testifies Rose, "Detective Wandling, while coming up . . . the hall, said that I should play
ball with the District Attorney and to make sure that I said
that I had given the gun to Beansy and that I didn't give it
to Footke, that I had given it to Beansy." Again, contends
Rose, he recounts "almost the identical story that I had told
previous" to Rosenblum.

On his third and last pre-trial visit to Rosenblum's office
—March 5, thirteen days before the beginning of the trial—
testifies Rose, "Detective Wandling this time told me that if
I didn't play ball and do what he told me, that he would see
that I would fry and get the chair . . ." Before Rose enters
Rosenblum's office, "for a half-hour or so . . . he sort of told
me that when Mr. Rosenblum asked me who I had given . . .
the gun to, I should say that I had given it to Mr. Zimmerman

. . . and I seen Beansy take them and put them in his pocket and walk away with them. That is about all I can remember."

After this conversation with Wandling, says Rose, he was ushered into Rosenblum's office. No stenographer was present, though one was to be admitted later to take his statement. In Rose's recollection: "[I was asked] did I recall . . . giving the gun to Beansy and that I didn't give it to Footke; and I sort of hesitated there for a while, and . . . Mr. Rosenblum passed a remark to Detective Wandling—I don't know the exact words—because I remember Detective Wandling grabbed me on the shoulder and took me out into the next room, sort of was a little mad, and he said, 'Now, you do what I told you,' he says, 'or I'll make sure that you go to jail or fry,' or whatever it was . . . and he brought me back in again and that is when I changed my story completely and said that I had given the gun to Beany, whatever Mr. Detective Wandling wanted me to say, and then, as I recall, then the stenographer was brought in and it was taken down."

Nineteen days later Rose was to take the stand as a key witness for the prosecution's case against Zimmerman. Questions Burlakoff, eighteen years and three months later: "Now, Mr. Rose, the story that you testified to at the trial, was that the truth?" Objection by the Assistant District Attorney; overruled by the judge. Burlakoff: "Was that the truth . . . with respect to Zimmerman?" Rose: "With respect to Zimmerman, no, sir, it wasn't the truth . . ."

Why the change? Some months before the present hearing, declares Rose, "I happened to be downtown and passed by the neighborhood [the section of the East Side which he left in 1938], stopped off to say hello to a friend of mine, and asked him about the old gang . . . And then I asked him if . . . Isidore Zimmerman ever got out of jail and how long he has been out; and I was told that he is still in. I thought that he was kidding me." It was food for thought. District Attorney Herman: "Was your conscience bothering you?" Rose: "Well, my conscience bothered me a little bit, yes." Herman: "Had your conscience ever bothered you since 1938?" Rose: "No, because I did not think he was going to be in that long."

Carl Zimmerman, trying to establish his brother's innocence, is anxious to talk with Rose; Rose is willing. The meeting takes place one evening in Rose's uptown apartment. Carl asks Rose "if I would help . . . They wanted me to help get Beany out of jail, and I thought he was out already. Jesus, it's a long time. I said, 'He shouldn't be in there.' And he says, 'Well, will you tell it to the lawyer?' I said, 'Well, if I could help him, I will help him.' "

Tevyah Hanover too has changed. His thin hair is graying; he wears rimless glasses now; and his health is none too good. He is sixty-two. His command of English has not improved, nor has his accent diminished with the years. The candy store is gone, but he now works for the Krimgor Cigar Store at 570 Eighth Avenue; his boss begrudges him the time off to appear in court. Down the years since his testimony helped convict Zimmerman, Hanover has had unpleasant reminders of the case. When Benny Ertel was extradited to New York for trial, he recalls, Detective Wandling dropped by the store. " 'We got Ertel, and be ready to be in court again,' that's what he told me . . . I testified." Ertel will get the chair, but, says Hanover, "I didn't have to testify in a lie, because he was there that night [the night of Foley's murder] with all the boys."

Tevyah's acquaintance with Wandling is a long one. His shop is in Wandling's precinct, and even before the Boulevard holdup his visits are routine. On the Monday following the shooting of Foley, Wandling visits him in search of leads on Chaleff, on Friedman, and on Guariglia. (There is no mention yet of Zimmerman. Wandling's first reference to him, says Hanover, will be "about seven or eight months later," that is, not before the fall of 1937.) Wandling returns, again and again, and Hanover, whom the police know to have been involved in taking policy slips, finds the visits disquieting:

running the store leaves him little leisure for interviews with police officers. "He [Wandling] kept me awake for the whole time what I was supposed to sleep, between two and five," mentions Hanover. "He was every day in my house . . . He left me a telephone number. I told him, 'Don't come up because I got to sleep a little. If I'll hear anything, I'll call for you.' " In time "he served me with a subpoena. He says, 'You come to the District Attorney's office.' . . . He promised me he wouldn't take me long." Hanover is asked to identify mug shots, answer questions, make statements, sign statements. "I was doing anything they asked me just to get out of the office, because I left my store all alone." He never examines any of the statements after they are transcribed, "because I can't read too much, and I never bothered with it . . . I was for weeks and weeks there [at the District Attorney's office]. I used to be there as far as five days a week on the bench there in the corridor, and at four o'clock they used to say, 'Go home and we will call you tomorrow.' "

Like Rose, Hanover has provided Burlakoff with an affidavit in support of these affirmations. Its text, beginning at the bottom of page 2, reads: "I was . . . taken to the district attorney's office by Detective Wandling where I was interviewed by Assistant District Attorney Joseph Sarafite. Mr. Sarafite asked me to describe the boys who were seated around the table having sodas. I did so. He asked me if Zimmerman was with them. I told him that he was not. Mr. Zimmerman on the night in question was not inside my store at all and . . . he had nothing at all to do with the boys. He then told me to sit outside and . . . Detective Wandling came and made various threats to me about what he would do if I did not co-operate with him and the district attorney with reference to Zimmerman . . . Finally I was brought in before Assistant District Attorney Rosenblum. Mr. Rosenblum told me point-blank that he can subpoena anyone, including the Governor, to come before him and that if I did not bring Zimmerman into the picture I would be sitting outside on the bench for as long as months and months to come, that he would see to it that I would go to jail as a material witness, that I would lose my business and be disgraced with my family in the neighborhood . . . I testified at the trial that Zimmerman had a soda at the counter and that the boys called him over to talk to him, that he went over, stood by the edge of the table and then went out of the store. That was not the truth. The Assistant District Attorney and the police officers all knew that it was not the truth. I had told them that Zimmerman came into my store, had a soda, and went out of the store by himself. He had nothing at all to do with the other boys nor did he talk to them that night. The only reason that I testified as I did at the trial was because I was intimidated by Assistant District Attorney Rosenblum and Detective Wandling . . . When I was in the district attorney's office . . . I heard . . . Wandling say to . . . Rosenblum, 'Make it one case and mix Beany in with the bunch too . . . I'm going to fix him good.' I couldn't understand why they wanted to mix Zimmerman in with the other boys since they knew and I knew that Zimmerman had nothing at all to do with them. But when Wandling stated that he 'wanted to fix' Zimmerman . . . I understood what I will have to do in order to escape from their clutches. I did it, but it has been on my conscience ever since. It has made me sick. I have been under a doctor's care, but nothing will help me until I tell the truth."

On redirect examination Hanover reaffirms from the witness stand the contentions of his affidavit: until 1938 no one mentioned Zimmerman's name to him in connection with the Foley case. Then, after "a conference before District Attorney Rosenblum and Sarafite" early in the year, Wandling began talking of him to Hanover. Burlakoff: "Now, what did Detective Wandling say to you about Mr. Zimmerman?" Hanover: "He says, 'I want you to tell me the truth that he was there.' I said, 'I don't know.' He says, 'I want to get through with that case . . .' And I said, 'No,' and 'No,' and finally he says, 'I am taking you to the District Attorney's office and you got to say whatever I want, because that means to me a promotion and I want to get through with the case.' "

Question: "What did Detective Wandling . . . [want] you to say about Zimmerman?" Answer: "That . . . he was there . . . that night with the other boys in my store."

———————

But Hanover is well beyond his depth. Bewildered by court procedure, hampered by his imperfect command of English, concerned—as he was eighteen years earlier—at the idea of losing time from work even in the interest of justice ("I've got a letter here, your Honor, what the boss said the Court should sign that I was here yesterday and today"), he proves to be the weakest of possible witnesses on Zimmerman's behalf. Under cross-examination he is a natural target, a born loser, a sitting duck. Moreover, months in advance of the present hearing, the value of Hanover's revelations has been so vitiated by the District Attorney's office that now, in court, only a casual *coup de grâce* is required.

In January of the current year—1956—Mr. Herman, representing the People of New York County, assigns Manuel Graymore to an investigation in connection with Isidore Zimmerman's *coram nobis* petition. So it is that Graymore, who has spent two of his three years as a member of the District Attorney's staff working with the Homicide Bureau, meets with Tobias Hanover on two occasions in the witness room— 606: on February 28, and then again on March 1. Statements are taken both times; and both times there are conversational exchanges between the Assistant District Attorney, Graymore, and the ex-storekeeper that the stenographer does not record.

At the first meeting, says Graymore, "I apologized for having kept him waiting for such a long time, and I explained to him that I was interested in getting some information in connection with the affidavit which he had executed [in Zimmerman's behalf] . . . and that I was going to ask him some questions about it." There ensues a question-and-answer period. At its conclusion, continues Graymore, "I spoke to him [Hanover] and asked him when it would be convenient for him to come down again to resume our interview. And he explained to me that he worked during the daytime and that his employer objected to his taking time off from the afternoon; that it would be best after he gets through with work. So I made an appointment with him for March 1 in the evening, and he said he would come down."

At the second meeting, after another question-and-answer session, the stenographer is dismissed and Graymore has another conversation with Hanover. "The gist . . . was," testifies Graymore, "that from what Hanover had related to me, I gathered that he was under the impression that the conviction of Zimmerman at the first trial . . . depended solely on his testimony; and I told him that, for his own benefit, I would like to indicate to him that there was other testimony [that is, the testimony of Cooperman and Rose] connecting this defendant to the crime with which he was charged, and it wasn't his [Hanover's] sole responsibility that Zimmerman had been convicted . . . I thought that he was sincerely mistaken as to what . . . he thought he had testified to during the trial. In his statement I recall . . . that he had the idea that he testified during the trial that the petitioner Zimmerman left the candy store in the company of . . . the other defendants; and he was very insistent in telling me that Zimmerman had left alone, as he recalled. And I had examined the record previously to interviewing him, so I knew that he was mistaken as to what he had thought he said. And I thought perhaps this was the important thing . . . since he did make such a point about it and didn't negate anything else that he testified to . . ." In another view, "the important thing" might be deemed not that Hanover was "mistaken as to what he had thought he said" back in 1937, but that he was stressing, in 1956, that what he said earlier was false. And while Graymore feels justified in reminding Hanover "that Zimmerman was convicted not solely on Hanover's testimony, but on the testimony of other witnesses," he sees no need to recall that Cooperman's complicity in the Foley murder was officially recognized, and that Rose's complicity was not, by only the narrowest of margins. Whatever the spirit in which Graymore offers these reassurances to Hanover, their effect—even on a character stronger than Tevyah's—may well cancel out what pangs of conscience Hanover feels as a consequence of his role at Zimmerman's trial. Viewed in another light, Graymore's handling of Hanover can be likened to that of an officer in charge of a firing squad: don't feel bad about executing people, he can always say to the tender-hearted rifleman; you're not the only man pulling a trigger.

By his affidavit Hanover has certified to giving false testimony about Zimmerman at the time of the trial; and by his two statements to Mr. Graymore he has managed, to all intents and purposes, to impair the value of the affidavit and, by extension, reaffirm the validity of his trial testimony. Under cross-examination at the *coram nobis* hearings Hanover completes the nullification of his affidavit in the course of skirmishes like this with the Assistant District Attorney, Mr. Herman. Question: "Did you say that you told Mr. Graymore that Zimmerman was not in your store in '37?" Hanover: "Mr. Graymore I said [told] he had a soda and he went out. That is what I said." Herman: "Didn't you also tell Mr Graymore . . . that, before he went out, he stopped over to talk to the boys at the table there?" Hanover: "Well, that is what I said." Herman: "Well, *did* you tell that to Mr. Graymore?" (He wants a yes or no answer.) Hanover: "Yes, that is what I said *according to the first statement*." (Herman is talking about Hanover's declarations to Graymore; Hanover, about his original testimony at the trial. For Hanover, at any rate, the confusion is never properly dispelled; his answers are blurred and sufficiently contradictory to require an intervention by Judge Mullen; and the upshot of Hanover's confusion is a clear victory for Herman, a clear defeat for Zimmerman.) Judge Mullen: "Did you say anything to Mr. Graymore about 'according to the first statement'?" Hanover: "I made the same statement what I made in '38 to Mr. Graymore." Judge Mullen: "Please listen to my question. Did you tell Mr. Graymore that 'I am saying this because I said it before,' or did you just tell it to Mr. Graymore?" Hanover: "I just told him, yes; I just

told him." Judge Mullen: "You didn't mention to him anything about that prior statement?" Hanover: "I didn't mention,
no. No, this I didn't mention." Assistant District Attorney
Herman, resuming: "And did you tell the truth to Mr.
Graymore?" (If Hanover's answer to this question is Yes,
then the value of his affidavit in support of Zimmerman is
canceled out. If he answers No, he admits to lying to a
member of the District Attorney's office.) Hanover: "Well, I
told him what—" (Vaguely aware of the inconsistency of his
testimony, he is nonetheless incapable of escaping from it.)
Herman: "Did you tell him the truth?" Judge Mullen: "Make
up your mind." Hanover: "I told him what I recall." (He may
mean "what he recalls from his trial testimony," but it is
possible he simply has no idea of an appropriate answer at
this point.) Judge Mullen: " 'Did you tell Mr. Graymore the
truth?' is the question that is being asked of you now." Hanover, aware he cannot rationally claim to have lied to Graymore: "That's what I told him." Judge Mullen: "What is
that?" Hanover: "I told him that he had a soda and he walked
out." Judge Mullen: "Was that the truth?" Hanover: "Yes, sir,
but according the [*sic*] last [1938] statement—" Judge Mullen:
"No, never mind about 'according to the last statement.' I am
asking you, Was that the truth?" Hanover: "That was not the
truth." (Hanover means that his trial testimony was not the
truth; Judge Mullen, however, is concerned with his declarations to Graymore. The confusion continues.) Judge Mullen:
"Then you state now that you lied to Mr. Graymore?" Hanover: "To Mr. Graymore I followed the same statement what
[*sic*] I did before [in 1938]." Judge Mullen: "Did you lie oɪ
did you tell the truth?" Hanover: "Now I had to lie, because
according [*sic*] he [Graymore] had a statement [from 1938]."
Judge Mullen: "Did you lie or did you tell the truth?" Hanover: "I told the truth what I recollect [meaning in the
affidavit, as opposed to his false statements in 1938]." Judge
Mullen, again: "Did you lie or did you tell the truth?" Hanover, bewildered: "I don't know what you mean, your Honor,
by did I lie or told the truth." Judge Mullen: "You know

the difference between a lie and the truth?" Hanover: "I know I was lying the first time [at the trial]." Judge Mullen, again: "Do you know the difference between a lie and the truth?" Hanover: "Yes, sir." (This question, at any rate, is easy for him to answer: no one in his senses is likely to tell a judge on the bench that lies are good and the truth bad.) Judge Mullen, returning to his original point, of which Hanover has by now lost sight: "All right. Did you tell Mr. Graymore a lie or did you tell him the truth?" The judge's point is simple: if Hanover's statements to Graymore—which at this point are tantamount to a repetition of his trial testimony—are the truth, then Hanover's statements in the affidavit are false. Hanover's understanding of the question is much simpler: he is being asked whether or not he is a liar. And so he replies, "I told him the truth."

Mr. Herman, now that the uncomprehending Hanover has been thoroughly demolished by the judge, shows he can be modest in victory. "That's all," he says: Hanover can return, without further harassment, to his occupations at the Krimgor Cigar Store.

———————

Assistant District Attorney Manuel Graymore, called as a witness on behalf of the People on June 19, has not confined his preparation for the *coram nobis* hearing to discussions with Tobias Hanover. Because of Daniel Rose's affidavit in support of Zimmerman's petition, he too has been interviewed by Graymore on two occasions during the month of March. The first Graymore-Rose meeting lasts two hours; the second between ninety and one hundred twenty minutes, compared to a total of forty-seven minutes for the two Graymore-Hanover sessions. For both meetings with Rose, Graymore dispenses with the services of a stenographer. Why? "The reason," testifies Graymore, "was that I was never satisfied that what Rose was telling me was true. He told me any number of accounts, so I never could be satisfied that any one of them was a correct account." Although Counselor Burlakoff, pressing Zimmerman's case, does not raise the question in so many words, it suggests itself at once: since Rose, from the beginning of his involvement in the Foley case, has been conspicuous for giving "any number of accounts," how can the District Attorney's office, which is not now "satisfied that one of them was . . . correct," have been satisfied to the contrary at the time of the trial? If Mr. Graymore feels that Rose may be lying in 1956, is there not some reason to suppose that he may have been lying in 1938—or 1937—as well?

In the courtroom Burlakoff takes a slightly different tack. Before Graymore's meetings with Hanover, arrangements were made for a stenographer to be available. But before Graymore's meetings with Rose, no such arrangement were made. Why? asks Burlakoff. Graymore's answer: he was acting on the basis of information furnished by a Detective Kelley of the Homicide Bureau. "I asked him," testifies Graymore, "first to speak to Rose informally about the reason why I wanted to talk to him, just to feel him out and see what his attitude was, and Detective Kelly told me that he was very antagonistic and he was a bit of a screwball, so I thought it best not to take his statement from him, without actually finding out what he did in fact have to say." No such problem arose in the case of Hanover.

Now Burlakoff has two telling questions for Graymore. First: "With respect to the witness Hanover, you desired to perpetuate his testimony?" Graymore: "Yes, I did." Second: "Now, with respect to the witness Rose, can you tell us, please, why you did *not* perpetuate his testimony?" An interjection from the bench here provides the answer which Graymore may have been on the point of giving. Judge Mullen: "I think he [Graymore] told you on the record that Rose told four or five different accounts of what happened. Is that what you said?" Graymore: "That is correct, your Honor."

Assistant District Attorney Graymore concedes in this exchange that during the investigation necessitated by Zimmerman's *coram nobis* action he has taken statements from Hanover amounting to a repetition of his 1938 testimony, and refused statements from Rose in contradiction with his 1938 testimony. If this course of action simplifies the task of the District Attorney's office, it all but nullifies Zimmerman's appeal: because of it the *coram nobis* hearings may be judged to bring absolutely no new elements to the case. If Hanover is easy to confound in a courtroom—or even in casual conversation—Rose is another matter altogether. He has produced an affidavit in support of Zimmerman whch can only be embarrassing for the District Attorney's office: suddenly, unexpectedly, the man who was the People's witness in 1938 has become, for the People's representatives in 1956, "very antagonistic . . . a bit of a screwball," apt to give "any number of accounts" of a given set of facts. In plainer language, a liar. In the vocabulary of the courts a man who lies under oath— last year, this year, or next—is a perjurer.

Accordingly, a good three months before the beginning of the present hearings, Graymore issues a subpoena calling for Rose to appear—March 9, 1956—before a Grand Jury. Grounds: "investigation [in] to the possible crime of subordination of perjury." The District Attorney's office feels it is time for Rose to learn—never too late—that perjury calls for punishment. But on Rose the antagonistic the lesson seems lost. On June 13 he charges from the witness stand: "I was threatened . . . with perjury. He [Graymore] said if I went ahead with the case [i.e., testified for Zimmerman in the present hearings] he would see that I had a perjury rap against me . . . He said that in front of a detective . . . I swear on my kids I was threatened with perjury no more than ten weeks ago if I went ahead with this case, and I told him, 'I am going ahead with it.' "

Now, six days after Rose's outburst, Graymore is concluding the account of his preparation of the People's case for the present hearings. Most of the ground has been covered; the afternoon is drawing to a close; and Burlakoff, like a fighter anxious to finish his opponent before the bell, moves in to inflict a final dose of punishment on Graymore. "Were you interested," he asks, "in preparing the case for hearing or in ascertaining whether or not the facts contained in the affidavits were true or not?" Clarification from the bench: "I take it you [Graymore] were a lawyer and you were acting as a lawyer for the People, whose position was antagonistic to . . . [Zimmerman's]; is that correct?" Graymore: "That's correct, your Honor." Burlakoff: "Now, Mr. Graymore, were you acting as an attorney for the People of the State of New York, whose position was antagonistic to that of . . . [Zimmerman], or as an assistant district attorney interested in finding out where the truth lies and particularly whether or not a crime had been committed as against this defendant Zimmerman which had resulted in his conviction of the crime of murder?" Graymore: "I was interested in both of those functions."

Burlakoff, stalking: "Now . . . in connection with your interest in whether or not the defendant Zimmerman had been unjustly convicted, were you interested in obtaining a statement from any witness, whether you agreed with it or not, or whether . . . it supported the People's contention or not? . . . Were you interested in obtaining statements only from those witnesses who would support the People's contention or were you interested in obtaining statements from any witness who had any knowledge of the facts surrounding this case?" Graymore: "I was primarily interested in investigating the truth or lack of truth of the allegations in Zimmerman's [coram nobis] petition and the allegations in the affidavits submitted by the witnesses Rose and Hanover. I assumed that all the other witnesses were going to adhere to their previous testimony, in which case there would be no point in speaking to them about it."

Burlakoff, finding the answer unsatisfactory, phrases his question more directly: "Would you have taken the statement from any witness who did not support the People's contention?" Graymore's handling of the witness Rose—first, dispensing with stenographic statements such as he was willing to take from Hanover, and second, issuing Rose a subpoena in connection with "possible subornation of perjury"—makes the question difficult to answer with a Yes, and a No would seem incompatible with justice. Judge Mullen intervenes, without making the question less dangerous: "Counsel [Burlakoff] wants to know would you take statements only from persons who supported the conviction of this man by a jury and affirmed by the Court of Appeals, or would you take statements from anybody whose testimony might upset that through a *coram nobis* proceeding?" Graymore: ". . . The only way I can answer that question is that the general practice is to take statements from witnesses where you desire for some reason or other to perpetuate their testimony. If a witness, say, would make statements unfavorable to our defense of the charges made in this [Zimmerman's] petition, it wouldn't be necessary to take the statement of that testimony because we would assume that the person would repeat that same thing on the stand, or perhaps add to it. It would depend on the witness, what the situation was and how it occurred. There is really no general rule."

Correction: there is a general rule, and Graymore has stated it. The prosecution is interested solely in elements which convict, or which maintain a conviction once acquired. Anything else is not worth recording.

―――

On June 19, Isidore Zimmerman takes the stand in his own behalf. Without his initiative there would have been no *coram nobis* hearing; the testimony of Rose, of Hanover, of Graymore—indeed, each of the ten days of court sessions—relates, directly or indirectly, to him; and yet less than a day will be given to his testimony. Though most intimately concerned with the outcome of the proceedings, he is the least questioned: from the time of his arrest in 1937 he has been assigned, by law, the passive role, the role of the man to whom things are done. But Zimmerman has no illusions about the importance of the present hearing: it is, literally, his last chance at life. An exchange with Assistant District Attorney Herman reflects his awareness of the stakes: "Don't put words in my mouth . . . Don't try to browbeat me in this court. I am fighting for my life and you know I should not be here."

What Zimmerman has to say, then, is short, and, to the extent that it does not go over ground already covered by Rose and Hanover, startling. In January, 1938, some two months before the trial of the East Side boys, Zimmerman's counsel, James Murray, visited him in the Tombs Prison. As lawyer to client, testifies Zimmerman, "Mr. Murray told me that my indictment was going to be dismissed before the end of February."

In the course of the same month, ". . . a detective came down to the Tombs to see me . . . and told me to sign a paper which would enable him to take me to the district attorney's office." Zimmerman declines to go without his lawyer's approval, but Murray has no objection; the matter has nothing to do with the Foley case. "Probably a few days later I was brought to the district attorney's office . . . To the best of my recollection it was in January of 1938." Present, recalls Zimmerman, were Murray and Mr. James Neary, an Assistant District Attorney.

Now Zimmerman learns the purpose of the visit. Six months earlier—in June, 1937—he had been placed in a cell in the Tombs when "about five minutes later a man was brought in, put into the cell with me. His name was Lawrence Sullivan. The man was a mass of bruises, practically from the top of his head to the tip of his toes, and I had to nurse him . . ." There Zimmerman had supposed—mistakenly— the incident closed. But now, in January, Neary brings up the episode again. "He wants to ask me some questions about the Sullivan case. During the questioning he told me, '. . . Isn't it true that you had a fight with Sullivan?' and . . . 'If he had bruises on him you put them there?' I said, 'That is definitely not the truth.' He says, 'Would you want to help us in this case?' I told him that if I was to help him I'd be telling a lie. And there was some other words to the conversation, I don't recall just what, but that was probably the heart of the matter. And then he told me if I would not help the district attorney's office that it would be extremely hard for me, that I could be very sorry. There wasn't much I could say. I told him I had no intentions of testifying for Sullivan or anybody else."

On the same occasion, testifies Zimmerman, there occurs a second incident which remains fresh in his memory. "When I was brought out of the district attorney's office, Mr. Rosenblum came over toward me." Burlakoff inquires if this is the same Mr. Rosenblum who has been present in the courtroom at the District Attorney's table since the beginning of this hearing: the former Assistant District Attorney, Jacob Rosenblum. Zimmerman: "Yes, sir. He asked Mr. Neary if I was going to co-operate, and Mr. Neary answered, 'No, he's not. He doesn't want to help himself either.' Mr. Neary left, and then Mr. Rosenblum told me that if I step into the courtroom as a winess for Sullivan that I would regret it . . . every day I lived."

Now when the case of the People versus Lawrence Sullivan comes to trial in February, 1938, Zimmerman is subpoenaed by the defense after an appeal by Sullivan's attorney to Zimmerman. "He told me, without my testimony the man hasn't got a chance. I decided to testify. I felt it my moral duty to do so. In fact, I had made my mind up before that, and told Sullivan that I would testify. I did. I testified as to various bruises he had, his entire physical condition, how long I nursed him, what I had to do . . ." Sullivan—who told Zimmerman of having signed a confession just before being put in the cell with him—was acquitted of the charge of murder and freed. Zimmerman went on trial for his life in the course of the following month.

What of Murray's assurance to Zimmerman that the "indictment was going to be dismissed before the end of February?" In the light of what was to happen, it can be judged—at best—erroneous. What of the threats Zimmerman attributes to Neary and to Rosenblum for his refusal to "co-operate" on the Sullivan case? Both men, on the witness stand, deny not only the conversations but the physical possibility—for administrative reasons—of their taking place. Further, all records in the Tombs antedating 1940 that might serve to corroborate the transfer of a prisoner—Zimmerman—to the office of the District Attorney were destroyed five or six years before the *coram nobis* hearing. For Zimmerman's charge that he is being punished for refusing to "co-operate" on the Sullivan case, one witness already heard has furnished corroboration of a sort: Hanover. In his affidavit he states: ". . . When I was in the district attorney's office . . . I heard . . . Wandling say to . . . Rosenblum, 'Make it one case and mix Beansy in with the bunch too. He made me lose my case again Sullivan and I'm going to fix him good.' . . . When Wandling stated that he 'wanted to fix' Zimmerman because Zimmerman made him lose the Sullivan case, I understood what I will have to do . . ."

Something like a pattern seems to be emerging now. In 1939 Zimmerman is paid a visit—authorized by prison officials—in his cell at Auburn by a man whose name he does not recall but whose title is that of Assistant District Attorney. "He asked me . . . in connection with another case, if I would be a witness for the State. A case [involving] Isidore Engel. I told him I knew nothing about the case and I therefore couldn't help him. He questioned me along that line and he decided I didn't know anything. At the end of the conversation I asked him would he look into my conviction, that I had been convicted on perjured testimony. He asked me what do I base that on. I went on to explain . . . threw up his hands and didn't want to hear any more about it."

Still in Auburn Prison, Zimmerman receives still another visit in 1940 from still another Assistant District Attorney and some detectives. Among them is Detective Wandling. "The assistant district attorney told me that Bennie Ertel had been captured . . . Would I be a witness for the prosecution? I told him I had known nothing of the case from the start. Therefore I could not help him now . . . I was left in the room with Detective Wandling, and I said to him, 'How can you have the audacity to come to see me after what you did to me, after you helped frame me into prison?' He agreed that he did and told me that I still had a chance to help myself if I would be a witness for the prosecution. I says, 'I know nothing about the case; therefore I can not be a witness . . .' "

The professional credentials of Jacob Rosenblum are impressive, and he begins his testimony with a recital of them. The light glints off his rimless glasses; the dark hair, streaked now with gray, is as thick as ever; the manner may be gentler now but it can turn waspish when the middle-sized, middle-aged man on the stand feels called upon to move from an attitude of cool self-possession to a posture of attack: once a prosecutor, always a prosecutor.

Today he is a member—in time, the senior partner—of a Wall Street law firm, but his career begins in 1923 with eight years of private practice in the office of George Medalie, a well-known New York lawyer. By 1931 he has become an Assistant United States Attorney for the Southern District of New York, resigning in September of the following year to become Chief Assistant to Thomas E. Dewey in Special Rackets Investigation. He holds the post, along with the title of Deputy Assistant District Attorney of New York County, until its expiration on the last day of 1937. On January 1, 1938, Dewey, New York County's District Attorney, names Rosenblum head of the Homicide Bureau. He continues in that post until December 31, 1941, at which time he resigns to join the Wall Street firm.

A simple frontation of these dates—a matter of record—with dates mentioned in the affidavits of Rose and Hanover is defense against certain of the charges made against Rosenblum. He took no part in the questioning of Rose during the period when Rose states he was not implicating Zimmerman. "I point out to the Court that . . . the statement of Rose which he gave to Delehanty and McGuire on June 4, 1937 . . . was approximately seven months before I took office in the

District Attorney's office in New York County, at which time
he gave his testimony with reference to the guns which he
said he either gave or made available to . . . [Zimmerman]
in the hallway at 201 Clinton Street."

Judge Mullen: "After you came into the picture [beginning
January 1, 1938] was there anything that transpired to your
knowledge that would support that alleged statement by
Rose [the statement from Zimmerman's affidavit that, beginning 'February 18, 1938, almost a year after the crime . . .
Rose falsely implicated . . . (Zimmerman) in the commission
of the crime . . . in order to avoid imminent indictment and
punishment']?" Rosenblum: "Nothing that would support this
statement here by . . . [Zimmerman]." Mr. Herman: "And
that part of it is completely false?" Rosenblum: "That's completely false."

Mr. Herman: "In this Zimmerman trial of March, 1938,
in any preparation and the examination of witnesses in connection with that preliminarily to the trial, did you make any
threats or exert any pressure by way of coercion or attempt
to or duress upon any of the witnesses, and specifically the
witnesses Rose and Hanover?" Rosenblum: "Definitely not."
Herman: "Did anyone in your presence, and, of course, I
include by 'anyone' District Attorneys, police officers, detectives and specifically Detective Wandling, in your presence
or to your knowledge, in connection with any of the witnesses,
in preparation for the Zimmerman trial, and specifically Hanover and Rose, exert any threats, pressure or exert any duress
upon any of those witnesses?" Rosenblum: "They did not."

In his *coram nobis* petition Zimmerman has charged that
his conviction "was procured principally by the utilization of
perjured testimony and the facts . . . manifest that the prosecution was well aware that the witnesses mustered to testify
against . . . [him] were committing perjury." The affidavits
of Rose and Hanover are offered in corroboration of the
charge. Rosenblum's reply: "That is false. . . . I never saw
[Zimmerman] or any of the other defendants [Guariglia,
O'Loughlin, Friedman, and Chaleff] whom I tried prior to the

time that they appeared in court . . . when the trial started."

In his *coram nobis* petition Zimmerman has charged that he was not inside Hanover's store in conference with the conspirators, that "Detective Wandling and District Attorney Rosenblum were so told by Hanover; that nevertheless in spite of Hanover's desire to tell the District Attorney the truth . . . Hanover was threatened that he would be sent to jail, that his business would be taken away from him, that past police records [Hanover's involvement with policy slips] would be made public, that he never would be permitted to obtain gainful employment and that he would be put in jail and kept there, first as a material witness and then as a defendant in connection with the concealment of a conspiracy."

Regarding any possible promise by Neary to quash the indictment against Zimmerman in exchange for his "co-operation" on the Sullivan case, Rosenblum expresses disbelief. "I say I don't believe it because . . . [Neary] had no authority. It was my case . . . I never at any time said to him or to any other person that . . . [Zimmerman's] indictment would be dismissed."

Regarding Popeye Cooperman, Zimmerman has charged in his *coram nobis* petition that, "This . . . accomplice Popeye was given every consideration by the District Attorney, and although he had admitted to the District Attorney that he had actually participated in the crime and was the weapons carrier, he was not indicted, but was permitted to remain at large [even leaving the state for an eight-month period] shortly before the trial . . . Popeye Cooperman was testifying under a promise or prospect of immunity and . . . because of his co-operation with Detective Wandling and District Attorney Rosenblum was permitted to have his freedom, while his crime was foisted upon . . . [Zimmerman's] shoulders." Rosenblum's answer: he knows nothing of the fashion in which Cooperman was treated during the seven- or eight-month period before he himself took office in 1937. But insofar as Zimmerman's charge relates to his treatment of Cooperman

after the first of January, 1938, "That statement is untrue."
He himself never promised immunity to Cooperman, whose
role in the Foley killing was assessed by a grand jury in
the summer of 1937 "before I came into office. Now, why
they didn't indict him . . . is something I can't pass on. I
had nothing to do with that."

Denying any feeling of animosity toward Zimmerman and
the other East Side boys, Rosenblum declares: "It was just the
reverse. I felt sorry for the people I was trying. I had a duty
to do and I was doing it fairly to them and fairly to the
People of the State of New York . . . I didn't care what the
outcome was so long as the facts were presented to a jury
properly." Down the line goes Rosenblum—with appropriate
corroboration from Detective Gallagher, from Neary, from
Sarafite—refuting, denying, point after point, claim after
claim. False, says Rosenblum, are Hanover's charges of in-
timidation by him and by Wandling; false, Hanover's claim
of having informed the District Attorney that Zimmerman
was not inside his store on the night of the conspiracy; false,
that he or Wandling knew Hanover's trial testimony to be
perjured; false that he and Wandling concocted Rose's trial
testimony, coached Rose to say he had given the guns to
Zimmerman; false he had stated in January or February of
1938 "that it was necessary . . . to obtain the testimony of
a witness who was not an accomplice [that is, someone besides
Rose and Cooperman] in order to hold Zimmerman"; false,
finally, that in the course of prosecuting the case against
Zimmerman he withheld information which might have
helped the defendant. Rosenblum gives the impression of
being unassailable.

But on June 20, two days from the end of the *coram
nobis* proceedings, Burlakoff, cross-examining Rosenblum,
starts an extraordinary counteroffensive. The beginning is
modest, inauspicious, all but imperceptible in the still air of
the courtroom: it is the faint rumble, the heat lightning on
the horizon, that portends the coming storm. Do you, Burlakoff asks Rosenblum, recall the following question-and-

answer exchange from the 1938 trial, as Zimmerman's lawyer, Murray, cross-examined Rose?

> MURRAY: "And you never told any Assistant District Attorney or anybody in authority before a couple of weeks ago [that is, before April, 1938, when trial was begun] that Zimmerman had anything to do with guns?"
> ROSE: "That's right."
> MURRAY: "Is that correct?"
> ROSE: "That's right."

Burlakoff's question is rhetorical: though Rosenblum may not recall the Murray-Rose dialogue vividly enough to quote it from memory, he cannot ignore that it is to be found in the trial record, nor can he deny he was present in the courtroom, in his capacity of prosecutor, when the words were spoken. Burlakoff's question, despite its innocent appearance, is in reality a time bomb with a very long fuse; answering, as he must, with a "Yes," Rosenblum lights the fuse. And the explosion, six long years away, will open a breach in the prison walls for Zimmerman.

Now, asks Burlakoff—with the advantage of knowing in advance what Rosenblum's answer must be—did Rosenblum produce before the court Rose's statement of June, 1937, implicating Zimmerman? Rosenblum shows perplexity. The statement was in his possession, yes; but "exhibit it to whom"? Assistant District Attorney Herman objects to Burlakoff's question, contending, ". . . It would not be a proper way to try a case, to offer [the statement] at that moment, in the middle of cross-examination . . ." And Judge Mullen intervenes with an objection to the direction the proceedings are taking. The purpose of the *coram nobis* hearing is not retrying the original case, but "trying to establish here whether or not this man, in some way, was deprived of a constitutional right, and, principally, had witnesses who would have normally testified otherwise, falsely testify against him." The decision as to when Rose's statement of June, 1937, should have been produced "is a matter for each counsel on each side to conduct as he sees fit, according to the exigencies of the circumstances at the particular moment."

Burlakoff reminds the court of the purpose of his cross-examination: it is directed to Rosenblum's affirmation, a moment earlier, that if he had information indicating that testimony given was false, he would reveal that information. (Question: "If you had testimony contrary to the testimony of the People's witnesses, would you make that available to the Court and to defense counsel?" Rosenblum: ". . . You mean, if I had testimony which would show . . . that certain facts were not true? . . . Yes, I would.") Now Burlakoff moves in for the knockdown. ". . . Did you understand Rose to testify that he had never . . . given a statement or never said to any Assistant District Attorney prior to a couple of weeks before the trial that Zimmerman had anything to do with guns? And was that statement true?"

The question is deadly, though its full significance will not be realized until later. Rosenblum's answer is less assured than usual: "At the trial, during cross-examination, you say that Mr. Murray developed that Rose had made a statement about the guns some short period before the trial, and you say that, in fact . . . [Rose] had made such a statement a number of months before that. Frankly, if that were the fact, and, as I see now, it is the fact, it certainly escaped me. But it would make no difference. I don't think I would bring it out, because it certainly wouldn't hurt Zimmerman. Now, if I knew it at the time, in all likelihood, I would bring it to the Court's attention. But I don't recall that on cross-examination, when the attorney for the defendant examines the People's witnesses, as he says, You said it for the first time a couple of weeks or a couple of months ago, when, in fact, he had previously said the same thing some months before that, it undoubtedly escaped me. It is cross-examination. You can't follow every detail, unless there is something that is material. Now, if it was something material, which would make this false in the sense that it would affect Zimmerman's rights, you could be certain anything I had in my possession and I knew of, was within my control and to my knowledge at the moment, I would bring it to the Court's attention."

Burlakoff, with satisfaction: "I can be certain of that. Very well . . ." Now, after the discursive answer, there is evidence of pique in Rosenblum's retort: "Sarcasm with me doesn't mean a thing, you know." And in the later dialogue between Burlakoff and Rosenblum there is evidence of something more than pique. "I noticed," throws out Rosenblum, "some of the witnesses [for Zimmerman] cutely or very definitely said that [Detective] Gallagher wasn't there [to witness this or that incident], because Wandling is dead." Burlakoff: "But you are alive, Mr. Rosenblum, and they say you were there, do they not?" Rosenblum's counter is the charge that Burlakoff's preparation of affidavits for the *coram nobis* hearing is marked by negligence. Burlakoff: "Mr. Rosenblum, you are the one that's in this witness stand because of what occurred eighteen years ago and not I." Rosenblum: "That's what you say. You don't know a thing about it." Burlakoff: "Mr. Rosenblum, I don't want to argue with you. Please answer the questions." Rosenblum: "I am here because of your carelessness in making the statements [affidavits] and charges against Mr. Neary, against me and Mr. Sarafite." The last word, however, belongs to Burlakoff: "Mr. Rosenblum, the Court will decide that . . ." "Of course . . ." concurs Rosenblum.

In the closing minutes of the hearing Assistant District Attorney Herman requests permission to read into the record the Court's exhibit J: two single sheets of yellow notepaper. They bear notes taken by Mr. Sarafite, Rosenblum's assistant, on 2/24/38 in connection with a statement given by Hanover. Judge Mullen, assenting, inquires whether the two sheets are separate or attached, and Mr. Herman replies that they "are still in the original binding as they came from the pad." Two sheets of yellow paper, covered with notations: eighteen years earlier they were part of the vast machine which caught up, drew in, swallowed, and all but destroyed

Isidore Zimmerman. Mindful of the impermanence of archives and the weight of the years, Judge Mullen directs: ". . . They will be fastened together; they are fragile paper now." And Assistant District Attorney Herman answers, "That's right; the paste is beginning to come apart . . ."

The hearing is over. The date is June 22, 1956. The Court's decision is pending: until it can be rendered, Zimmerman is returned to his cell in Dannemora. He is now in his nineteenth year of imprisonment.

CHAPTER 6

THE
WAIT—part III

ON THE TRAIN BACK to Dannemora I felt I'd hit rock-bottom. It had taken me eighteen years to reach a point where the court would stop and listen. They'd listened and all but said No: an easy little word to say, short and to the point. It would cancel everything out: the thousands of words that had gone into the re-examination of Rose and Hanover, cancel out the very meaning of those words—"We lied about a man when he was on trial for his life"—cancel out the months, the years of waiting, the marshaling of the evidence, the study of the minutes, the preparation of the motion, cancel out the money Papa had managed to scrape together, the subways taken, the phone calls made, the city blocks walked by Carl and Papa and the others on the spadework that had to be done to prepare for my new "day in court." Somehow I knew that No was what they'd say. Why else would they have said, now that they had heard me after years of silence, #31063, back to your cage in Siberia. Dannemora was Siberia to anyone who spent a winter there: we were thirty-odd miles from Canada, and for a good eight months of the year the thermometer acted accordingly. I put my forehead against the cool glass of the coach window, closed my eyes to the blur of the landscape rushing by, and wondered how I could ever stand another winter in Siberia.

206

I'd figured it dead right. The last day of the hearing was a Friday. Monday morning I got a telegram advising me the judge had rejected my petition. I'd been so near, and now, again, I seemed so far from freedom. In theory, I knew, an unfavorable decision still left room for appeal. But theory didn't mean much: in theory, I shouldn't have been convicted in the first place. An appeal could take forever, or at least until I was too old to care; court calendars were jammed and the waiting list for trial dates was giving nightmares to the New York judges. Besides the time involved, an appeal would take money: another dead end. And without a bushel basket full of dollar bills, I had no attorney. Burlakoff had explained to me on the last day of the *coram nobis* hearing that, win or lose, he was withdrawing from the case. Theoretically—again —I could handle my own appeal; lots of men in prison tried to. But without proper legal training, without the freedom of operation any lawyer has on the outside as a matter of course, I'd just be stacking the deck against myself. Zimmerman, you were born lucky.

Back in Dannemora there were raised eyebrows, expressions of surprise and sympathy, and many a cigarette offered to console me for the setback, temporary or not. The consensus among the inmates with some knowledge of the law was that my case was a solid one, and that I'd be sure to make it "next time." But from where I stood I wasn't so sure there would be a next time; and besides, as a matter of course I discounted half the reassurances I got: it isn't kind to kill a man's hope in prison, and they were being kind. And back in Dannemora there was the routine, the endless, pointless prison routine. I buried myself in it: at least it kept a man from thinking.

But even though there was nothing to announce it in advance, my life was going to take another turn now. For days—days that grew into months—after my return I'd wandered around the yard, tossed and turned on my cot, wool-gathered in the mess hall, saying, to nobody in particular, "What do I do now? Where do I go from here?"

Mr. Burlakoff had done a superb job of preparing for the *coram nobis* hearing, but now he felt it was impossible to get any further action on my case, and I could see why. Judge Mullen, after what I suppose was due reflection, denied our motion for a writ of error: my conviction for murder in the first degree was not going to be set aside because of any revelations by Rose and Hanover at the *coram nobis* hearing. Burlakoff didn't see what else could be done, and I didn't see how I could pay him, whatever he did, so we terminated our lawyer-client relationship. So after six months or so without a lawyer I'd reached the stage of asking the question, "What do I do now?" without really expecting an answer.

The answer came, though—unexpectedly—one morning when I was walking in the yard with a friend, trying to fend off the Siberian chill. "My attorney's up here today on a visit," said the friend. "Why not talk to him? Maybe he'll take your case." At first I didn't pay much attention, beyond rewording my automatic questions a little: "Why should he take my case? How would I pay him if he did?" "Never mind about that; let me talk to him. He's a good man. Let's see what he says." "Sure," I said, "sure," and thought, What has Lucky Zimmerman got to lose?

At 3:00 P.M. I heard the PA system calling my name. What for? I'd all but forgotten the conversation in the yard until the loudspeaker sounded off: Report to the room reserved for conversations between inmates and their lawyers. I reported: a wooden table, three wooden chairs—one reserved for the guard posted at the door throughout—cheerless gray walls, barred windows overlooking the yard. The man across the table from me was short, chunky, powerful-looking. There was power in the handshake too. And there was something in his manner—the taut way he listened, the incisive way he talked, the rapid way his eyes appraised me from behind the big black-framed glasses, the short, choppy gestures of the hands, the fingers. I was impressed. Was it his energy? No, I decided, though there was clearly energy there; it was intelligence, first and foremost. He listened to me, and nothing interfered with his listening; there was a kind of barely controlled tension to it. He gave the impression of knowing what I was going to say before I got it out, nodding his head as if I were only confirming what he knew; but he *listened*, and lots of lawyers never take the trouble. The intelligence was almost audible, like the hum of a generator, in the little room. As he listened I could sense he was thinking, weighing alternatives, anticipating difficulties, calculating probabilities. "He's a good man," my friend had said. He was an impressive man.

He was a no-nonsense man, too. No smiling, no jollying me along. Right from the word go he took a chance on scaring me away. "I hear you want to see me," he said, with what might have been a frown. "Here I am. But first I want to tell you something: I've heard a million stories from innocent men in prison. They break your heart when you hear them, but they have a way of breaking down, of coming apart at the seams when you listen to them twice." I knew a good lawyer had to be a no-nonsense man, but this one was hard as nails. "So don't try to break my heart, Mr. Zimmerman," he went on. "Don't tell me any fairy tales. Don't kid yourself and don't kid me. And be brief—I'm catching a train back to New York this afternoon."

I knew what he meant, but his way of saying it knocked the breath out of me. He might be intelligent, but he didn't know much about handling people. Or care how he handled them. I decided I didn't like him: he could go to hell. But somewhere in the back of my head there was a memory of my friend in the yard that morning, leaning his head back as he took a drag on his cigarette and saying, "He's a good man, Beany. Talk to him." What the hell, I thought: talk to him.

I talked. That was the day Lucky Zimmerman got lucky. Maybe I even managed to be eloquent; the words were suddenly coming faster and faster—the past . . . Cooperman . . . Foley . . . Rose . . . the death house . . . Hanover . . . the Court of Appeals . . . *coram nobis*. Every disappointed hope, every setback, the fears, the bitterness, the days and nights in solitary, the shame, the longing for my family, my freedom—it all welled out. And as I talked the man across the table began to change before my eyes: the frown softened, disappeared; the coldness left his face; the features relaxed. But the look of intelligence remained; it was the only thing about him that remained unchanged as I talked.

Then, suddenly, his hand was raised, palm towards me, to stop the flow of words. Up to now he'd listened, but it was over; he was through; he had a train to catch. My voice died in the middle of a sentence. Lucky Zimmerman, I thought, you've done it again. Let the man catch his train.

But the man across the table remained seated; he didn't seem hurried he didn't even look like the hard-faced character who'd told me, twenty minutes before, in a voice that chilled, "Don't tell me fairy tales, Mr. Zimmerman; don't waste my time." This man was different: he looked downright gentle, benevolent; his hand was raised almost in the gesture of a man giving his blessing. "Slow down, Mr. Zimmerman," he said. "Slow down. Forget about that train I was going to catch. Give me a chance to take some notes." He was smiling.

He never did make the train. When the note-taking was over, he gave me another smile—I was surprised at the warmth of it, but I remembered I was dealing with a different man now, the "good man" my friend had told me about—and he said, "Mr. Zimmerman, you're a man on his way out of prison."

He was right. That was the turning point, but nobody knew it then. That night I wrote a letter to the family with the news: a lawyer by the name of Maurice Edelbaum was going to take my case.

———

Mama and Papa had been driven up to Dannemora for a visit in the fall of 1958. The *coram nobis* hearing was ancient history, but I'd appealed the decision, and Mr. Edelbaum's confidence was downright contagious. There was

every reason, I told them, for optimism. "I have every hope
of winning the decision in a higher court. It's just a matter
of time now." Mama shrugged and smiled a little sadly.
"You've been telling me this for so many years . . ." She was
right; Mama was always right.

So many years. It came as a shock to me, then, to see how
my parents had aged. A man serving time in prison imagines
his family, his friends outside the walls, will remain somehow as he left them: his wife faithful, his children children.
No matter how slowly the clocks tick for him, he thinks,
they will have stopped for them. I knew how much older I
was, but until that visit I'd never thought of them as changing.
Yet there was the evidence: the white of the hair, the lines
etched in the face by a thousand disappointments, a thousand
fatigues, the look in the eyes, resigned to more disappointment, more fatigue.

She looked older, but physically she seemed as spry as
ever—that's what I told myself, but I didn't carry much conviction. Every postponed hearing, every motion before the
court that was deferred or delayed—the courts were over-
crowded; Mr. Edelbaum was overworked; and the District
Attorney's office, for which my case was something of an
annoyance, was not unhappy when, for one reason or another, the annoyance was put off—everything and anything
that slowed down or stalled the machinery of my release was
a blow to her, and her physical reserves—she was seventy-one
—were nothing like mine, and the endless delays used to
drive me mad. On more than one occasion, when the waiting
was too much to endure, I'd written letters to my lawyer telling
him to give up my case, telling him I'd ask the court to appoint someone else to defend me, telling him that with every
postponement I died a little more. The letters never changed
anything: I never sent them. But writing them was an outlet
for my frustrations, and when they were written I'd reread
them and tear them up and try not to think about these
things until the pressure built up again. But what could
Mama do to let off steam?

She could pound pavements, ring doorbells, buttonhole ward heelers to get her son out of prison, and she did. For weeks on end, I remembered, she'd walked twelve or so blocks to the D.A.'s office—Papa with her on his days off—and haunted the anterooms on the chance she'd find someone to tell my story—her story—to. Of course the D.A.'s staff found out who she was, and it was easier for them to ignore her than talk to her. But she kept right on coming. When Mama heard a man from the D.A.'s office was scheduled to make a speech at the New Era Club down on Montgomery Street, she made a point of attending, listening politely, and then, working her way up the line of people waiting to shake hands with the speaker, asking him point-blank: "Would you like to help in correcting a great wrong?" And before he could answer, she made a speech of her own about her son Isidore. He was a politician, so he backed off, but you always had to give Mama credit for trying.

So, when they came to Dannemora in 1958, I fell back into the old routine. "Don't worry, Mama, it's just a matter of time. Everybody says so now. When I get out—any day now—I'll get money enough to buy a house for you and Papa. A house with every kind of modern gadget—you won't have to lift a finger." Mama was still Mama. "I wouldn't like that, Beany. You know I like to do my own housework." "Yes, but Mama, it's about time you got a little rest; you've been working all your life. And for Papa I'm going to get a big black car with a chauffeur, so you can visit all the kids every day in the week. And suits with pockets full of quarters you can give away to them." "Look at him," Mama said. "He's making us millionaires already." Her smile was just the same as it always had been. By the time she waved good-bye to me I'd managed to persuade myself that everything else was just the same.

The black day came in September, 1959. I was working in the mess hall; our shift was on its morning break, and I was sitting at one of the empty tables with two friends. We were talking about my appeal: by all indications it was in the hopper now, ready to come through almost any day. I knew there were delays to be expected, but I hadn't heard from Mr. Edelbaum or the family, and I figured no news was good news. When the officer showed up asking for Zimmerman, I was keyed up: a message from the chief clerk's office saying I was wanted up front. I knew what it was for— official notification that my case was won. All the way to the chief clerk's office I was walking on air.

There was a little wait, and then I was ushered into the inner office. They'd be asking me to sign something, I knew —papers, a release. I had the pen in my hand when I crossed the threshold. The chief clerk looked up from his desk. He didn't look happy, but I suppose they're never happy to lose a star boarder. "Zimmerman, when did your family see you last?" "What? You mean my parents?" "When was the last time you saw your mother?" "I don't understand. What does that have to do with my appeal?" For months I'd been thinking of nothing else; I couldn't adjust my thinking that fast. "I regret to inform you . . ." began the chief clerk. Then the news hit me right between the eyes like a piece of lead pipe. Mama was dead; she'd grown tired of waiting for me.

There was a pen in my hand. I snapped it in two and let the pieces fall to the floor. Then I found a way out. "There's another Zimmerman here. He's the one you want. You've made a mistake." "I'm sorry; we've checked it out. You're the man." "This is a mistake, I tell you." I could feel a wave of anger mounting in me: trust some quill-driver in an office to mess up the record every time. "My mother's OK; she's just fine. If she was sick I'd have heard from the family." By this time I was fighting mad—this was a hell of a way to treat a man. The chief clerk found a way to cool me down. He read me the telegram. "We regret . . ." it began, and it ended, "She asked that you do not come to the funeral." The signature was my brother-in-law's.

"Somebody forged that," I said, and went on saying it all

the way back to the mess hall; anybody can sign a telegram—
Mussolini, Robert Wagner, Dwight Eisenhower. But before
I got there I'd stopped believing it myself. The officer gave
me permission to go back to my cell: the word must have
traveled fast. The block officer, too, waving me to my cell:
"If you want, I can leave the door open." Door open, door
closed: I didn't care, was past caring. I threw myself face
down on the cot and pulled the pillow over my head. Great
racking sobs began to shake my body, but there were no
tears. For too many years I'd bottled up my feelings, hardened myself to take the shock of one disappointment after another. I wanted to cry; I wanted to—it would have been a
relief—but I couldn't. I just lay on the bed, shaking like a
leaf, like a man in the grip of a fever.

At dinnertime one of the boys from the mess hall came
with a tray of food for me. "Get away from the door; don't
bring me anything; just leave me alone." I managed to grate
the words out, but I couldn't have said one syllable more.
More of the mess-hall crew came when their "tour" was over
to express their sympathy. "I don't want to talk," I said. "I
don't want to talk." I wasn't hungry; I couldn't think; my
mind was reeling. Mama hadn't waited for me, and now I'd
never see her again. She hadn't even wanted me at the
funeral. I wasn't much of a son: all her life I'd brought her
pain and shame, and now she'd wanted an end to it. She
hadn't wanted to say good-bye to me, not even the kind of
poor good-bye you can say in a cemetery. Or was it the family
—not Mama—who didn't want me? Not Papa, no; not Carl,
who had given every free minute of his life to my appeal. Who
hadn't wanted me at the funeral? Who? Did they care what
the neighbors thought? Were they ashamed of me now, after
all these years of loyalty? To hell with the neighbors. To hell
with everything.

Then I made up my mind. Over and over I said to myself,
grinding my teeth, biting off the words: I've got to kill myself
now, kill myself and end this endless misery . . . misery for
me and for my people. A man shouldn't have all that misery

packed into one short lifetime; a man couldn't stand it. Perhaps I slept a little in my cell. Perhaps. It was a little confused
in my mind. But now I found myself sitting on the edge of my
cot, chain-smoking. How long had I been sitting there? It
didn't matter. I was going to kill myself. I ground out the
cigarette butt.

How to kill myself? More than one man in prison had had
ideas like that, but it wasn't an easy trick to pull off. With a
piece of rope or even strong cord I could hang myself, or at
least work out some way to choke myself to death. I began to
search the cell for something that would do the job. Nothing.
Nothing. Then I thought of making a kind of cord by tearing
a bedsheet into strips and knotting them together. I must
have been something to see: grinding my teeth, cursing my
life, sobbing dry-eyed, tearing at the sheets. And then a great
fatigue set in—at least I think it happened that way. A great
fatigue and then a kind of dull sleep.

Whether I dreamed it or whether it was a hallucination
that took hold of me before sleep came, or whether it really
happened as it seemed to, I don't know. I felt something cool
and soft on my forehead, like my mother's hand. There was
a voice, heard or imagined, like my mother's voice: "Quiet,
quiet now, my son . . . you'll be going home soon. If you
harm yourself it will only bring me more pain . . ." I slept.

The next morning my dream was less vivid than the reality
I remembered: Mama was dead. And I was ready, again, to
die. But in prison, where a man is free only to suffer, he isn't
free to kill himself. There was an officer there by the name
of John Quinn, a good Irishman, a regular guy. He showed
up with a tray of food first thing in the morning: rare steak
and black coffee. "Beansy, I want you to eat this. Come on,
now. It'll do you good." "John, I'd choke if I tried to eat. I
can't. I'm not going on." But John was a stubborn Irishman.
He told me I had everything to live for. He told me my case
was all but won—everybody knew it—that I'd be leaving
prison soon as a free man to begin a new life. "Your family
needs you, Beansy. Your father needs you. Now more than

ever. Be a man." I got the message. When he left I took out
my patchwork rope and flushed it, piece by piece, down the
toilet.

It was another turning point, even though the subject of
death was still very much in my mind, and my depression
blacker than any I'd ever known. What hurt the most now
was the knowledge I'd been considered unworthy to say a
last good-bye to Mama: it was something I just couldn't grasp.
All my life she'd fought for me, believed in me, and now . . .
My heart was full of the deepest sadness. If there was one
thing that symbolized, more than any other, the release I'd
hoped for, it was to go home to Mama, whom I imagined
smiling, standing in the doorway, her arms stretched out to
welcome me. That dream was finished, and I knew that nothing would restore it now, not even my death.

Johnny Quinn wasn't the only one who helped. Kennison,
the kitchen keeper, came with a sack of sandwiches and a big
carton of cold milk he insisted on leaving. Another friend
gave me his tobacco ration for the entire week, which was a
good thing, because most of my waking moments were spent
chain-smoking and staring at the ceiling of my cell. Another
of the boys managed somehow to get me five boxes of Hershey
bars, and my locker in the mess hall was crammed full of
provisions; but if I got down Kennison's carton of milk, I still
couldn't bring myself to eat. Then, five days after that awful
morning in the chief clerk's office, I got a special delivery
letter from home. It was signed by every member of the
family; it told me about Mama's illness, and the last days;
and it spelled out the reasons they'd wanted me to stay away
from the funeral. Mama had gone, years before, to the funeral
of a friend whose son was a convict. He was a long-termer,
and the prison authorities decided to keep handcuffs on him
even at the cemetery, and nobody looked at anything else,
or thought or talked about anything else throughout the ceremony but those handcuffs. It made a terrible impression on
Mama; and when she lay dying she said to Papa, "I don't
want Beany at the funeral . . . I don't want him to come and

have fingers pointed at him . . . Promise me . . ." So they promised her.

It was some comfort for me to know she hadn't been ashamed of her son, but only anxious that a humiliating, demeaning incident should be avoided. Later, too, much later, I learned how long she'd been ill before the end came: a long time. She hadn't wanted me to know that either, and no one in the family had told me. In a way it was hard for me to understand, and yet, finally, I did: it was out of love for me. But that love almost destroyed me. I had come very close to the edge, closer than at any point in the long ordeal of arrest, trial, and imprisonment. In spite of the letter, it seemed to me still that my heart was broken; and if I'd given up the idea of suicide, I couldn't see, now, how it made much difference whether I lived or died

I must have continued in that frame of mind for another week or so. I still wasn't eating, but Johnny Quinn kept bringing me quarts and quarts of milk that the officer on night duty in the block stashed away in his icebox for me. And then one day the guard asked me if I didn't want to shave. I didn't want to and I hadn't, for something over ten days. "Why?" I asked, as though shaving was something out of science fiction. "Because you've got a visit." So I shaved—no sense looking like a wild man—and went off, dragging my feet, to the visiting room.

I had two visitors: Papa and my sister Celia. When she saw me she started to cry; then they were both telling me at once how much they loved me, how important I was to them, how terrible it would be for them if anything were to happen to me. I still couldn't cry tears—only great dry sobs came at first; Papa was crying too; and we were all talking at the top of our voices. It was quite a while before any of us paid much attention to what was being said. The whole family had wanted to come, they told me, but finally they'd settle on delegating just Papa and Celia. They told me about Mama toward the end, and I told them about what the news had done to me. "If only I'd known she was ill, I could have prepared myself for the inevitable; but the news coming out of a clear sky like that was too much. If it hadn't been for your letter . . ."

They, with their grief, had simply failed to realize how the news would hit me in prison. That they knew at all, I learned, was due to the rabbi. He'd come to see me in my cell, done his best to console me, and understood it wasn't going to be enough. "I'm giving up, now," I told him. "I'm giving up." He'd gone from my cell straight to a telephone and called New York. "You'd better get someone from the family up to visit him, and make it fast," he'd said. "I'm very much afraid of what he may do." And if they couldn't afford the train fare, he said, he'd take it out of his own pocket. For all my bad luck, I thought, I had some pretty lucky breaks.

At the end of the visit—we must have talked for a good two hours—I kissed Papa and Celia through the wire screen that separated us and watched them as they walked away, Papa shuffling, dragging his bad leg, the slope of his shoulders spelling out his grief, his age, his vulnerability. I prayed that a little more waiting wouldn't do to him what it had done to Mama. I felt sorrow for him, for the ordeal I'd brought into his life, sadness too that Mama was gone, leaving him alone. I even felt a little sorry to be living: it made things harder on everybody. But in the minutes just passed, in the words spoken, the love they had shown me and the love I felt for them dissolved the clot around my heart. I was making the journey back.

The upper left-hand corner of the envelope bears the printed instruction: "After five days return to Box B, Dannemora, N.Y.," but there is no name of sender given. Inside, a sheet of white letter paper eight inches by eight and a half: twenty-four ruled lines on one side, twenty-eight on the other. At the top of the page, on the left: three dotted lines for the name and address of the recipient; a line on the right for the date; and, in italics at the upper right-hand corner of the page, the notation: "When replying sign your full name and address. Give inmate's full name and number." Prison stationery: you used it or nothing, and you wrote in ink, between the lines, as you were told to.

Dear Mr. Edelbaum,

In the spirit of humanity, may I make a personal plea of you? Not so much for myself, but very much for my father.

On September 28th, 1959, my blessed mother passed away. She and my father have been inseparable for fifty years. I very much fear that if he is not given any incentive for the near future the results could easily be another great tragedy. I was always his favorite son and if [he] were given hope that I could soon be with him, some of the bleakness could easily evaporate.

As you know, the facts more than prove my innocence. No doubt as you read all of the minutes you begin to see that mine was a grave miscarriage of justice. But I am not trying to impress you—no matter what I say, the record speaks for itself.

From the last report I got the appeal was supposed to be argued either in late September or early October. I pray that this is so. But if it is not, then my plea is to you to try to rectify the situation. My father's life could very easily be at stake. In the years you have handled my case, as you can remember, I made no demands upon you, knew that you were the man for the job and at the right time you would move rapidly and win. Yet the choice is not mine any more. I desperately need to be with my father and give him some great incentive for going on. I'm sure you can understand that. If it is in your power to do so, please make sure the appeal will be argued in October. Needless to say, I'd be grateful in more ways than one. My mother and father suffered twenty-two and a half years for nothing. At least let me try to make some amends to my father. It will be a great blessing for you.

I know you do not make a practice of answering letters, but in this case won't you make an exception? I desperately need some reassurance.

Thank you very much!

Your client,
Isidore Zimmerman
#31063

The letter that came back included a clipping from the **Law Journal**:

103. People, &c., v. Isidore Zimmerman—Motion granted in so far as to permit the appeal to be heard on the original record without printing the same, and upon typewritten or mimeographed appellant's points, on condition that the appellant serves one copy of the typewritten or mimeographed appellant's points on the district attorney of New York County, and files six typewritten or nineteen mimeographed copies thereof, together with the original record, with this court on or before March 1, 1960, with notice of argument for the April, 1960, term of this court, said appeal to be argued or submitted when reached. Order filed.

It was encouraging. Printing cost $2,500 for each 1,000 pages of testimony, and the original record ran to over 2,300 printed *pages*—more money than I'd ever seen. And they'd named the date: the April term. I'd waited this long; I'd wait a little longer.

April came and went, then summer. Then it was fall. In October, 1960, the First Department of the Appellate Division of the New York Supreme Court, in a brief signed by Frank S. Hogan, District Attorney of New York County, rejected my appeal. The brief concluded that the decision to deny my *coram nobis* petition was "amply supported by the record [and] should not be disturbed."

I'd waited this long; I'd wait a little longer.

———————

Living without hope makes it easy for the strongest man to go over the edge after a while. There were times, I know, I must have been over it myself, but I always managed to wander back. Maybe it helped me to know that in most prisons Section A—the slot where they put the cons that are demonstrably out of their minds—has a long waiting list. My religion was a sheet anchor for me too; and all around me there were men trying to live without it. Then there was the knowledge that my family was fighting for me still, believed in my inno-

cence; that helpcd sustain me too, and all around me there
were men deprived of that kind of support. There was a kind
of confidence too—although God knows what grounds I had
for it—that sooner or later somebody would notice the mistake that had been made and correct it; and, especially after
my meeting with Mr. Edelbaum, the confidence that, alone of
the half-dozen lawyers who'd defended me, he would get the
job done. In any case, it was a combination of things that
preserved me from the sin of giving way to absolute despair—
or at least giving way for very long. And although I can't
sort them all out in my mind, one of the lot turned out to be—
as silly as it may sound—an elliptical spheroid made of pig-
skin and empty of everything but air: a football. Or the game
of football. Robert Bruce had his spider, and I had my football. It kept me from going over the edge.

It began, I suppose, with the strike in Auburn Prison; and
the strike calls for a little history lesson. It grew out of a basic
injustice in the sentencing system. There was a time when it
was mandatory for a judge in New York State to give a maximum sentence. Armed robbery, for example, called for a sentence of thirty to sixty years, and some judges would do the
law one better: make it forty or fifty to sixty. (The maximum
and minimum figures were meant to encourage good behavior;
if you were a troublemaker you could count on doing the
maximum.) Now, the prisoner sentenced under this system,
no matter how good his conduct in prison, had the date at
which he was first entitled to come up before the parole board
figured on the basis of the maximum. A man serving sixty
years, say, was—theoretically—able to be considered for
parole after serving the first third of his maximum, that is,
twenty years.

Then the law was changed, and sentence became discretionary with the judge, who used the lower of the two figures as
his point of departure, so that entitlement to parole came up
much sooner. The result was that, side by side in prison, you
might have a "discretionary" man doing five to seven years
for the same offense as a "mandatory" who was doing thirty.

Naturally this made for considerable unhappiness among the mandatories, and lots of them wrote to Albany asking for changes in the law. Some of the people in the state legislature could see it their way, and would promise to vote the changes; but the state governor—a former District Attorney by the name of Dewey—would always veto them.

After being disappointed time and time again, the mandatories decided the only solution was a strike to call attention to their predicament. The organizational work began in the yard: you were asked if you sympathized, if you'd go along with the movement. They asked me on a Monday if I'd go along with the strike set for Thursday, and I said Yes. As a lifer I had nothing to gain, but the inequality in sentencing between the mandatories and the others struck me as a hell of an injustice: one more for the collection. Then, having said Yes to the strike, I forgot all about it until Wednesday evening, when two guards escorted me—and a number of other prisoners—to the PK's office; they'd got wind of what was coming. Did I intend to strike the next day? Yes, I said. That earned me a little talking-to: it made no sense for me, a lifer, to go on strike; I'd lose my privileges; I'd be put in isolation. I still said Yes to the strike; it was a matter of principle. So they put twenty-six of us—including Isidore Zimmerman—in the box. We were supposed to be the ringleaders, the "hard-core strikers."

Next morning, when the cell doors opened for the rest of the inmates, some eight hundred men just stayed in their cells. That was the kind of strike it was—no violence, just a show of solidarity. There was a roll call by cell; each man was asked whether he, individually, was willing to go back to work, and a record was made of the answers. In three days' time those who'd said they were willing were allowed to leave their cells. The others, running out of steam, stayed as long as their convictions would sustain them, and that wasn't very long; the strike movement fell apart at the seams before the week was out, and things were back to normal. Normal for a prison, that is.

Normal for the others, that is. The twenty-six of us in the

box decided to show them now how hard the hard core was. We folded our arms, trying hard not to think about tobacco and other amenities of gracious living, and sat back firmly on our principles to wait. We sat there for eighty-seven days, which is a long time even if you're having fun. They saw to it that we didn't. Every privilege was taken away from us, and after a while the guards make a point of blowing tobacco smoke into our cells. That may not sound downright inhuman, but some of us would have been happier with the third degree. On the eighty-seventh day one of the boys in Albany on whom the mandatories had been counting for support stood up to be counted out. They read us his letter: "If you men don't call off your strike, I will never sponsor another such bill—to rationalize the sentencing procedures—as long as I sit in the legislature."

Did we still want to strike, they asked us. We took a vote. It didn't make sense to go on, and the majority was for giving in. We could smoke again, read again, have visitors again, and after a time the "hard core" would even find its way back to the yard with the others. But not Zimmerman: too hard-headed, too much of a troublemaker. They put me on a draft to Attica State Prison. They had me figured for a bad apple, and my part in the strike made it official. Imagine a lifer going on strike for a matter of principle! They must have been glad to get rid of me.

As things turned out, they'd done me a favor. This was in July of 1947. I'd been in prison for ten years or so, and it hadn't done much for my faith in humanity. But so long as I had to be in prison—and by now I'd begun to feel I was born for it—Attica was the best thing that could have happened to me. Like Greenhaven, it had four separate yards—which, for the con, means four separate prisons, and being separated, artificially, from friends whose mailing address is the same as yours; and like Greenhaven—and all the others built by man—it was a prison: the deadly routine, the purposeless work, the constant friction—blacks and whites, Jews and Gentiles, homosexuals and non-homosexuals, habitual criminals and first offenders, "organization men" and loners, the kids and the old men, the "in" group and the "out" group. There were tensions enough to blow up Fort Knox. But there were compensations. The food, for one thing. Most prison food is the cheapest money can buy and still keep your teeth from falling out. But Attica is probably the best feeding prison in the state. The steward there was a good man who knew his job and who did his best to plan good meals on the limited budget with which all prisons are afflicted. The facilities for visits were, compared to other prisons, downright beautiful. I could lean over the low barrier separating us and kiss my sisters, hug Papa in my arms, without having to shout at them through a double thickness of murky wire mesh that all but made them invisible. The inmates too, for reasons I never tried to fathom, were a nicer bunch—at least at that time—than those I'd been thrown in with earlier. Besides the bad ones there were good ones; in prison or out, there are good men, friends, people you can trust, people you can count on. Is anybody shocked to learn there can be good men in prison? It was my universe, prison: all I really knew of the world. And it came as good news to me. I made a new friend or two. And—it took a while—I managed to forget about the frustrations of the strike and the eighty-seven-day stretch in solitary.

Attica had a sports program, too: softball, basketball, football, volleyball, handball, and a rec room full of equipment: barbells, dumbbells, rings, bars. I was still pretty much locked up inside myself; team sports didn't interest me so much as working out alone. I started working out with weights, doing push-ups, and in no time at all I burned off the fat I'd picked up in Auburn sitting in solitary. I began to look—and feel— like one of those pictures in the physical culture magazines: all bone and muscle, healthy as a horse, sleeping better, feeling better, looking better than I had in years. It showed; the family remarked on it when they came up for visits. I turned into a kind of walking ad for the benefits of the good life in prison. Sure, the unhappiness was still there, but I managed to keep it in the back of my mind.

By the time fall came around, and football practice started,

I had more energy than I knew what to do with. I could have mopped up the floor with a cage of lions every afternoon, but lions were in short supply. One afternoon I found myself —without knowing why—out on the B Block athletic field. It was football weather, cold and dry, with a nip in the air. My memory went back to the days at school when my life still had a purpose, like other lives: blocking, passing with the other kids, our fingers stiff with the cold and our cheeks flushed with the autumn air, the excitement. Suddenly I found my legs carrying me forward in a run; my muscles were doing the thinking for me, thinking maybe I could run back into my childhood. Then I was charging down the field in a kind of fury, feeling the cold air on my face, driving with my legs at the ball carrier, bringing him down hard on the damp ground, so hard the breath was knocked out of me. It hurt, and at the same time it felt good. I got up and walked back to the line. There was nothing in my mind but the next play. What the hell, I thought; let my muscles do all the thinking from now on.

Signals again: I was off, tearing at the ball carrier. Maybe he was the District Attorney; maybe he was the guard blowing smoke through the bars into the box; maybe he was Cooperman; maybe he was the guard who told me one day, with a leer, "I hate Jews, all Jews." I didn't stop to analyze. The game, the play, was all that counted. And with every play, more and more came back to me from the past: the high-school coach standing there in the long fall afternoons and saying, "Hit them low, Zimmerman, low, low, low when you block!" or "Knees high—knees high when you move forward." At the end of the day I ached in every muscle, but of all the days I'd spent in prison until then, it was probably the happiest.

I went back the next day, and the next. The season ran for a little more than six weeks, and I began to wonder how I'd survived before it, and then how I'd survive when it was over. From each block—with five hundred men or so—there'd be a hundred-odd candidates for the team, and of those only thirty-three would make it, so competition within the block was stiff. We played one game a week, and two weeks out of three. If B Block played A Block on Saturday, then we'd go as spectators to watch C take on D on Sunday: it gave us a chance to recover from the pounding we'd taken—there were rocks galore and very little turf on our playing field—and see our friends from the other blocks. We played hard, but clean; nobody tried to hurt anybody, but nobody tried to lose. I always hit the opposing linesmen as hard as the rules allow. It mightn't have been good for them, but I knew it was good for me. On offense, I played tackle, and sometimes guard; on defense, guard. Every now and again I'd find myself in the backfield, but I wasn't happy there. Charging a wall of linesmen, though, was the best therapy I knew. Fairly early on, the head coach—nicknamed "Dash"—watching me block, asked me where and when I'd played before and told me he'd like me to help him as line coach. I wasn't keen on the idea at first, but the game was already beginning to get under my skin: I accepted. If some of my teammates had reservations about the competence of the new line coach, they lost them after I'd bounced them off the line of scrimmage a few times. And, after every workout, every game, I could go back to my cell dead tired, but easy in my mind—too tired for bitterness or worry or even for pleasant thoughts—and fall into a deep dreamless sleep: no baby in a crib could sleep better. And when the six-thirty bell blasted me awake next morning I'd find myself, refreshed in mind and body, with just one overriding concern in my mind—how to make the time go fast until I got my hands on a football again.

From time to time it occurred to me that this was one hell of a note: here I was, Zimmerman, the bad apple, the fighter, the fomenter of strikes, the man who'd cheated the electric chair, turning into a model prisoner, taking part in community activities like some raw kid doing a six-month stretch for stealing a bicycle. The next step for me would be to start a prison glee club or crochet doilies in my cell. Watch yourself, Zimmerman, I said; you're getting soft in your old age.

That was the first step. The simple fact of being able to play football—it sounds like nothing. Objectively, I suppose, it is nothing; I could have been singing hymns or building model airplanes. And I knew very well society didn't build prisons and fill them so that the inmates could play football together. No, the important thing was that I had finally managed to get out from under the weight of the world's injustice; I'd carried it around on my shoulders for so long . . . too long, maybe. Maybe, after all those years, I was used to prison, but I don't think a man ever really gets used to it, not even the most incorrigible of lifers. And I know that, however discouraged I got on occasion, I never really lost the hope that one day—one day—the wrong would be righted and the doors would open up for me again. Maybe I just needed a chance to think about somebody else than me, about something else than my own troubles. Whatever the reasons, the process was under way, inside me, without my knowing. That was the first step.

The second step could come now. It wasn't so much something I did as something that happened to me, something I didn't try to fight. We were resting between scrimmages. The afternoon was almost over; it was downright cold in the shadow and not much sun left on the field; and I was nursing a charley horse. A stocky, fresh-faced kid named Pat—playing guard—came up and asked to speak to me in private. I was tired; my leg ached; I didn't want to talk about anything, even football. So in my best "Big House" manner I stopped it before it got off the ground. "Don't bother me, kid," I said. "Tell it to the coach."

He didn't say anything, just walked away. Suddenly I found myself wondering if that look in his eyes meant he was hurt, and then I wondered why I was wondering. Suppose he was hurt, I thought: things are bad all over. If he was hurt, he wouldn't be the first. But he was young, awfully young; it's harder to take when you're young and full of illusions. Besides, I reminded myself, you don't even know what the kid wanted to talk about. To hell with it, I thought; to hell with it. And then, a little later, telling myself I was a damn fool, I called him over. A good thing, too. For him. A good thing for me.

He was going to tell me about it after we'd showered and

changed. I found him waiting at the door; he fell into step alongside me and began to talk. Why to me? I wondered as I listened. Then the thought occurred: the kid's so young, so young . . . I'm not old, not yet, not in spite of all the years I've lost here in prison; but I suppose to him I must seem old enough to be his father, very old, very wise. If things had been different I might have had a kid coming to me for help with his homework, help with his electric trains, help with the tough kid down the block. But Pat had a problem. Most men in prison do. "Look," he began, "this is a hell of a thing to ask, but . . . I'm having trouble with my wife." Like most men in prison, I thought. "Help me," he said. It came as a surprise that anyone should come to me for help. "How?" I asked.

It was pretty simple, really, except that for the man "inside" nothing is simple. When he'd started serving time she told him she loved him and she'd wait. Now in her letters she was talking divorce. Why the change? Pat was unhappy in prison, unhappier than he'd ever been in his life—nothing was right with the world, no one was right in the world. It showed in his letters: bitterness, recrimination, suspicion, reproach. She thought it was meant for her—the bitterness, the reproach. What else could she think?

What I told him was pretty simple, just like his problem. Write her a letter, I said, and apologize. Tell her you're a damn fool to have made her feel that way. And tell her how it happened that you did—you're not the first man to have done it from prison. Prison can do these things to a man. And tell her she's the universe for you, your only reason to go on living. He did what I told him to, and showed me the letter. I didn't like the way it read—what he was trying so hard to say didn't come across the way I felt it should—so I took a pencil and changed things here and there, added this and subtracted that. He recopied it and sent it out.

It did the job. He showed me the letter she wrote in reply. No more talk of divorce; she'd wait for him forever, or longer. When you do time it can be longer than forever. It came through in every line of her letter that she was happy, happier than she'd been in a long time: she knew now she hadn't lost her Pat. And Pat was happy too. Showing me the letter, he looked even younger than he was. Even I was kind of happy, but I couldn't afford to show it. Zimmerman, I thought, you've come a long way from the day when they hung a rap for Murder One around your neck. Now you're in charge of Advice to the Lovelorn.

That wasn't far from the truth. Pat spread the word. Everybody in jail has at least one problem, and Pat started a small mass movement in my direction of people with problems. They weren't always as easy to solve as his, but I did what I could. I remember one kid—as young as Pat—who wasn't a queen and didn't want to become one. That was his problem. Or rather, the problem was that there were people around who had no intention of respecting his natural preferences. Prisons being what they are, the problem always arises. And the terrible thing is that there are places where nobody, least of all the authorities, tries to solve it. The attitude can be, "So long as it keeps the men quiet . . ." This particular kid was frightened. When I say, "It was only a matter of time," I'm just telling the truth: he had every right to be frightened. But I'd been inside long enough to know who to talk to, and to know what to say. They left him alone; he served his term and found himself a life outside the walls—a wife and kids. I still get letters from him.

So there it was: Zimmerman, Stage Two. All of a sudden I was acting as a kind of Den Mother to a lot of unhappy guys with no one to talk to. They had their families, sure, but the families had no idea of the nightmare they were living, and most inmates preferred to keep it that way. And the believers had their faith—I wasn't trying to replace the chaplain— but you can't talk to the deity the way you can to the man from the next cell block, with the same uniform as yours, the same working hours, the same problems. I don't lay claim to any special knowledge, and I probably couldn't have told them a thing they didn't know already. But because I was one of them, they were inclined to listen—maybe just because they needed confirmation from someone they trusted. Any-

way, it wasn't long before older men began to come to me too
—not just the young ones. Two men on the verge of a fight
would come and ask me to arbitrate, or to decide who had
prior claim to a lawbook that was circulating from cell to cell;
I'd be asked to organize a collection for somebody's widow
or how to go about getting permission for a Christmas raffle.
And every night, when I went back to the cell, I'd have half
a dozen letters with me, from somebody else's wife, or sweetheart or mother or sister, with more problems: should we
move to another neighborhood? should Johnny or Joany quit
school? how can I pay the rent? why doesn't the lawyer get in
touch with me? why don't you love me any more? I'd try to
give honest thought to every answer. Sometimes it was a job
for King Solomon, but writing every night to all those strange
women, I felt a little like Don Juan. In time I picked up a
nickname: "Judge." Judge Zimmerman.

The funny thing was that I felt better for it all. Just because
one day after football practice a kid had wanted to tell me
his troubles, I was getting all kinds of unexpected fringe benefits. There were floods of people waiting to tell me their
troubles. They looked so sad, so sad. I had to listen. And
talking to them, thinking about their problems, made me forget my own. Not long, but long enough to sleep nights. Looking back, it seems simple: take on somebody else's worries
and you won't have time for your own. It worked, but it can't
be that simple. All I know is that it helped me. It helped them
too; I may be wrong, but I don't know of a case where what
I said didn't help a little.

So helping the others helped me, to my surprise. In prison
I always made a point of hiding my real feelings from the
family—it didn't help for them to know just how miserable
it was. I didn't lie; I just didn't bother to spell out the misery.
My letters during this period weren't exactly those of a man
overjoyed to be spending his life in prison; but, reading between the lines, the family realized there was a change for the
better in me. And that knowledge made things a little easier
for them to bear.

The prison library: two books at a time, one fiction, one non-fiction. Maximum holding time, two weeks. No books on crime, no books on sex, no books on prisons. Lawbooks were in a special category: permitted in theory, they were discouraged in practice. They gave the men ideas. At the least, they could lead to flooding the chief clerk's office with writs, and at the worst they might—after a long, uphill fight—lead to somebody's release. The cons who weren't reconciled to the idea of dying in their cells of old age fell into two categories: those who were looking for a file in every package from home, and those who were reading lawbooks. Up-to-date lawbooks were hard to come by; you had to find your own ways of getting them, and you did. They circulated clandestinely from cell to cell and block to block. After lights out I'd throw a cloth bag attached to a string out of my cell; friendly cons would work it down the corridor to a neighbor's door; he'd put the book in the bag and I'd draw it in like a fish. Night after night I'd study the texts in the dim light from the corridor, making notes on precedents I thought might apply, encoding them sometimes to minimize the danger of detection. I'd use my laundry bag for a combination desk and pillow, and keep one ear cocked for the slam of a door somewhere, the sound of footsteps, a guard on his rounds: anyone telegraphing his arrival found Isidore Zimmerman sound asleep under a mound of blankets. Under Zimmerman, of course, was the book. During the day I sometimes took the chance of mixing a lawbook in with the others in my cell—there was safety in numbers, and the guards were unlikely to be suspicious of something right out in the open. Some prisoners managed to wangle official permission to have lawbooks, but every authorized volume was registered to its owner, and it was strictly forbidden for inmates to "help" each other with their cases. If you were caught with an unauthorized book, then you faced the usual punishment—the box, for example— which was bearable, but they confiscated the book as well. For some of us that was heart-breaking.

The law business began for me when an East Side neighbor of mine turned up in Dannemora: a real prison lawyer. He asked me to fill him in on my case, all but guaranteed me a successful appeal—"It's just a question of time, Beansy"—and drew up with me a *coram nobis* writ in 1952. I submitted it to the Court of General Sessions—the court which had pronounced my conviction—and it was denied without a hearing, even though we found a recent ruling that stated a hearing was mandatory. We weren't particularly discouraged—everything comes hard in prison—and we went right on looking for the legal key that would open the door; it made more sense than getting into fistfights in the yard. All in all, I worked with my "prison lawyer" friend some four years before he was transferred out of Dannemora. It was no substitute for law school, but it was a very practical course of law: wherever, whenever we met—the mess hall, the rec block, the yard— we'd talk law. I was sorry to lose him. All that reading after hours had begun to play hell with my eyes, but now, thanks to him, I had at last begun to realize how I might help myself.

———

Transfer to Greenhaven: from the inmates' point of view probably the worst prison in the state. In every respect. The warden reads in my record that I have been active in the prison sports program. He questions me: how do we go about organizing a football team? The first step, I say, is to get uniforms. How, he asks. Write to a pro team like the New York Giants and ask for their cast-offs—uniforms and equipment they'd be throwing out otherwise. No, says the warden. Why, I ask. We won't ask for charity, he says, not from anyone. I try to explain that uniforms are necessary to distinguish the players of one team from the players of the other; that equipment— some equipment: helmets, shoulder pads—is necessary because football is a rough game. But the warden has the answers: one team can wear their prison-issue caps, the other team not; the players can use rolled-up underwear for padding. Otherwise, he says, the whole thing will cost too much money. I make one last try. When I was in Attica Prison, I tell him, coaches from the professional teams would come up for nothing, just to help the prison teams, to help the convicts. No charge; just like the old uniforms. But before he came to

Greenhaven, the warden had been superintendent of Woodburn, an institution for retarded criminals; for him all cons
were retarded, as a matter of principle. Up to a point, he was
right: any con who tried to substitute rolled-up underwear for
shoulder pads was pretty clearly retarded. Not surprisingly,
the warden had the last word. He refused to authorize anything that involved begging. Besides, he said, I'm sure we can
find someone just as good as you or better to organize the
team. End of interview.

═══════════

The news reaches me that Chaleff is dead in prison—a diabetic coma they couldn't bring him out of. I remember my
last glimpse of him four years or so ago in Greenhaven. It
was 1950. I hadn't seen him for nine years. Thinner, balder,
his cheeks sunken, he looked more sickly than ever. Prison life
and diabetes had combined to slow him down terribly; even
his mind didn't seem to be what it had been. Like me, he was
studying the legal aspects of his conviction, and like me he
was hoping to organize an appeal that would lead to his release. But he was terribly pessimistic—he talked as though
the effort was hardly worth making. "I'll try," he said. "I'll
try, but I don't know why." It was damned depressing.

Was it two years later? In 1956 somebody told me Little
Chemey was dead now too—in his bed, of natural causes.
Never brought to trial for Foley's killing, never a day in prison.
Never a seat in the electric chair, like Dominick and Hutch
and Harvey. I was reminded of Chaleff, and then, suddenly, I
realized. Foley, Harvey, Hutch, Dominick, Little Benny—
electrocuted in 1940—Sonny Chaleff, dying in prison, and
now Little Chemey, dying in bed. Even Wandling and McGuire
gone. Isidore Zimmerman was the last one left, the last man
to die.

═══════════

The parole system: sometimes you wonder if it isn't a
diabolical part of the pattern of punishment. If it is intended
to hold out hope to the prisoner anxious to earn another
chance at life, why does it so often drive men to despair?

In Auburn I am invited by two men—both married, with

families—to participate in an escape attempt: commandeer a truck unloading provisions inside the walls, ram it through a side gate—less massive than the main doors—and break out to freedom. I am depressed, desperate, but not to that extent; I refuse the offer. The attempt is made; the gate holds; the truck is demolished; my friends are in the hospital, one with a broken leg, the other with concussion of the brain. For the attempt to escape, their sentences are increased. The reason for this madness? Both men, technically eligible for parole, had simply given up all hope the board would ever grant it.

In Auburn I meet a man who is serving his fifty-second year in prison for a murder committed in 1910. Twenty-five years after his crime, in 1935, the District Attorney's office recommends that his life sentence be reduced. The parole board ignores the recommendation.

In Attica another escape attempt misfires: two men with provisions, money, civilian clothing, and a key of their manufacture which will open a little iron door in the prison power plant are caught at the last minute with the help of an informer. In justification they say they are convinced the parole board will never allow them a favorable hearing. "So what have we got to lose?" The question, asked time and time again, compels an answer. If the parole board does not perform the functions it is intended to serve, the convict who tries to break out has nothing to lose.

The parole board's members are appointed by the governor. The salary is handsome. The job is a political plum; the Democratic governors appoint Democrats, and the Republican governors Republicans. Qualifications (a knowledge of penology, psychology, sociology, medicine) are reduced to the purely political. Five men are appointed: three sitting when the board meets, and the other two "roving"—inspecting prisons, on vacation, or home sick. They are answerable only to the governor, unless, of course, they happen to be violating the law. (On occasion they do violate the spirit, if not the letter, of the law. Their refusal at one period to grant "good time"—time off the sentence for good behavior—necessitated a special emendation of the law sponsored by the Commissioner of Correction, and triggered strikes in prisons all over the state until the legislature spelled out the fact that the "good time" provision was obligatory.) As a general thing they know little about the law, less about prisons, and nothing about men. What knowledge they do have comes from two sources: an interview with the prospective parolee, and the report of the "parole officer" attached to the board. Three or four months before the prisoner sees the board, he is interviewed at length and in depth to determine his prospects for parole—his mental attitude, his prison record, the nature of his offense, his prospects of earning an honest livelihood. The parole officer may even interview the prisoner's family and friends outside before he turns his report over to the board, recommending, or not, that he be released. But in time a positive recommendation from the parole officer came to mean less and less: the board would sit back, fold its collective arms, and ignore it. Interviewing the prisoner about a parole wasn't necessarily significant either. They'd send you right back to your cell with an RO—for "reconsideration only"—notice. A three-year RO just meant they'd think about it and maybe see you again when three years had elapsed. And in time the parole officer—seeing that his recommendations didn't carry any weight unless they were negative—left off making recommendations altogether, and just handed in a report on the prisoner. That made it even easier to the board to reach its conclusions: no action, or six months' RO or six years' RO. The principle seems to be: better keep 99 potential parolees under lock and key than let out that hundreth who might cost us our jobs.

Every now and again events prove just how right the parole board is. The hundredth man turns out to be somebody like Frederick Charles Wood, who committed a double murder out on Long Island while on parole. Somebody told me it's the only instance in the penal history of the state of a paroled murderer committing a murder on parole. Be that as it may, the Wood case scared the hell out of every parole board in New York; they'd sit on their hands and say No from dawn to dusk and hand out RO notices for five and seven years— five to seven years before they'd even talk to you about parole again—the way Rockefeller used to hand out dimes. I remember a businessman who'd gone broke the wrong way; with a little better luck it would have been considered a civil offense, but the District Attorney managed to send him away for fraud. It was a short term and he was a good risk; no parole board in he country would have turned him down. Along came Frederick Charles Wood, and the board gave him eighteen months' RO. It was like adding eighteen years to his sentence.

Trouble started in Greenhaven, when a prospective parolee serving a short term came up before the board in what amounted to a test case and was refused. Two hundred fifty inmates went on strike; the strike spread, and before it was over there were sit-downs and small riots and cracked heads in every prison in the state. It was all traceable to the parole boards, but nobody could persuade them not to run scared for months and months after. And for a while nobody—but nobody—got paroled.

I remember Tom. He'd been inside forty-three years. Maybe it helped pass the time: he was always cleaning up his cell, washing clothes, scrubbing floors; his uniforms were spotless; his cell was spotless. Now, after forty-three years, even the parole board agreed that Tom was morally spotless too. "You've been in a long time, Tom, and changed for the better. You're a model prisoner, and we're recommending your release on that basis just as soon as we check the psychiatric report on you." Tom leaves the board all smiles, and when he comes before them three months later, he's still smiling: today's the day they tell him his release date, the day he's dreamed of for forty-three years. But the board isn't smiling. The psychiatric report is favorable, but there's a new element to consider now. In the three-month interval since Tom's last appearance, a parolee named Wood has murdered two elderly men in Queens. "We've been reviewing the case . . . No." Depressed, Tom makes his way back to the cell. It's a six-month "hit," he thinks; the parole board will see him again in six months and then everything will be all right. What's six months more, now, after forty-three years? The slip comes down from the board giving official notification of the RO period. It's a two-year hit. Tom hangs his head, begins to brood. His friends do their best to talk him out of it, but Tom's not in a talking mood now. He is sick with disappointment; he feels a bar of pain pressing on his chest. A friend in the neighboring cell calls out: "Tom boy, give me your cup; I've made coffee." No answer. The friend angles a hand mirror through the bars at arm's length for a view of the cell: Tom is sitting on the bed, arms folded tight across his chest, rocking back and forth, mute. The friend, alarmed, calls for a guard: "Hack! Hey, hack! Man sick!" The cry is taken up from other cells. "When I'm ready," snarls the hack. "Not before." He is startled by the quantity and quality of abusive language in reply: he calls the hospital. Two hours pass—no word from the hospital. The whole block is shrieking its indignation now, and the disquiet spreads to neighboring blocks whose inmates hear the noise and can only speculate on the reason for it. Two hours later—four after the first call to the hospital—a nurse reaches Tom's cell. The men all around in the block are furious, cursing, spitting, shouting their hatred. There is no help for Tom: he is dead now. A hypodermic might have saved him for another appointment with the board. They said he died—literally—of a broken heart.

———

Edelbaum had written to tell me of it, and today I was advised officially: I'm being moved from Dannemora to the Tombs. They may set aside my conviction, but I don't count on it. Don't count on anything, and you'll never be disappointed. Prison has taught me that, if nothing else. All I know is that I'll be on the train tomorrow to New York, and see Papa, and Carl and maybe Louis, and talk to them if I'm lucky for a few minutes. And there'll be scenery to look at out of the train window: trees, fields, billboards, people. Pretty girls: I remember a girl I saw on the train up to Sing Sing in 1938. By rights that should have been my last train ride. Will I ever see another girl as pretty? I'm lucky to be taking a train ride tomorrow, the luckiest man in the world.

Rabbi Oster heard the news somehow. He came to my cell to kiss me and to say he was happy for me, and say good-bye and wish me luck. Surely goodness and mercy . . .

CHAPTER 7

THE
KEY

WITH THE CONCLUSION of the *coram nobis* hearings in June, 1956, Zimmerman is returned by judgment of the Court to his place of exile, behind walls of stone and bars of steel. Neither the affidavits and testimony of Hanover and Rose that their trial testimony against Zimmerman was perjured, nor the candor of Graymore's admission that, for the District Attorney's office, some testimony was to be "perpetuated" and some to be ignored—depending "on the witness, [and] what the situation was"—is considered grounds for giving him his freedom. Perpetuating Zimmerman's imprisonment is procedurally simpler. The idea that he may have been arrested by error, tried by error, convicted by error, sentenced to die by error, and live out his life in prison by error is less embarrassing to society than the uglier charge which suggests itself: that this has occurred not by error, but by design. Error perpetuated acquires a kind of sanctity in time, the force of tradition. The District Attorney's office need not be anxious to violate the sanctity, break with the tradition; such a position is understandable, if not praiseworthy. So the arguments for keeping Zimmerman in prison are rationalized: Rose's 1956 testimony can be disregarded, because Rose is given to perjury (although there is no reason to doubt the truth of what he said in 1937); and Hanover's 1956 testimony can be disregarded, because Hanover disavowed it all to Graymore before the *coram nobis*
238

hearings (although there is no reason to doubt the truth of what he said in 1937).

So Zimmerman has gone back to live on hope again, back behind the wall. But something has been changed. The wall contains a tiny flaw, a fissure that will widen into a breach; and the day is coming when Zimmerman will step through it to freedom.

The beginnings are modest, unmarked by portents. On the morning of June 21, in the opening minutes of the *coram nobis* hearing, Mr. Herman offers "for identification" a statement given by Rose on May 25, 1937, upon questioning by District Attorney Ambrose Delehanty in the presence of Detectives Gallagher, Bambrick, and Wandling. The document—a carbon copy of eighteen typewritten pages which reflect the questioning of Buddy Boyles and Ralph Scalogna as well as of Rose— was misfiled, explains Mr. Herman, under Scalogna's name rather than Rose's. Judge Mullen directs that it be "marked for identification as Court's Exhibit H." Burlakoff, after inspecting it, asks that pages 6 to 11, and 15 to 18, covering specifically the declarations made by Rose under questioning, be marked as Exhibit F for the petitioner, Zimmerman. Judge Mullen accedes.

Moments later Mr. Herman offers, and Judge Mullen receives, as People's Exhibit 9 the transcript of another statement given by Daniel Rose, this time on June 4, 1937, under questioning by the Assistant District Attorneys Delehanty and McGuire in the presence of Detectives Gallagher and Wandling, and Acting Lieutenant Vincent Kiernan of the Ninth Squad.

The two statements read into the record by Herman are intended to point up past vacillations in the testimony of Rose, and thereby demolish the credibility of Rose's affidavit in Zimmerman's behalf, but their introduction is an unlooked-for windfall for Zimmerman's counsel. Up to now the defense has never had access to these statements, never known, in fact, of their existence. Because of their availability a new situation has arisen. In his haste to repudiate the witness Rose, the Assistant District Attorney is offering, as it were, to take

Zimmerman's lawyer on a guided tour of "the enemy camp." "The witness is not worthy of belief," he is saying. "Look at this skeleton in Rose's closet, and this, and this." What he overlooks is that the skeletons belong as much to the office of the District Attorney as to Daniel Rose, welder-mechanic.

That two such documents exist is no grounds for disbelieving in the existence of others useful to the defense. A search is undertaken, and a third statement, similar in character, made by Rose on March 5, 1938, is turned up. After the close of the *coram nobis* hearing, the Court of Appeals will direct that it be made available to Zimmerman's counsel.

The means, at long last, are at hand: buried in the welter of fact and forgetting, contradiction, confusion, interruption and objections that go to make up any court proceeding are the elements of Zimmerman's deliverance. They are not easy to see—except for the kind of mind trained to suspect their presence and the kind of energy capable of bringing about their rational fusion, the fact of their existence would be meaningless, purposeless, useless. To utilize them requires special knowledge, special skills, and above all, time. Burlakoff has begun the work. Edelbaum will finish it. In his hands the three statements withheld by the prosecution become a redoubtable weapon: the instrument of Zimmerman's liberation.

———

Daniel Rose was first called to the stand as a witness for the prosecution on March 24, 1938, six days after the beginning of the trial of the East Side boys. In the course of his questioning by Assistant District Attorney Rosenblum, no mention is made of any pre-trial statements. Zimmerman's lawyer, Murray, cross-examining the witness immediately directs his questioning toward the discovery of such statements. He suspects—rightly—their existence, and hopes to turn them to the advantage of the accused; but he can make no headway against Rose. On the stand and under oath Rose declares, among other things, that the first time he made a statement concerning the Foley case was "about three or four days ago . . . approximately a week"—that is to say, at the latest about a day or so before the beginning of the trial. But the first of the three "suppressed" statements brought to light by the *coram nobis* hearings is dated May 25 of the previous year—a good ten months earlier; the second is dated June 4, also of 1937; and even the third, made on March 5, 1938, antedates the beginning of the trial by ten or eleven days: lie number one. Next, Rose declares to Murray that the only time he made a statement concerning the Foley case *in the presence of a stenographer* was the occasion earlier mentioned as being "about three or four days ago . . . approximately a week"— that is, a day or so before the beginning of the trial. But Rose's three pre-trial statements dated May 25 and June 4, 1937, and March 5, 1938, were—precisely—made to members of the District Attorney's office in the presence of stenographers: lie number two. Now for lie number three: Rose testifies to Murray that his first incrimination of Zimmerman, in the course of a dozen or more periods of interrogation in 1937 and 1938 by the police and members of the District Attorney's staff, was "a couple of weeks ago." But Rose's first statement incriminating Zimmerman is in fact the one dated June 4, 1937, twenty-four days after the crime and ten months before the trial opens. Finally, though Rose declares on the stand that the only statement he has "signed" is the one made by him in Mr. Rosenblum's office at a date he can situate only as coming after the first of January, 1938—that is, the statement of March 5—it is evident that the value to the District Attorney's office of the statements dated May 25 and June 4 would be nil unless they too were signed by Rose: lie number four.

So it is established beyond contestation, with the aid of the three suppressed statements, that Rose has given false testimony at the time of the trial. Now, that Rose should give false testimony is hardly news to Zimmerman; as far back as 1938 he heard himself being sentenced to the electric chair because of it. Nor should it come as a surprise to the District Attorney's office which considered hauling Rose before a grand jury in 1956 on the ground of possible "subornation of perjury." For Rose, perjury is a reflex. He is not the first, nor will he be the last, of those who—even without malice or an eye to self-interest—are simply incapable of telling the truth, incapable of recognizing it, incapable of recalling it. As a native Congolese may acquire immunity from a tropical virus, so Rose has, over the years, built up an immunity to the truth. There is no real ground for being surprised at Rose's perjury. There is, however, grounds for surprise at the facilities granted a perjurer to send men to the electric chair, or, failing that, to prison for the rest of their days. Surprising too, for a well-ordered society, is the demonstration that the prosecutors of the People's case against Isidore Zimmerman found it unnecessary, at the very least, to acknowledge perjury in the courtroom by a key witness and thereby to grant to Isidore Zimmerman his constitutional entitlement as a citizen: the right to a fair trial.

In effect: it is demonstrated that Rose made three pre-trial statements to members of the District Attorney's office; that the prosecution, in possession of those statements—which were rich in inconsistencies—permitted false testimony to be given by Rose at the trial denying their existence; and by its failure to make known to the Court, the jury, and the defense its knowledge of the falsity of that testimony and the existence of those statements, the prosecution has been guilty of nothing less than suppressing evidence. The consequence, for Zimmerman, is literally a matter of life or death: acquittal or conviction.

At least one man of law is able to condone the District Attorney's failure to produce Rose's inconsistent pre-trial statements, and the prosecution's permissive attitude toward perjury in this language: "In the heat of preparing and pleading a case, a lawyer is pretty much like a troop commander on the firing line, being shot at, shooting back at the opposition, trying to press an advantage in this area of the battlefield, shore up the defenses in that sector, anticipate here, improvise there. In all the smoke and shouting and confusion he's trying his best to do the impossible: forget nothing, neglect nothing, make no mistakes. And even with the best will in the world, and the best brain, he'll make a mistake." But the acknowledgment of error—of which those who suffer from it may take a less lenient view—is hardly sufficient to deter the law from its ponderous and continuing march: the machinery may be breaking down, but the wheels go on spinning. A judgment of the New York Court of Appeals seems more pertinent to the idea of justice than arguments proceeding from the fallibility of prosecutors: "A lie is a lie, no matter what its subject, and, if it is in any way relevant to the case, the district attorney has the responsibility and duty to correct what he knows to be false and elicit the truth . . . That the district attorney's silence was not the result of guile or a desire to prejudice matters little, for its impact was the same, preventing as it did a trial that could in any real sense be termed fair."

———

On the record, Rose has provided a different version of the facts—as recalled by him or as understood by him—for every time he has been questioned concerning them. The very wealth of variations he provides on any given theme is, perversely, a kind of proof of purity: a calculating scoundrel will make an effort to be consistent in his fabrications, but this effort seems to be beyond Rose's powers or intent. Accordingly, there is no purpose to be served by setting down—elsewhere than in a legal brief—point by point, without omissions, all the contradictions, confusions, and collisions between Rose's trial testimony in 1937 and the three pre-trial statements to which he put his signature. But even a cursory examination of the salient features of those three statements makes clear the extent to which they would have given Murray the means of defending Zimmerman, and Zimmerman the chance to have lived another life.

In the first of the three statements, dated May 25, 1937, Rose discusses the shuttling of the guns from person to person in considerable detail. There is mention of Footke, of Buddy Boyles, of Scalogna, of 201 Clinton Street: there is no mention whatever of Zimmerman. Boyles—declares Rose—is the party who turned Scalogna's .38 over to Footke; Boyles is the last party to have had custody of Scalogna's gun; Boyles, not Footke, is the party to whom he loaned his overcoat. In any case, says Rose, he himself returned the pistol to Scalogna before Foley's shooting. Further, maintains Rose, after Footke has "bunked" the guns in the hallway, "about a half hour later

I went home and went to bed," and sets the time when he and Footke hid the guns at 11:30 or 11:45 P.M. This chronology rules out Rose's peregrinations to and from the Scammel Street Boys' Club, to Hanover's Candy Store, to the two Clinton Street hallways where the weapons were transferred, the episode of the coat, and the conversations with Zimmerman and Cooperman—there is simply no time for these things to happen. Nevertheless, Rose will testify unchallenged at the trial that they did happen; Zimmerman's defender, Murray, unaware that Rose's statement exists, will be unable to confound him with it; and the prosecution, with the statement safely in its dossier, will maintain silence. Moreover, in the interval between this statement and his trial testimony, Rose will have fixed the hiding of the guns to 7:00 or 7:30 that evening—a clear gain of three or three and a half hours—in order to allow time for the alleged conversations with Zimmerman concerning the guns, the alleged pick-up and transfer of the guns from Zimmerman to Cooperman, and the conspiratorial discussion in Hanover's store with Zimmerman's alleged participation. But all of the aforementioned details from Rose's statement of May 25 are incompatible with his trial testimony.

Now ten days elapse, during which it is reasonable to suppose that members of the District Attorney's office continue to question young Danny Rose. The grounds for the supposition are simply that the second recorded statement, dated June 4, 1937, and read into the minutes of the 1956 *coram nobis* hearing on Assistant District Attorney Herman's initiative, bears so little resemblance to Rose's first statement, and conflicts not only with Rose's trial testimony, but also with the third statement he will make on March 5, 1938. Twice the second statement is interrupted by "off the record discussions" between Rose and those questioning him; and twice the direction on resumption of the question-and-answer session suggests that Rose is, to put it charitably, being oriented to reply in a certain fashion. Now Rose speaks of Zimmerman as participating in the transfer of the guns, but still maintains he and Footke hid the weapons about 11:30 P.M., far too

late in the evening to be reconciled with Zimmerman's timetable as the prosecution will present it at the trial: Zimmerman
has still not the time, nor is he in the right places physically
to perform various activities—conferring with O'Loughlin
and the others at Hanover's, negotiating for the guns, picking
them up, and transferring them. Nor has Rose yet placed
Footke and Zimmerman together in his presence to discuss the
guns—Footke, he claims, dropped out of sight for the rest of
the evening after hiding them in the hallway—but he will
rectify this omission in his trial testimony.

Now, for the first time, Rose is putting Zimmerman into
the picture, but the chronology of his movements will still
not bear examination. Rose begins to repeat his earlier version
of events: that, half an hour after hiding the guns with Footke
—around 11:30 P.M.—he has reached home or is well on
his way there. But now his interrogator elicits the information
that he did not go "exactly home." Now, says Rose, he went
to the corner of Clinton Street, where he loitered until about
half-past twelve, met Zimmerman, discussed the existence of
the guns with him, and indicated their hiding place, before
parting in opposite directions. At this juncture—according to
the transcript—Rose, questioned as to the direction taken by
Zimmerman, suddenly "volunteers" the information: "The
two guns were taken out by Beansy." The revelation comes
as a surprise in this context; it is not offered in reply to any
direct question in the transcript but, to all appearances, gratui-
tously. (But Rose is not the sort to furnish information gratui-
tously. Any lawyer who questions him will certify that the exercise has more in common with painless dentistry than with
classical forensics. Zimmerman's counsel would have been
justifiably curious as to what, in the ten-day interval between
the first and second statements, provoked such gratuitous information—would have been, that is, if he had known the
statements existed.) Continuing on the same tack, Rose volunteers further that Zimmerman took the guns with the intention of hiding them in the poolroom. Again, none of this is
compatible with Rose's trial testimony: that he first told Zim-

merman of the existence of the guns—but not their hiding place—in Hanover's store at around 9:30, that Zimmerman *and Cooperman*—who has not been mentioned in either statement up to this point—sought out Rose at the Scammel Street Boys' Club to find out where the guns were located.

The second statement introduces still another element tying Zimmerman to knowledge of the felony: meeting Rose on the morning after Foley's shooting, he asks—*dixit* Rose—if he has heard "what the stupids went and done," and buys him a newspaper to read about the holdup. Rose becomes almost eloquent on the subject: "While walking down to buy the paper I asked him about the guns. I asked him if they used the guns. He said all he knows is that the big one they dumped; the big one, see. He didn't want to tell me who was there. He just said the big one is dumped." An examination of the transcript reveals the question triggering this answer: "Didn't you forget to ask him something? What about the guns that he took away with him?" The form of the question suggests a schoolteacher prompting a backward pupil: familiar ground must be covered again, until it becomes more familiar; the lesson presumed learned requires more study.

For Edelbaum the witness is being cued, like an actor who does not yet have his lines down pat. There are other indications in the "script" of the second statement that seem to bear him out. For example, immediately after Rose's "He just said the big one is dumped" comes an off-the-record discussion. For what purpose? Curiously, when Rose's testimony resumes, immediately after the off-the-record exchange, it takes the form not of laconic, chaotic answers to questions, but the recapitulative form of a narrative run, and includes even the modification of an earlier statement—introduced by the self-conscious phrase, uncharacteristic of Rose: "This I didn't say before"—which suggests that little by little, by dint of adding this and changing that, a statement, revised and corrected to suit the questioner's requirements, is being methodically worked out.

A few minutes later the second off-the-record discussion supervenes, and again the transcript resumes with a detailed

recapitulation of the ground covered so far. For whose benefit? Surely it is not required by Rose's sense of logic. For
Maurice Edelbaum the case is clear: "The prosecutor-ventrilo-
quist himself speaks the lines and has the witness ratify the
concocted recapitulation." What is Rose's rejoinder, at the
close of the recapitulation? A fervent, "Right." Of what
notion is "Right" the semantic abridgment? Of: "You are
right; what you have just said is so; I am in agreement with,
I subscribe to, what you have just said."

Again: after Rose's sudden, "This I didn't say before," there
is a new development in contradiction with Rose's first statement. Now he acknowledges seeing Footke after Zimmerman
is supposed to have taken the guns, and lying to Footke about
their disappearance. Why? Because the lie suggested by Zimmerman serves to stress Zimmerman's conscious role in their
disappearance: Zimmerman, Rose is trying to say, was aware,
therefore guilty. The point is further spelled out, for the record,
in Rose's reprise after the second "off-the-record" discussion.

Lastly, of cardinal importance among the new elements in-
terjected into Rose's second statement is the first pre-trial
mention of Cooperman. The coincidence is troubling: once
again this important modification follows an off-the-record discussion—the second—and is incorporated in the detailed
"narrative" resumption by the questioner; and once again, it
is worth noting, the first allusion to Popeye Cooperman is to
be found in the mouth of the questioner.

QUESTION: "We'll go back to the point where the guns had
been hidden, 201 Clinton Street. You left that locality after
the guns were bunked and eventually you came back to
this point . . . and there you saw Beansy; and then you
told Beansy the guns were bunked . . . for Footke who was
going to pick them up . . . that he was going to do a job;
and if the job was successful you were going to get something out of it. Beansy then . . . went in and got the guns,
walked to the corner and then he met a man named Elly
or Popeye coming around the corner and you saw them
from where you were standing . . . step into a hallway on
Clinton Street and when they came out Elly walked around
the corner of Henry Street out of your sight entirely, and

Beansy came back and told you that he had given the guns to Elly to hide and that when Footke came to look for the guns for you to tell him that somebody had taken them?"

The only reason for accepting the foregoing as a question, rather than a recitation, is the presence—at the end of the passage stenographically recorded—of a question mark rather than a period; alter the punctuation and you transform the text into a briefing. Now, at this juncture, the prosecution is well aware that Cooperman will testify against Zimmerman and well aware of the advantage of having Rose—another foundation witness—and Cooperman corroborate each other's testimony; yet even this version of events will have to be improved on before Rose's trial testimony, with which it is still at variance.

———

With the third and last of the three "suppressed" pre-trial statements—dated March 5, 1938, thirteen days before the opening of the trial—time is clearly beginning to run out. The People's case against O'Loughlin, Guariglia, and Friedman seems as strong as the general sense of outrage over Foley's killing; Chaleff's guilt leaves little room for doubt; and the absence of Little Benny and Chemey is presumptive of their guilt. Only Zimmerman's connection with the case may seem —without the testimony of Hanover, Cooperman, and Rose— to be tenuous: hence the importance of Rose's last pre-trial statement for the prosecution. In the words of Maurice Edelbaum: "This statement, after certain perfunctory preliminaries, begins with a pious exchange between the questioner [now Assistant District Attorney Jacob Rosenblum, in the final stages of preparing the case for trial] and Rose in which the witness obediently agreed that part of his previous statement was incorrect and that it was now his 'desire to change that portion' of his previous statement."

The first major "correction" is the declaration by Rose that on Wednesday, two days before Detective Foley's shooting, he had a conversation with Footke, who promised him $10 for procuring a gun "to take (that is, hold up) a whorehouse."

Rose, in his third statement, admits he was agreeable to the project, but to allow him to make such an admission on the witness stand, before a jury, is to present him in a distinctly unflattering light; if Rose lends himself to robbing whorehouses, he may be presumed capable of lending himself to other unsavory enterprises, such as incriminating others to save himself. So Rose's third statement is never produced at the trial, nor does he ever testify to Footke's projected holdup of a whorehouse. If he borrows Scalogna's .38, he will testify, it is for the noble motive of forestalling another holdup, rumored to be plotted, of the Scammel Street Boys' Club. As Edelbaum puts it: "Had the jury in the 1938 trial known that Rose was in so unattractive a complicity with Footke as is spelled out in the Rose statement of March 5, 1938—indeed, had the jury learned of this through an impeaching cross-examination of Rose based on the March 5, 1938 statement—the outcome of the trial for Zimmerman might well have been different. The People deliberately concealed this dismal episode involving their star witness, Danny Rose." A corollary falsification in the same area of questioning: Rose admits, in the third statement, having fabricated rumors about a holdup of the boys' club in order to borrow the gun from Scalogna, but on the stand at the trial he is permitted by the prosecution to present these rumors as the truth.

Still another touch is employed to prettify the portrait of Rose for jurors who may feel his character leaves something to be desired. In the March statement he admits lending his coat to Footke "for the purpose of a job," that is to say, a holdup or some other criminal undertaking linked with the gun; but at the trial Rose will state, with no fear of correction by the prosecution, that Footke has borrowed the coat to wear on a date. The result is simply that the "partnership in crime" of Footke and of Rose, first glossed over and then disguised, finally disappears altogether from the eventual disapproval of the jury.

A major discrepancy with Rose's trial testimony continues to mar the March statement, and will require further "correction" before Rose takes the stand: he is still maintaining he turned his gun over to Footke at 11:00 P.M. In time this too will change, and by resetting the transfer to 7:00 or 7:30 Rose will present the prosecution with a gift of an additional three and a half to four hours in which to demonstrate Zimmerman's involvement with the conspirators.

The gist of Rose's first two pre-trial statements: he hides the guns with Footke, meets Zimmerman across the street from the hiding place, and tells him where they are hidden, after which Zimmerman enters the hallway and takes possession of the guns, all between 11:00 and 11:45 P.M. The gist of Rose's trial testimony: between 7:00 and 7:30 the guns are hidden; around 9:30 he meets Zimmerman at Hanover's store and tells him of the guns, after which Zimmerman, accompanied by Cooperman—another star witness for the prosecution—seeks him out at the Scammel Street Boys' Club in order to get possession of the guns. But between the trial testimony and the first two pre-trial statements intervenes the third statement, dated March 5, and it contains such blatant contradictions that —far from being the next-to-last "draft" of Rose's story, and therefore nearly perfect—no effort is made to refine Rose's trial testimony from it. Why? In Edelbaum's words, Rose makes declarations in the March statement which "are obviously and ineptly designed to conform with the subsequent trial testimony of Cooperman and Hanover, but which are so entirely irreconcilable with Rose's prior pre-trial statements that it is hardly to be wondered at that the prosecution did not let Rose, at the trial, testify in line with this portion of his statement . . ."

In his March statement to Rosenblum, Danny Rose declares that he goes, shortly before midnight, to Hanover's Candy Store after hiding the guns, and there sees, occupying booth number one (about which Hanover will testify at the trial) not only Zimmerman, but all the "East Side boys" involved in the Foley murder—O'Loughlin, Little Benny, Little Chemey, Guariglia, Friedman, Chaleff, and Cooperman; Cooperman and Zimmerman then and there—in Hanover's—leave the others to ask him, Rose, about procuring guns. Situating all the conspirators together with Zimmerman in their midst;

changing the place where Rose and Zimmerman allegedly discuss the guns from the Scammel Street club to Hanover's store,
where all three prosecution witnesses—Hanover and Cooperman as well as Rose—can place Zimmerman; and adjusting
the timetable of events to coincide with the physical availability of persons purportedly participating in them: from the
prosecution's point of view, this is all too good to be true. Yet
no reference will be made to these damning "revelations"
during the trial by a prosecutor attempting to demonstrate
Zimmerman's guilt; Rosc's trial testimony against Zimmerman
will be alogether different from this version of events set forth
in the last of the pre-trial statements. Why? Edelbaum makes
it clear: "In view of the obvious benefit that such testimony
would have brought to the prosecution if it had been at all
worthy of reliance, i.e., in view of the fact that such testimony
by Rose would have fitted in most beautifully with the testimony of Hanover and Cooperman, the voluntary decision of
the prosecution not to use this . . . story is the best indication
of its falsity." In other words, it is too pat to be credible: the
kind of neat tying-up-and-gift-wrapping of a case that district
attorneys dream about, but hardly expect to find in their
stocking even on Christmas morning. Edelbaum concludes:
"It is not difficult to imagine what would have been the sen-
sational effect upon the minds of the jury if this portion of
Rose's statement . . . plus the fact of the prosecution's election
not to have Rose testify along those lines, had been available
to the defense cross-examiner at the trial of Zimmerman."

A final crucial point emerges from examination of Rose's
statement of March 5. At the time of the trial Rose will testify
under oath that he has no memory of declaring—to Harry
Levy and Hyman Liebowitz, both of whom testify, in Zimmerman's defense, to statements by Rose at Madison House ex-
culpating Zimmerman—that Zimmerman has nothing to do
with the crime. Not only—testifies Rose—does he have no
memory of such declarations; he has no memory of such a
meeting at Madison House. But, under interrogation by District
Attorney Jacob Rosenblum on March 5, Rose recalls the conversation, and recalls it very well. He told a story, he says, to

"cover" Zimmerman. Now, much to Zimmerman's detriment, this particular detail will be purely and simply suppressed; and by its suppression the prosecution manages, in Edelbaum's words, "to water down the glaring conflict of credibility as between the accomplice witness Rose and the unimpeachably credible and reputable witnesses [Levy and Liebowitz, both members of the New York Bar with an aggregate of thirteen years of professional experience, and whose civism can be measured by the time and energy they devote to voluntary work at the Madison House] who testified for Zimmerman concerning the Madison House exculpation of Zimmerman by Rose." Moreover, points out Edelbaum, by suppressing the two statements (June and March) which inculpate Zimmerman and which were made at the same time Rose was giving directly opposite statements (to Levy and Liebowitz) absolving Zimmerman, the prosecution "deprived Zimmerman's defense at the trial of what would probably have been its single most striking means of demonstrating to the jury that Rose, the witness who was not loath simultaneously to condemn and to exonerate another person, was absolutely unworthy of belief when testifying against that person as an accomplice who had the mortal self-interest of saving his own life."

The doors are opening for Isidore Zimmerman, but his freedom is not yet an accomplished fact. The labyrinthine machinery into which he has been drawn by error, ignorance, mischance, which snatched him up, drew him in, mangled, maimed, and all but destroyed him, is never casily emerged from. The perjury of the prosecution's witnesses is established; established too the suppression of evidence which makes a further mockery of his trial. But of its own terrifying momentum the machinery continues to grind.

Zimmerman appeals an order, dated January 31, 1961, of the Appellate Division of the First Judicial Department, affirming the order of the Court of General Sessions of New

York County by the Honorable John Mullen denying, after hearing, his motion for a writ of error *coram nobis* vacating the 1938 judgment against him.

May 1, 1961, Charles S. Desmond, Chief Judge of the Court of Appeals, grants permission for the appellant Zimmerman to take his case to the Court of Appeals.

On January 1, 1962 the New York Court of Appeals reverses the order of the Court of General Sessions denying Zimmerman's motion for a writ of error on these grounds: "When the defendant was on trial in 1938 under an indictment charging murder in the first degree, the witness Rose called in behalf of the People, falsely denied upon cross-examination that he had made any statements in the presence of a district attorney's stenographer more than a week before the trial when, in fact, he had previously made such statements, containing material inconsistencies, on May 25, 1937, on June 4, 1937, and on March 5, 1938. The failure of the prosecutor to make any effort to correct this falsehood and to afford the court or defense counsel an opportunity to examine those statements, which were in his possession, in effect amounted to a suppression of such material and prejudiced the defendant in his right to a fair trial."

Zimmerman, by order of the Court of Appeals, is remanded for a new trial.

On January 30, 1962, Isidore Zimmerman is re-arraigned for the murder of Detective Foley. Asked if his financial circumstances allow him to pay for the services of a lawyer, Zimmerman must reply negatively; he is destitute. The Honorable Thomas Dickens, of the Court of General Sessions, assigns Robert Ellison, Fred Samuel, and Maurice Edelbaum to represent Zimmerman.

He has served twenty-four years and eight months in prison. In three years and six months he will be eligible for parole. Maurice Edelbaum moves for an order dismissing the indictment against Zimmerman on grounds that the interest of justice requires his release.

On February 2, 1962, court is convened by the Honorable Thomas Dickens, Judge of the Court of General Sessions.

CHAPTER 8

THE
WAIT—part IV

I COULDN'T BELIEVE it was ending. Why should I have believed it? When it all began, twenty-four years back, I hadn't been able to believe it either, for a while. But when I saw Mama for what they told me was the last time; when the death house barber gave me the "dance hall special"—short on the crown and on the calf, where the electrodes fit—I'd finally begun to believe it was happening to me; and when, night after long night, I sat on the cell floor with my head against the cold steel of the bars, waiting for them to come and tell me there'd been a mistake, that I could go home now—I knew then, in the ache of my heart and my bones, that prison would be my lot forever. What reason was there to believe now that the trap would open, that I could leave? No reason at all. I was a lifer, and when I died it would be in a cell.

Why did I appeal? Why did I keep on trying to win a fight I'd lost years back, when my parents were still young, and I had brothers and sisters who were, literally, children, when the best years of my life lay before me, available for my own particular pursuit of happiness? No one had listened to me then; why should they listen now to my appeal, when memories had grown dim and uncertain and half the actors in the tragedy —McGuire, Chaleff, Little Benny, Wandling, my mother— gone? Who remembered? Who cared?

I remembered. I cared. If I stopped caring, it would mean

254

they had won: that the wrong man could be sentenced to death, or to life-in-death, and the universe would go right on spinning. We all knew it could happen—I thought of Hitler and the camps and my father's family, left behind in Europe, who would never write us letters again—but the mind refuses such knowledge. My father remembered, too; my father cared. He was seventy-five now, but he'd never stopped believing I'd come home one day, and he believed it now as much as ever. Why did he believe? The last day in the death house—the day I knew would be my last on earth—he simply wouldn't believe they'd execute his son, and he'd been right. I remembered trying to talk to him about arrangements for my funeral. He'd grown impatient, shaken his head. "Why talk about it, sonny? I'm sure you're not going to the electric chair, as sure as I am that today is Thursday. There's no need even to talk about these things." He was my father; I loved him and I could see why he was talking like that—but I'd known I was going to burn as sure as there was a sunrise. And he'd been right after all.

They'd operated on him twice: in 1954 and then again in 1955. It was serious. They'd all but given him up, but he wasn't worried. "I knew I would be around to open the door for you when you come home from prison," he told me later. "Mama will be lighting candles to welcome you, and we'll all sit down together and have a good long talk." Now Mama was gone, but as long as she drew breath she'd believed that day was coming. They were so close—we used to say it to kid them— that anything Papa believed, Mama believed too. And it worked both ways. Throughout the trial, when Papa came home in the evening he'd find Mama praying. She'd spend the day in court, suffering, and the night in prayer. "She made me into a good Jew," he'd say, remembering their ordeal together; what she believed, he believed too. But how he found the strength, the courage, day after day . . .

He needed courage. There were the letters from cranks: advice, abuse, threats. After my sentencing someone left a pistol on the landing just outside our door, a pistol with a note attached. Take the gun to your son in prison, it said; he can

kill himself and beat the chair. Then there was the mother of
one of the boys they executed—she came and all but ordered
Papa to give her the money for her son's burial. Like the other
parents, she took my commutation as a deliberate affront for
which the whole Zimmerman family was somehow responsible.
Papa didn't have the money she asked for, but it wasn't in
his nature to refuse; for him, we'd all been visited by the same
misfortune and we were all equal before it. So he took the
subway up to Harlem and asked Father Divine—whom he'd
met a couple of years earlier at a Labor Day parade he helped
organize—and Father Divine gave him the money like that,
with no questions asked. Then there were the extortionists: on
two occasions Papa got death threats. "Pay up," they said,
"or else . . ." probably on grounds that somebody in his position would be too crushed to do anything but comply. But
Papa didn't scare easy. If he took the precaution of notifying
friends—among them a municipal assemblyman—"just in
case," he never tried to buy off the extortionists, and they
never tried to carry out their threats.

Papa had the courage to stand up to threats, but he could
never handle the sweet-talkers. "Mr. Zimmerman," they'd
say, "we're going to manage a fund-raising campaign, the
proceeds of which will go to finance your son's appeal and
eventual release." Papa would contribute from his own pocket,
ring doorbells with the best of them, and turn whatever he
collected over to the sweet-talkers. They'd deduct 99 percent
or so for "campaign expenses" and drop out of sight forever,
but it never seemed to hurt Papa's optimism: he was convinced
they were fighting the good fight.

It didn't hurt his faith in human nature either when the
mother of one of the boys—one who was executed—threw a
rock at him in the street one day: what right did he have to
be the father of the one that got away? After the special
hearing in Albany the families of the "East Side boys" all
dined together in a restaurant on East Broadway to discuss
their prospects, and somehow they all felt the Zimmerman
family—Papa and Mama in particular—were primarily responsible for what was happening. And they showed it: Mrs.

Friedman even told my parents I was a "killer," which didn't make things easier for anybody. Maybe even then she had a premonition of what was going to happen—an attendant at the hearing remarked that in twenty-five years he'd never seen a governor give so much time to such a proceeding—and maybe even then it might have seemed painfully evident that Chaleff and I were the only ones to stand an outside chance of commutation.

For twenty-four years Papa had had patience, too, with the lawyers and with the law. Of the half-dozen men who'd handled my case from the beginning, some had been indifferent, and some bad, and some good. If there hadn't been good ones in the lot, I realized, I wouldn't still be around to regret the others. But the law moves as slowly as a glacier: there are motions and cancellations and trial calendars to be respected; there are briefs to be drawn up and submitted and replied to; and time is needed—always more time—for deliberation and decision and disposition. And time, of course, was my enemy—the enemy of every man in prison.

There were lawyers who'd take on the case with all the energy of an Olympic runner entered in the hundred-yard dash; but with the passage of time and the expense of effort their optimism would vanish and their pace would slacken— when they discovered we were on a cross-country run, with no finish line in sight—and their action on my behalf would become less and less vigorous, more and more sporadic, until they dropped out of the race against time. But there was no dropping out of the race for me, and the fact that I understood what was happening—why they were doing it—didn't take the edge off my disappointment. But Papa too had been living with disappointment for close to a quarter of a century, and he was still going strong.

Lawyers needed money; I knew that. The law is as expensive as it is slow; and lawyers, even the philanthropic kind, have to pay rent, secretaries, carfare. Papa didn't have any money to offer—just the conviction that I had to be brought back home as soon as possible. That conviction had taken him a long way. At its best it was downright con-

tagious. And somehow, too, over the years, with the rest of
the family helping, he managed to scrape up enough here and
there to retain that lawyer or this, for six months or a year or
two years—long enough to get the wheels moving again.

Now it was Edelbaum who was working for us to get
the ponderous legal machinery off dead center. He knew his
business. I knew he'd long since been paying for the prosecution of my appeal out of his own pocket; and he was as tire-
less as a long-distance runner. Papa had written to tell me
how, five or six weeks back, Edelbaum had sent for him. In
the book-lined, green-carpeted office, hands folded in his lap,
he waited. "I am the happiest lawyer in the state of New
York, Mr. Zimmerman. Your son is going to come home in
a matter of weeks." Suddenly Papa was afraid to be optimistic
any longer. After twenty-four years of bad news, good news
is kind of hard to take. "When?" "In a few weeks, at most a
few months," said Edelbaum. "Have patience, just a little
more patience." "I have no patience now," Papa said. "Six
years ago his mother died. Now I am waiting alone. But I
have no patience."

Just six weeks ago Papa had gone to Bellevue again with
double pneumonia. Edelbaum had said, "Take good care of
yourself, Papa. I'm bringing your boy home to you." Papa
must have believed him then, judging by the way he pestered
the doctors to let him out of the hospital. It was just a week
ago, I knew, they'd discharged him. Now it was Friday, eight
days later, and on the strength of Edelbaum's promise he'd
be in court again, waiting—one more day's wait tacked onto
twenty-four years—and somebody else from the family—
Celia, maybe, or Carl, or my brother Louis, if he could get
off work that day—would be there to wait with him. Through
the dirty barred window with its wire netting I could see the
weather: half snow, half rain, all gray. I hoped the damp
wouldn't kick off another round of pneumonia for him.

Papa told me later the day had been like all the other
days, almost. He had breakfast in the apartment—eggs and
black coffee in the little kitchen—watching the early-morning

traffic on the bridge to Brooklyn. The subway to court. Edelbaum was there, telling him for the thousandth time, "These
things take time, Papa." Papa wasn't exactly overjoyed to hear
that; he knew it already. Celia was there, and she began to
cry the way women do—on general principles. It was Papa's
fifth straight day in court, she knew; and for the fifth straight
day she was afraid the District Attorney would manage not to
make the recommendation we were all praying for. Then, at
the end of the afternoon, Papa would turn away again, put his
coat collar up against the drizzle, and go back to the little
apartment on Columbia Street again, alone. Maybe that was
what made her cry. Maybe not. She might have been crying
because she felt that the long wait was finally over, that today
was the day when Papa wouldn't go home alone.

Nothing happened. Lunch hour came and went. Papa didn't
go out to eat; he was afraid of missing something, without
quite knowing what. A half-dozen reporters in the corridor
had buttonholed him and begun to ask questions about the
case. Who was Isidore Zimmerman? Who was Foley? What
was the Boulevard Restaurant? Papa didn't give them much
satisfaction. Like a lot of New Yorkers, he was given to
answering questions with questions of his own. "Where were
you while he was in prison?" he'd ask. "Why should you be
interested now? You weren't interested then."

It wasn't until later that I found out what had been going
on. I'd been taken from the Tombs that morning and de-
posited in the "bullpen" outside the General Sessions courtroom, dressed like a free man: single-breasted reddish-brown
tweed, white shirt, red tie, tan top coat. No number in sight:
a novelty for 31063. There was no way for me to spend the
time but pace, pace, up and down, back and forth. Planning
ahead didn't make sense. The disappointment was sure to
come, and it would only be harder to bear if I started making
plans. Edelbaum had come to see me in the bullpen early,
said, "I think today's the day," and disappeared to attend to
another case due for hearing that morning. I paced.

Around ten-thirty they came to get me, but right away I

could feel there was something wrong. Everyone was there in court—everyone but Mr. Edelbaum. "Is your attorney present, Mr. Zimmerman?" the judge asked me as only a judge can ask. "I don't see him your Honor," I managed to answer, and thought to myself, "Not today, Zimmerman, not ever—it's a bad dream, but you'll never wake up from it." A court attendant passed a note to the judge. He frowned, cleared his throat: Mr. Edelbaum's absence was unavoidable; because of the "other case" his presence was required elsewhere in the courthouse. The judge ordered me back to the bullpen as only a judge can order. I was physically numb. Was it disappointment? Over and over I told myself, "You expected this—it had to happen—you knew it would happen." I paced, up and down, back and forth.

Thirty minutes later they came for me again. I felt thirty years older. Edelbaum was in court now, presenting his apologies to the judge. There were the members of the District Attorney's staff: Mr. Herman, of the Homicide Bureau, and two other Assistant District Attorneys. Mr. Edelbaum made a motion on my behalf. It was eloquent; it was moving. I remember there were spectators moved enough to applaud when he finished, but I can't remember the words, just the sense: he was asking that all the charges against me be dropped. Then there was silence, and the silence was unbearable.

This was the day, the hour, the minute, the moment toward which all my hopes and energies had been directed for twenty-four years. It had taken six years of writs and motions and appeals to bring about the present hearing, to make the wheels of the vast machine move ever so slightly. And now, I realized, my life—what it had been, what it was, what it might still be—hung on the first word to pass the judge's lips. After that it was over. Over forever: a man's life against one word from a man's mouth. That word could never be recalled in a man's lifetime. Even if the word was wrong, there wasn't time to call it back. It was final.

He didn't say the word. One of the Assistant District Attorneys sitting next to Mr. Herman got up and handed a slip of paper to the judge. He read it and returned it to be read aloud. Now I felt again as I had while Mr. Edelbaum was making the motion in my behalf: the words, I knew, meant everything to me, but what were the words? Not the ones I feared, not the single word the judge could say—"Denied"— that would send me back to die in prison. What were the words? I remember their sense, nothing more: the District Attorney was joining with counsel for the defense in recommending that the original indictment against the defendant Zimmerman be dismissed.

That meant it was over, over at last. No: only that it might be over, if the judge, black-robed and forbidding, saw it the same way. I couldn't take my eyes off him. What kind of man was he? Gentle? Hard? Compassionate? Unforgiving? A father, a grandfather? A man who smoked cigars, remembered his wife's birthday, kept goldfish, walked the dog, liked a drink before dinner? I realized with a kind of terror that a perfect stranger was about to dispose of my life—a man I didn't know, and who knew of me nothing but what was in the record, filtered across the courtroom through direct examination and cross-examination and objections sustained and objections overruled. That was what had happened to me before, twenty-four years ago, and now it was happening all over again. I prayed the judge was a wise man, wise enough to know there was more to the case than the record—any record—could show.

The word I dreaded did not come. The judge, I realized, was listening still to the man from the District Attorney's office. They recommended dismissal of the indictment, yes. "But we do not concede this man's innocence. We are supporting the motion made by counsel because it is apparent that certain witnesses have given perjurious testimony . . ." something like that. Certain witnesses: Danny Rose, Hanover, Cooperman. Twenty-four years back, when I was on trial for my life, Mr. Murray in his defense had brought it out that witnesses against me were perjuring themselves. How had he put it? Something about how the law did not allow men—

like Rose and Cooperman, whom Judge Nott had recognized, even then, as accomplices to the felony—to fight their way to safety at the expense of a third. A third man like me, for instance. But the law did allow it. Cooperman, I knew, had never been indicted for his role in Foley's murder, never served a day in prison in his life. Where was he living? What was he doing? How did he sleep nights, knowing what Danny Rose had known, and what Danny had finally had the courage to admit? And Rose: a seventeen-year-old kid at the time of my trial, afraid of what could happen, afraid of prison, he'd fought himself clear at my expense, even though the law claimed he couldn't. He'd grown up, grown older, got married, had a family, a job—everything everyone had in the wonderful world outside the walls, and took for granted—while for twenty-four years I lived like an animal.

Outside of prison: on a hot summer night a man could walk down to the corner drugstore and buy a pack of cigarettes, a paper, drink a soda; a man could go for a walk in the rain, to a movie; sit in the park on a bench and feed the pigeons; play poker all night with his friends; move to California; join the Merchant Marine. All these things they could have done, or did, while every night for twenty-four years they shut the steel doors on me at night like an animal in the zoo.

I thought of Hanover. How many sodas had he served; how many times had he wiped the marble-topped counter with a wet rag; how many times swept out the store at the end of the day; how many times had he rung up the cash register? How many times, in twenty-four years, had he thought of me in my cage? And how many nightmares had he had, remembering how they'd questioned him and questioned him until he didn't know what to believe about that April night and the boys in booth one. All he wanted was a little peace— for them to stop asking questions about things he didn't understand and let him go back to his candy store, ringing up nickles and dimes in the register and wiping the marble-topped counter with a wet rag. I didn't hate him—hadn't hated even during the trial—but I wished he'd had a little more imagination, a little better understanding of the damage he was doing to another life just so they wouldn't ask him questions any more.

So there it was, finally: perjury admitted. I didn't really care, at this point, whether they conceded my innocence. What I wanted more than anything else in the world was to go home now, with Papa, to the little apartment off Delancey Street, where you could hear the traffic rolling over the bridge to Brooklyn. Not back to prison: just to go home, finally, to go home again. And all this time the judge hadn't said the word I was afraid of. He could raise his eyes from the record he was reading, look right through me and say, "Denied," and it would be another death sentence for me—this time, with no reprieve. He could say it, and I was terrified he would.

He didn't say it, but he almost broke my heart. Take him away, he said. Bring him back to court at two-thirty this afternoon. I'll announce my decision then.

As I left the courtroom I got a glimpse of Papa's face.

In the bullpen again: pacing, pacing, pacing. I was ready to give up. I'd come this far, and it was a long way, but it had taken too much out of me. If I had to wait any more . . . No, going back to prison was easier; I knew the routine there. But I hated like hell what they were doing to Papa; they had no right to subject him, at his age, to this kind of torture. Twelve-thirty.

What they did to me didn't matter much any more. It was part of my punishment; they'd figured it that way. But my father couldn't be expected to stand much more. I'd tell Mr. Edelbaum it would have to stop. We could all stop fooling ourselves. One o'clock.

What did the judge need the time for? Why couldn't he have announced it then and there? Why did everything in law take hours, days, months, years? One-thirty: pacing. Two o'clock: pacing. In half an hour I'd know the worst again. If I was lucky they'd let me talk with Papa before they sent me back. I'd try to cheer him up. Should I tell him I'd appeal again, work up some kind of story with Mr. Edelbaum, just so he'd have something left to hope for? It would be more honest, kinder perhaps, if I told him I was through fighting, tired out, resigned: if they could admit I'd been convicted with perjured testimony and still somehow manage to deny my innocence, then they were too strong for me. Too strong for anybody.

Two-thirty: footsteps outside. No, not for me. Two-forty: a pair of plainclothesmen stopped in the corridor just outside the cell; one lit a cigarette; they passed on. Two-thirty, they'd said: it was nearly three now. They were trying to drive me crazy, or they were crazy themselves. I mustn't get angry; I mustn't let it show: that's the best way to fight back. I'll pretend I don't care—that'll make them furious. Three-ten: I don't care; I don't really care. Three-twenty: how can a judge—a man whose profession it is to make decisions—spend this long "making a decision"? He doesn't know his own mind. No, he knew his decision perfectly well when he ordered the noon recess; it's the system. They're trying to drive me crazy, but I won't give them the satisfaction. When I get back home—to my cell in Dannemora—I'll build a new bookshelf and paint it. I'll try to stop smoking, or at least cut down: I smoke too much. My cell isn't so bad. Three-twenty: what the hell are they doing to me? My cell is downright pleasant compared to this one. In Dannemora I have my things: my books, the lamp I made. I'll cut down on smoking. This cell is cold, impersonal, uncomfortable. There's someone different in it every day. I wish I had a cigarette. Three-thirty: steps outside again. Steps: this time it's for me.

When I got back to court there was only Papa left. Celia had gone. She'd been lucky to get the morning off from work, and she was lucky not to be here now, to see her brother go down for the count again. I wished there was somebody from the family to comfort Papa; it wouldn't be easy for him to take after a week of waiting. He was standing up by the barrier separating the spectators from the officers of the court, facing the judge, his back to the left-hand row of seats, with a couple

of court attendants flanking him. I suppose they figured he
was going to make a scene when the judge lowered the boom
on me.

Mr. Edelbaum was asking for the floor again, and the judge
gave it to him. Again, I could hear the words, but I was too
upset to remember anything but their general drift: something
about how terrible a thing it would be if this man were to be
kept even another minute in prison. Then it was over, and the
judge announced his decision. "Upon recommendation of
the District Attorney I hereby order the indictment against
Isidore Zimmerman dismissed and further order that he be
released from custody." It was over.

The worst was over, anyway. Somehow I found the presence
of mind to stand up and thank the judge. Then Mr. Edelbaum
and I walked through the barrier separating us from the spectators: I was a cripple who could suddenly walk without
crutches. My father shot out from behind a line of benches like
a halfback on a power play and hugged Mr. Edelbaum and
kissed him. "Thank God for this day," he kept saying. "Thank
God." I realized he was crying, and how close I was to crying
myself. But only close. After all those years of waiting it had
finally happened too fast.

What happened in the corridor outside the courtroom wasn't
any easier to believe: a horde of photographers firing off
flashbulbs, and a half-dozen reporters, notebooks in hand,
asking questions simultaneously. Nobody remembered Foley,
or the East Side boys. It was all ancient history to them; it
might just as well never have happened. The questions were
reasonable enough, I suppose, given the circumstances, but
whatever answers I could manage probably didn't make for
good copy. When the judge pronounced those magic words,
my brain had all but stopped functioning, and nothing much
was filtering through. One question I do remember, if only
because of its consequences later on. A woman reporter asked
me if I planned to get married. Twenty-four years of prison
had done nothing to prepare me for my first press conference,
so I improvised what I thought was the one sensible answer:

"All things considered, I don't know whether any woman would have me as a husband." That, I thought, was the end of that, but I was wrong.

Arm in arm Papa and I walked down the long marble corridor to the bank of elevators, my brother Louis doing his best to fend off the press. We were on the seventeenth floor of the Criminal Courts Building, and in all my years of confinement I'd never taken an elevator from that altitude. I couldn't have been more nervous if they'd asked me to make the trip down by parachute. All the way I was fighting the impulse to shout "Stop!" to the operator.

Outside it was cold and damp, the pavements wet with a powder of snow. Not a trace of sunshine, but that didn't keep Papa from saying later, "It's the brightest day of my life." Fortunately, Louis was there to ride herd on us; at that point neither Papa nor I was level-headed enough to attend to practical matters, like finding a taxi. I stood in the wet in my thick prison shoes and my prison-made suit and sniffed the cold air and watched the people scurrying along the sidewalks. This was what it was like "outside"! The first "outside" air I'd smelled in twenty-four years: it made my head swim to think of it.

But my reflexes had been so conditioned by prison it would take more than fresh air and elevators to get them back to normal. In spite of myself I kept looking back over my shoulder, waiting for a blue uniform—and there were plenty in the neighborhood of the courthouse—to beckon me back. "Are you Isidore Zimmerman? There's been a mistake; you're going back to prison." It was an anxious ten minutes I spent there on the sidewalk, and my face must have showed it. "Relax, boy," Louis kept saying. "Relax—it's all over now."

We settled into a cab, Papa on my right and Louis on my left. That was a good thing, because I'd probably have tried to break out of the cab if I'd dared: every vehicle in sight seemed to be moving with the speed of light. Nothing in my memory told me we were traveling at a normal rate for New York traffic, and I was convinced we were headed for an

accident. "Take it easy—slow down," I called to the driver.
No cabbie in New York likes to be given that kind of advice.
"I *am* taking it easy," he answered, and he was probably telling the truth. Louis and Papa laughed, and Louis said, *"You
take it easy, boy,"* to me. But all the way home I was poised
on the edge of the seat, too worried about the traffic to notice
the changes in the city around us, the crowds on the street,
the shops, the ads.

Home was another shock. There wasn't much showing of
the East Side I remembered growing up in. Delancey Street
was still there, but the tenements were gone, or going. When
we got out of the cab at the housing project, I couldn't believe
my eyes: a cluster of huge apartment buildings, then another,
and then another, a dozen stories high, higher than any tenement, the kind of place where only rich people lived when I
was a kid. They were set in the middle of grass plots, with
trees around them, asphalt walks and playgrounds. On the
other side of the street a few surviving tenements, empty, with
boarded windows, waiting to be demolished; and between the
survivors vacant lots piled high with bricks and rubble and
scrap timber. Huge new buildings up; old ones—the only
familiar sight in the landscape—coming down; and nothing in
between. But a city—or even a neighborhood—doesn't
change like that overnight. I'd been away a long time.

The place had an elevator. When I was a kid, everybody
walked up the stairs, but there were too many stairs here.
Fortunately for me it was a good bit slower than the courthouse model: I took the trip like a veteran. When we got off
we found another bunch of newspaper people waiting at the
door. More questions; more pictures. They posed me by the
window, looking out; it was the first window without bars I'd
been able to look out for a long time, and I enjoyed it. From
way up on the seventh floor everything looked strangely tiny
except for the towers of the housing project. When somebody
asked me for my impressions of New York "after all these
years" I remember saying I didn't understand what had happened: "It's a city of little villages now. Everything's so

small." Why? I suppose because for twenty-four years my
world had been reduced to four walls, a rectangle eight feet
by five, so now I had to shrink the city to make it fit my own
shrunken vision.

More pictures: Papa with his arms around me, me with my
arms around Papa. More questions: what were my plans? did
I have a job? how did I feel about the witnesses whose perjury had sent me to the death house? At that point I didn't
feel much of anything but fatigue. It had been a very full day
for me. When the last of the reporters left I sank down into
the easy chair opposite my father, and we just looked at each
other across the little room: no glass between us now, no wire
grill, no guard watching the clock. Just the two of us. "This
is all I've ever wanted in life, Papa," I said. It didn't seem
like a lot to ask—to sit in a little room with your father and
talk. But it was more happiness than I thought I'd ever know.

We talked. First we talked about Mama. This was the day
she'd waited half a lifetime for, and it didn't seem right that
she wasn't there. What was done to her—to me, to all of us—
was a wrong, and for Mama now it was too late ever to set it
right.

I looked at Papa as he talked. He looked tired, and older
than I'd remembered, but most of all he looked happy. He
asked me about prison, about the kind of life I'd lived there,
but I didn't want to say anything that could hurt his happiness. God knows he'd had little enough of it in his life.
Besides, it's something you can't understand—existing in a
cage—unless you've lived it yourself, day after day, year after
year. Papa, like Mama, had known what it was to wait, while
the years passed; but for everybody life is a process of waiting. What he couldn't know was what it meant to be absolutely deprived of all the trivial little freedoms that, added
together, make a grand total of liberty: freedom to drink a
cold glass of beer on a hot day; freedom to sit on a bench in
the park and take the sun; freedom to say No or freedom to
say Yes. Not to be, like all the other cons around me, the
physical property of the Department of Correction, like the

blankets on the cot in my cell, or the tin trays in the mess hall. Never mind the killers; never mind the junkies; the mental defectives; the perverts; the thieves, the violent, the sexually obsessed; the liars, the informers, the sadists; never mind the brutality, the monotony, the ugliness; never mind the physical surroundings—one prison is pretty much like another, when all is said and done—and never mind the people —there were, after all, good ones among the bad and innocent ones among the guilty. But for all those years I had been deprived of my existence as a person, and reduced to the status of a thing: I belonged, literally, to the Department of Correction, in a way that no soldier belongs to an army and no citizen belongs to a state.

Sure, I'd survived the experience; and now, except for my memories, I was a free man, like the others—the ones who rode the subway to work, paid taxes, voted, married, raised families, worried about how to pay the bills. But I knew something the majority of my fellow citizens probably never thought about: I knew capital punishment was a good thing. Not a good thing in itself, but a better thing for most men, whether they know it or not, than life behind bars in the best of prisons. So when Papa said, "Tell me, now, what was it like?" I took the easy way out. "It wasn't too bad, Papa. I just bided my time and tried to make the best of it until the great day, until today. It wasn't too bad, Papa."

We talked about the family: Louis, Charles, Hilda, Ida. What were they doing? Where were they? I had relatives I'd never met: Carl's wife, Rose, who had never grudged her husband the time he spent away from her, working for my vindication and release—she'd taken my innocence for granted from the beginning, before their marriage, when Carl told her my story; my nephew Jay and my niece Fay, Hilda's children, and Rebecca, her oldest. I hadn't seen Hilda for twelve years, since I was in Greenhaven; a railway ticket to Dannemora was expensive, and there just hadn't been that much money to go round. Papa had organized a little party to celebrate my homecoming, and the first knock at the door

came at around eight-thirty: Hilda. Her elder daughter, Rebecca, had never set eyes on me—she was ten—but she flew
straight to my arms; Fay, her younger sister—barely a year
old—held off shyly, but Jay, their brother, gave me a big kiss
in welcome and called me "Uncle." It was the first time, and
it felt good to be called that. The doorbell again: Ida came,
and Louis; Celia; Carl and his wife and daughter Amy; Susan,
David, Brenda, Judy: everybody. There were tears and kisses
and more tears and more kisses and laughter and toasts
drunk and more tears and more kisses. When I closed the
door on the last departing guest it was after two in the morning.

Papa was ready for bed, and so was I, but it was too soon.
I needed time to sit and collect my thoughts, savor the occasion. Sprawled out on the living-room sofa in front of the
television set, I began to take the measure of my fatigue. But
the day was too wonderful ever to end—you didn't go to
sleep on a day like today no matter how tired you were. A
new life was beginning for me; it called for celebration. But
we'd been celebrating all evening: how much wine had I
drunk, how much whiskey? It didn't matter, I told myself.
In all those years in prison I'd never had a drop of alcohol;
even prisoners taking communion were given grapefruit juice
instead of wine. I was hardly used to drinking but I decided
I liked it. I'd have another drink and see what I could tune
in on TV. "So this is television," I remember mumbling to
myself, and, glass in hand, I began unsteadily fiddling with
the dials. For no particular reason I started to get the giggles:
trying to get the picture to hold still had suddenly become the
great adventure, my first in twenty-four years.

The next thing I remember was a loud crash followed by
the sound of breaking glass. I was sitting on the floor, not
standing. The drinks and my fatigue had combined to lay me
out over the long coffee table that had doubled as a bar during the party. The table was splintered, the glassware shat-
tered, the bottles broken. I still had the giggles, but I knew
I was in bad trouble for destroying all that property. There

was only one thing to do. Tiptoeing into Papa's bedroom, I woke him and told him what I'd done. It wasn't easy for him to grasp the seriousness of the situation. "We're in trouble, Papa," I kept saying. "I broke the table and all those glasses." Papa just said, "All right, we'll clean it up in the morning." And went back to sleep.

Papa didn't seem to understand the feeling of accountability I had. After all those years in prison I knew you couldn't destroy property like that and not be punished. I hadn't done it on purpose, no—but I knew I'd have to pay for it. Then I remembered. I wasn't in prison any more. I was in the wonderful world outside where a man was free to do undreamed-of things: break up the furniture, drink whiskey, stay up all night, sleep late in the morning. Nobody was going to punish me for making a mess in the living room. "We'll clean it up in the morning"; that was all. Freedom was a wonderful thing. I managed to find another bottle of something—unbroken—in the kitchen, and I toasted freedom a few more times, till the giggles came back.

I remember giving up on the TV set, settling into the armchair opposite the window, and dozing off at intervals, in spite of myself, for the rest of the night. Occasionally I'd snap broad-awake and, with a little effort, recall that it was all over, that I was home, with Papa sleeping in the next room; that the day I'd dreamed of for so many years had finally come, and that everything would be better from here on. That knowledge was too much to take sitting down, just as this night—my first night of liberty—was too wonderful to sleep through. I'd get up, then, and go to the window and look at the sleeping city, the scattered lights, and especially the stars. It was a sharp cold night, with snow on the ground but none in the clear air, and the stars fascinated me. Suddenly it occurred to me that in all those years of prison I'd never seen the stars, and suddenly it seemed the most wonderful of privileges to be able to stand at a window and look out at the winter night. Then back to the easy chair; I'd doze a little and then get up to look out the window again. The stars began

to grow pale; the light was coming up in the east, over the
river and the end of Delancey; the street lights went out—
puff! like candles on a cake. I saw my first sunrise at the age
of forty-two. I'll never forget it.

Papa got up around seven. I was still worried about the
coffee table and the broken glasses, but he just laughed it off.
And I had my first hangover, which couldn't be laughed off.
It was too much for me to swallow coffee, but I made a point
of getting breakfast for Papa: buttered toast and eggs. He
didn't want me to fuss—since Mama's death he'd been cooking his own meals—but he didn't know what a pleasure it
was for me. "Papa, this is what I dreamed of doing for years
—fixing breakfast for you at home."

The breakfast things were still on the table when the first
knock on the door came. I must have looked worried, as
worried as outside the courthouse the day before. It was a
policeman, I knew; he'd open the door and say, "You're
Zimmerman, aren't you? Well, you were released yesterday
by mistake, but you're going back to prison with me now."
But Papa just laughed. Yesterday it was the family; today it
was the turn of friends. While Papa went off to do the shopping for the Sabbath meal my sister would prepare later in
the day, I played host to people I hadn't seen for close to a
quarter of a century. Time is harder on some people than on
others; there were old friends I could barely recognize.
Twenty-five years can bring such a weight of misfortune—or
fortune, for that matter; some of the people I'd grown up
with, gone to school with, seen every day of my youth before
I went to prison, appeared like total strangers now. And yet
there were those of whom I could honestly say, "You haven't
changed a bit." And it was gratifying to see how many said
exactly that to me: in spite of my ordeal, I was still the Beansy
they remembered.

A lot of them went further in their remembrance. There
were presents: clothes, a wristwatch, a radio, an electric
razor. Those who had an idea of how little Papa's pension
brought him, and of how much he'd had to spend over the

years, with Carl and Louis and the others, so that one day I could come home from prison, gave us envelopes containing money; and though I was optimistic about finding work and supporting Papa from here on, I didn't see how we could refuse. During the Sabbath meal my brother Charles called from Las Vegas, where he lives, after getting the news of my release on television; he wanted Papa and me to fly out for a vacation as his guests. We decided to take a rain check, at least until I had a job lined up; and for the next week or so, when friends dropped by to reminisce, I'd let them know I was ready, willing, and able to work. Monday night there was another party in my honor at the Henry Street Synagogue, and another contingent of friends and another round of congratulations. All in all, a lot of fatted calves were slaughtered for the return of the prodigal. It was a wonderful week. If only there'd been a letter, or even a phone call, from a certain little snub-nosed Irish girl I'd known a hundred years back—just to say hello again after all these years—I'd have been walking on air. But I told myself the past was past. It was a wonderful week anyway.

Of course the letdown was inevitable. My liberty was still something I savored every waking moment, and even my dreams were different from what they'd been in prison. The joys of being with my father, my brothers and sisters—people who loved me and cared for me—were just as keen as ever; and playing with my nephew Jay and my niece Rebecca—little Fay was still on the shy side with me—was a pleasure I'd never known before. But the problem of finding a job began to preoccupy me. I had no illusions that the world owed me a living. When I left prison it was with exactly one suit of clothes, a pair of shoes, and my train ticket; and prison friends who'd written me after their discharge had told me what to expect on the outside: when the Department of Correction stops giving you those three meals a day, you're free to starve to death. I knew too, from what I'd heard in prison, how difficult it is for an ex-convict to get work, no matter how qualified he is. People are inclined to be afraid and mistrustful, and, logically, it's easy to see why they feel that way. Logically, though, the ex-prisoner means to be the best risk in the world for his employer. Having been in prison, he's anything but anxious to go back, and pathetically eager to do a good job for an employer willing to trust him. But few employers, I knew, would give an ex-prisoner the chance to prove himself. And, never having learned a trade—the prison authorities consider it a waste of time to teach a lifer a livelihood, on the grounds he'll never be able to use it—I knew my chance for finding interesting work, drawing a decent wage, were slim. Before the trial I'd worked as a truckman. I was young enough still, and in good physical condition: why not look in that direction as a starter?

There was nothing novel about my experience, except for me. And it was damned disagreeable. I asked friends and I asked acquaintances before I got around to asking strangers. The answers were always different in form, but they all came to the same thing: "Don't call us; we'll call you"; "No openings just now"; "This is the slack season; try us again in six months"; "Sorry, we only take union members." At first I believed in Santa Claus: from now on, I told myself, Isidore Zimmerman had to be lucky. After all, I'd had enough bad breaks for an average man's lifetime. But after collecting my first two dozen refusals I wasn't so sure. Were jobs really that hard to find? Or did people have reservations about hiring me because I'd spent twenty-four years in prison? They couldn't, I told myself, have those reservations. After all, a judge had quashed the indictment against me, and it had been officially recognized that my original conviction had been due to perjured testimony. It wasn't as though I'd committed a crime, been convicted, and as the phrase runs, "paid my debt to society" for my guilt: crime and punishment. That was the classical sequence. I'd gone to prison for someone else's crime, in which I had no part, protesting my innocence all along; I'd paid for someone else's guilt and almost paid with my life. As it was, I paid with a near-lifetime: punishment without crime.

Was it possible, I wondered, that for people outside of prison the important thing was not the crime, or even the guilt, but only the punishment? Was it possible, because of all those years I'd spent in prison, that I was marked somehow, with a mark like the mark of Cain—something hideous for all men to see, on my forehead—even though I hadn't slain my brother? And if I bore such a mark now, simply as a sign of my punishment, where was justice?

Stop thinking like that, I told myself. You're a lucky guy: if you hadn't been born lucky you'd have sat in the same chair as O'Loughlin and Friedman and Guariglia way back in 1938, and had your brains fried at 200° Fahrenheit. You're a lucky guy, full of self-pity right now and lacking in a sense of gratitude toward the universe, but you'll get over feeling sorry for yourself. Look at all the luck you've had: father, mother, family working year after year to bring you home, never losing faith in you; lawyers who fought for you, like Mr. Edelbaum, who believed in your innocence, who'd long since been taking the money for your case out of their own pockets, and whose efforts, month after month, year after year, finally added up to freedom for you. You were so damned lucky, Zimmerman, that you even had the governor of a great state in your corner, believing strongly enough in ˙your innocence to save your life, when another man might have been too busy, or too lazy or too careless to care. Stop feeling sorry for yourself, Zimmerman. Tomorrow you'll get a job and everything will look different; tomorrow you'll get a job and start trying to pay Papa back for all those years. Get a job and, just for a start, pay this month's rent for Papa: you'll be the happiest man in the world. Stop feeling sorry for yourself, Zimmerman—you're a man come back from the grave with a lot of years of good life coming to you. Stop feeling sorry for yourself, Zimmerman—you're a free man, and you know a man's freedom is his dearest possession.

So I stopped feeling sorry for myself and tried doing the rounds of the employment agencies, answering ads in the classified section of the newspapers. I walked a lot of pavement in this city of New York, grown strange to me now, and I answered a lot of questions and filled out a lot of forms, but nothing happened. There was always a point in the interview, or a space on the application, where I was asked something like "State reason for leaving previous employment," or "Give job history with dates for past ten years," or even "Note previous salary earned." What was I going to say? What could I write on a form, what could I say that wouldn't blow my application sky-high? My last job was in 1937. I hadn't worked for the last twenty-five years. Except in prison, and I wasn't considered to be on salary there. If you want to call Dannemora Prison my place of previous employment, why then I suppose my reason for leaving is just that they threw out the charges against me. The charges? Oh, yes, I was accused of murder in the first degree: the killing of a police officer. You probably wouldn't recognize the name, although the case caused a good deal of talk at the time; he was survived by his wife and his little girl. References? Names and addresses of people who will vouch for me, outside of the immediate family? Certainly, if you don't mind the fact that some of them have served prison terms for one thing or another. Some are still serving time, for that matter. They're not all bad, you know, just because they do time. Of course some go to prison because they're stupid, or hot-tempered, or lazy —too lazy to work at anything but crime—or because they never learned, while they were growing up, anything that would help keep them out of prison. And some men go to prison because they're bad clear through, from the cradle, and can't be trusted to walk the streets with the rest of the citizens. And some go to prison because they get one bad break and never manage to get over it and some go because they're framed. And some go because witnesses have been known to commit perjury. But inside that strange world of prison, you know, there are good men, brave men, friends: capable of laughter and generosity and loyalty, right in there with the thieves and the murderers and the extortionists and the rest. Men even capable of being character witnesses for

Zimmerman: I thought of Dash and Studdy and some of the men on the football team at Attica. Other character witnesses? Well, there would be Rabbi Katz from the death house at Sing Sing, or Father Martin; here a guard, there a keeper, here a clerk, there a con. I'm afraid that's the best I can do in the way of references: they were the only people I knew for twenty-four years. But they'll tell you I'm a good worker, strong, willing.

I never put it quite that way, of course. I never really got a chance to. I'd see their faces drop, their expression change, even though they tried to hide it, as soon as the question of my past came up. A man forty years old with no employment history and no references is pretty hard to find. When they realized they'd found me they were generally anxious to get rid of me fast. "We'll call you, Mr. Zimmerman, if anything turns up," they'd say. But they never did.

There was another solution, I suppose: not telling them the truth, not mentioning prison, making up another past they wouldn't find objectionable. But I couldn't bring myself to do it, somehow. For one thing, making false declarations was just the sort of thing that was expected of a man who'd spent even twenty-four hours in prison. I still had the feeling that "they" were looking over my shoulder and waiting, the first chance they got, to slap me back in solitary. For another thing, it isn't all that easy to invent yourself a believable past, and the people who make you fill out those forms know it. Places, dates, names—they were capable of calling me on any detail I furnished, and if it didn't check out, I was in trouble. And being in trouble was no way to start a new life.

It occurred to me now that there'd been something diabolical about the line taken by the District Attorney's office: they were willing to release me "in the interest of justice," and to concede I'd been sentenced on the basis of perjured testimony, but that was as far as they'd go. Maybe if they'd gone a little farther, made some sort of statement officially recognizing my innocence, it would have been easier for me to achieve acceptance, get a job, be reabsorbed into the world "outside."

But by going only that far and no farther, they hadn't made my readaptation any easier. So I went on collecting refusals from employment agencies until I began to feel like a squirrel running around and around in a cage and never gaining an inch of ground. A run of bad luck—the last of your bad luck, Zimmerman—I told myself. Change the scenery: now's the time to take Charlie up on his invitation.

So in March I packed up Papa—after all those years I didn't plan to let him out of my sight—and a couple of suitcases and flew to Las Vegas by jet—first flight, first jet—for a little vacation. All my life I've been frightened of heights, but the flight was smooth and uneventful; all things considered, the trip in the courthouse elevator on my first day of freedom had shaken me up more.

My brother Charles, his wife, and their two children met us at the airport: more tears, more laughter. He pressed a roll of bills on me. "Spend it," he said. "Spend it and ask me for more. Do whatever you want—just enjoy yourself. I want you to start making up for lost time." It was good advice. For the next three weeks—probably the best three in my life—I made up for lost time: lazying in the sun—it never seems to rain in Las Vegas—taking a plunge in the pool whenever I thought of it, eating steak, steak, steak, watching the people with money to burn trying hard to lose it on anything from one-armed bandits to roulette. And every night was a ball. Every hotel on the Strip had a spectacular show, with the biggest names in show business, and I saw them all. I followed Charlie's instructions to the letter: I enjoyed myself. Las Vegas may not be the place to live, but it's certainly wonderful to visit. When we boarded the plane for home I felt ten years younger, relaxed, optimistic. But before the jet set down in New York I was thinking again about my number-one problem: getting a job. Why should it be any easier because I'd had a three-week vacation?

There'd been a steady trickle of letters for Isidore Zimmerman ever since the papers carried the news of my release, but the mail waiting on my return from Vegas had reached flood

proportions: nearly 500 letters had accumulated in my absence, and I had my work cut out reading them. In the lot, I
figured, there had to be at least one job offer worth looking
into. But Lucky Zimmerman was wrong again. People wrote
to congratulate me; people wrote to tell me they knew of
cases like mine; people wrote to ask the name of my lawyer;
people wrote to say that, although they had no job to offer
me, I might try applying at X Company or talking to Mr. Y
or Mr. Z. I followed up all those leads because any one might
be the one I was hoping for, but all I ever got was polite
refusals.

There must have been twenty letters—real heart-breakers—
written by people in mental institutions. When they made
sense they all told pretty much the same story: I've been put
away here by mistake, or because of a plot; nobody listens
when I tell them I'm not mentally ill like the others; so please
put me in touch with your lawyer, who sounds like a wonderful man and who may be able to bring about my release.

A penciled letter addressed "Dear Isidore" began by stating that the writer had already written to my attorney

. . . and he never even answered my letter about him getting me out of this institution, now then I need your help
. . . I have never committed a crime in all my life and don't
belong here anymore than you belonged in the States
prisons I am a friendly kind, sober, honest man and I need
your help to get me out of the hospital the people of New
York have kept me here eighteen years and seven months
this place is probably much worse than a states prison I
have been good to the people of the world, and the free
attendants of the hospital have broke my finger, stole over
$100 worth of my property and have abused me very
much. I will pay you $25 a day and your transportation
from New York City [to X] if you will come here and get
me out. I am 55 years old and its worth just as much as you
are asking for . . . I have been abused probably much more
than you have been in the prison . . . I am just as innocent
as you was. The free attendants poisoned me here till I
nearly died from the effects of it. The Greyhound bus comes
from New York City [to the institution] . . . Please let me
know as soon as possible . . . I will pay your transportation

. . . plus $25 a day for your time . . . I am 100% innocent
same as you was so please come up and get me out.

It was signed "Yours truly, a friend." I answered it.

Two pages of lined paper, the margins filled with post-
scripts, were crushing to read.

> I was very much sorry to hear about your case but I have a
> very much similar case! My sister and widow mother had
> an unlawful arrest in a mental institution and now I have
> to find *someone* to help me get them out? *Please* write me
> a letter the name and address and phone no. of your attor-
> ney . . . he might be able to help me? If you know of
> anyone else who can help me and sign both my patients out
> for good to their houses for one year. *Please* give me the
> person's name, address and phone? If I don't get any help
> both my normal people will have to die in a state hospital
> after a frame-up! I will reward you in the end. I only hope
> that you will be our life saver? Pending a quick reply?
> Thank you very kindly! P.S. Both my two innocent patients
> haled under false arrest! P.S. After patients get out we will
> still need your attorney to sue. *Personal.* Please show this
> letter to your attorney for help. P.S. I need a New York
> lawyer and maybe your attorney can sign my patients out
> in his own custody with a Haybeus Corpus. Both my nor-
> mal patients can be released on their own.

Letters like these were proof, if proof is needed, that there
are a hell of a lot of unhappy people in the world. But if they
moved me to pity, there were those that sent chills up my
spine. Like the letter in fine, regular handwriting—full of
undecipherable words—whose author's sex I couldn't figure
out. It was signed "General," but the name on the return address was clearly a woman's.

> I would like too hire your firm. I've been listed here as
> something the doctors won't talk too me about it. They
> talk too my husband "when he comes." I would prefer talk-
> ing too one of your agents. They pulled a close motion on
> me and its very hard too get too see anyone. I was intro-
> duced too these doctors for the murder of me and I guess
> I'm the only one who believes it. I've been here for the past
> 5 years this May and only went on home on a 5 day passed
> and watched like a hawk. They have endangered and cost
> me my lives by holding on too me. My rank is United

States World International designer of War Material War head etc. etc. My credentials were stolen by a person I could identify. I don't want too write too much I would prefer a confidential arrangement of some sort or another.

The last line of the letter, after the signature, was, "It's out and out Murder Female."

There were letters from prison, too, asking for pretty much the same thing: everybody knows the jails are full of innocent people. For the innocents, and the boys who rejected the idea of breaking out by force, for those who told themselves that with a good lawyer and a break like Zimmerman's they could get their freedom back. I was a shining example, dramatic proof that it could happen, the way Lana Turner was proof you could become a movie star if only some Hollywood talent scout happened to see you drinking a soda after school. I could imagine the conversations in the yard, in the mess, from cell to cell, in prisons all over the country. Letters were coming to me from New York, California, Nevada (the Las Vegas papers interviewed me), Arizona, Chicago, and, before the press let go of the story, even from Germany and Israel. I could imagine the cons talking: "Did you hear about this fellow in New York? Lucky. Had a smart lawyer. What we need is a lawyer like that." "What's his name? Write him a letter: you were framed. A smart lawyer can get you out of anything." I could imagine, too, how many of those letters, conscientiously written, never saw the inside of a post office. They don't censor your mail in jail for the fun of it, and when the chief clerk runs across something in your correspondence that can spell trouble, or even mild inconvenience for him, he's inclined to bury it in your "dead letter file." After all, the prisoner doesn't have any rights. Just privileges. And writing letters is a privilege. I knew a lot of letters like that— addressed to Lucky Zimmerman, asking for the name of his smart lawyer—would stay buried in the files. So sometimes it was the relatives who wrote.

I am writing you because I . . . am interested in connecting or having some contact with your attorney . . . so as to bring to their attention another case similar to yours . . .

to see if they will handle this other case. This case is of my brother who was illegally sentenced to eighteen months in the pen and he did not commit the crime . . . Please excuse me for writing you whom I don't [know] but I feel you will give my letter some attention. Thanks for your courtesy and attention.

Still, whenever I got that kind of mail, or mail from people in mental institutions, I invariably forwarded it to my lawyer. And, more often than not, I tried to answer it myself. There was always a chance the claims were true; and even if that chance was only one in a million, I didn't like to think that some poor soul would have to go on suffering just because I didn't like the odds. After all, the odds against me had been pretty steep too. But even when I forwarded the letters as requested, or supplied the information myself, I'd get follow-up letters complaining that they hadn't heard from my lawyer, asking me for money, and generally taking me to task.

There was a little bit of everything in my mailbag.

> I've read in the newspaper about your sad experience and . . . the sad injustice that has been dealt upon you. But that is not new. It's in the book of Clarence Darrow how many people are even innocently electrocuted!

A Virginia schoolgirl wrote:

> Hi! How are you doing just fine I hope. I am doing just fine too. I would have written to you [sooner] . . . but I have had a lot of homework these past few days . . . School will be out soon and I can write you more often. I am maken [*sic*] good grades . . . this year. Hope I can keep it up . . . Send a picture of your girlfriend. Please.

A publisher of religious tracts, referring to himself as a "handicapped person," wrote:

> Enclosed three of my tracts in Hebrew published in Israel . . . Also one in English . . . Please read them all and pass on. If you should want more free let me know . . . Enclosed is one in Chinese that goes to Red China, Formosa and the offshore islands also Japan and many other countries. But Romans 1:16 is my first love. Please read it all . . . May Jesus be real to you and all your loved ones. Shall pray for you daily that you find a good position.

It was signed "Yours in Christ."

A woman wrote:

> . . . You only was always in my dreams. Don't laugh but I am not a chicken, I am too old for dreams I am 31 years old. I have a daughter six years old. I make this confession to you because when a person like me meet a friend (and this doesn't happen very soon) I tell the truth about my life so nobody start talking. Anyway I have nothing to be ashame [sic] of . . . Forgive my very bad English but I am Spanish and I don't know too much just a little. I learned in P.R. (Porto Rico).

After the signature came a P.S.:

> . . . With all my blessings falling over you and wishing the very best of all and for ever, Yours . . . I am dying to know you in person, so please come and kill my impatience.

I realized now I'd said the wrong thing to that woman reporter on the day of my release when she asked if I planned to marry. My reservations notwithstanding, the correspondence I was getting made it clear that there were women scattered all over the country who'd be delighted to have me for a husband. As nearly as I could tell from their letters, they came in every size, shape, and age group, from the teens to middle age. There were widows with families and widows who were single; there were women who'd never married at all and women who were just plain lonesome; and truth to tell, there were women who didn't care whether we married or not, just so long as they could be sure of having a man around the house.

In the lot—there were literally hundreds of marriage proposals in the mail before it was over—were certainly some fine women: attractive, selfless, tender, understanding, capable of bringing me happiness I'd never known, mothering my children, giving me a firm foundation on which to ground the rest of my life. And most of them, too, showed courage— they were willing to take their chance for happiness with a man whom they knew not at all, or knew only as a news item. I took all that into account, and yet there was something shocking in it for me. Marriage and all that goes with it is much too serious an affair to be embarked on by mail. Some of the letters simply suggested that if we should meet, and get along well together, it might lead to marriage. But there were women, too, for whom our marriage—once their letter was delivered—was a forgone conclusion. And that was a little alarming. I discussed the matter with friends—men friends—and found to my surprise they didn't shock quite as easily as I did. "Look into it," they'd say. "You never can tell." But I figured I had problems enough without looking for more, so most of those letters went unanswered, and all of them wound up eventually in the wastebasket.

But of all my correspondents, nobody put his finger more precisely on the problem than the man who wrote:

> I wish I can congratulate you in person after being saved . . . I follow your story in the newspaper and I see how the Law make mistakes. I know you were innocent. God never forgets his sons . . . *What are you going to do now?*

That was the question. My problem, now, was making a living. The people who run the prisons assume it never will be a problem for a lifer, so they never teach him a skill. The kind of work I'd done in prison—manual labor on the lowest level—had simply left me unfit to survive outside the walls. I could wash dishes or manhandle crates around a warehouse —it would keep me from starving while my strength held out, and it certainly beat being in prison—but I still couldn't seem to find an employer willing to take a chance on my honesty or trust me with responsibility. I remember one prospective employer saying to me: "Sure, you were the victim of circumstances; sure, you never should have gone to prison in the first place. But for the last twenty-four years you've been consorting with criminals, haven't you? How do I know some of it hadn't rubbed off on you?" And I remember answering, "If there's a man on this earth who's set to walk the straight and narrow no matter what happens, I'm that man. Because I know what prison is, and I can't even imagine going back." He couldn't see it.

Of course, there wasn't any money in the bank to tide me
over a rough period. What little Papa had been able to scrape
up was always spent on my appeal, and Mr. Edelbaum had
worked long months for me without a fee. Papa's doctor bills
and groceries took care of the rest. All things considered,
survival was an exploit I couldn't quite explain. I had no income. Friends had advanced me money, but they couldn't
go on doing that indefinitely. I'd planned to write a book
about my experience, and my publisher gave me an advance
against royalties, and then another, but I knew the book
couldn't be written overnight, and no more advances would
be forthcoming until it was delivered. Meanwhile, Papa was
still paying the rent, on nothing a month. It frightened me a
little to realize that, if I had a place to sleep nights, it was
just a lucky accident; without Papa and his apartment, I'd
probably be trying to keep warm on the Bowery with the
other vagrants. How many men, I wondered, released from
prison like me, unable to find work—like me—didn't give up
trying out of sheer fatigue? A man who is hungry, who is
homeless, who has lost all title to respect—or at very least
all hope of being accepted as a human being—is a man who
is close to doing something foolish. Something foolish enough,
for instance, to send him back to prison.

I said as much one day to my lawyer. Not because I felt I'd
reached that point myself, but simply to make him understand
the predicament I was in: I was the victim of a bad practical
joke carried on so long that it was physically painful. For a
quarter of a century the jokers had used a stone wall and steel
bars to keep me out of circulation; for a quarter of a century
I was a public ward, a wayward child, a corpse insofar as my
rights were concerned: I couldn't even make a valid will unless the Department of Correction agreed to countersign it.
Then, with the stroke of a pen, all my rights were restored—
on paper at any rate—and I was catapulted back into the
world of the living. The steel doors opened and the stone
wall came down: I could apply for a passport, travel abroad,
vote, pay taxes, and even breathe the same air as the rest of

the citizens. But somehow the wall wasn't down at all—just invisible; somehow the bad joke was going on and on; and somehow the jokers were still managing to keep me out of circulation. For fear of contamination? I was still whirling around in outer space where people were sent for punishment, and I couldn't solve the problem of reentry into society—not without help. That's why I spoke to Mr. Edelbaum as I did. Because he'd been able to work the miracle of my release, I hoped he could work just one more modest, everyday, common or garden variety of miracle: help me to my self-respect by helping me to a job.

He gave me a good scolding for being pessimistic enough to think about the kind of foolishness that took a man back to prison. And he promised to do his best to help me find a job. He did his best, too, but after a couple of months I realized that even he couldn't succeed at that undertaking. For one thing, I didn't have any skill that was readily marketable. If I'd been an electrician or a plumber or an accountant, someone might gamble on me in spite of the long lost years in prison. But I was just offering muscles and good intentions, which nobody seemed to need. For another thing, asking for a job, even under the best of circumstances, is just like asking somebody for a handout: pay me wages, you are saying, for the job I do. And nobody, I began to understand, was going to invent a job—give me money—just because I needed the work. I'd do better just panhandling for nickels and dimes; then, at least, people wouldn't have to worry about my "criminal associations."

There were lots of things about being a free man, I discovered, that hurt. What hurt most of all, though, now that Mama was gone, was not being able to make it all up to Papa. I knew I could never repay him for his devotion to me, for his suffering because of me; but I could try. With a job—that is, with money—I could try. All I wanted was to take him on a trip around the world, put him up at the best hotels, buy him a big white house in the country where the air was clean and cool, give him a Cadillac and chauffeur—two chauffeurs—for the days he went to visit his grandchildren, walk with him on my arm into a tailor shop and order a dozen suits to his measure. Or even take him out to dinner right now, tonight, in the best restaurant on the East Side. But without a job I couldn't even help him pay the rent. I couldn't pay my way. That hurt.

Despite his efforts Mr. Edelbaum hadn't been able to find a job for me, and it wasn't likely he would. But along about this time he gave me a kind of hope for the future. It was a legal matter, and so it would take patience, but patience was one thing life had taught me. It began with a short course of law: there was a time, he explained, when a man punished for a crime of which he was innocent was entitled, in New York, to bring suit for damages against the state. But the suit had to take a particular form. It had to be submitted, like a proposal for legislation, to the Assembly and to the Senate of the state, and be ratified by those bodies just like a bill for highway construction or slum clearance. The "bill" for compensation would then be submitted to the state governor for perusal. Provided the bill cleared these three hurdles—approval by Assembly, Senate, and governor—it would then be submitted to the New York Court of Claims, and the Court would fix what it considered suitable compensation. There was no appeal from the figure set by the Court of Claims—it was take it or leave it.

Now, explained Mr. Edelbaum, the New York Court of Appeals—the highest in the state—had recently ruled that any such suit for compensation must take place in the same locality as that in which it had been prosecuted. A man falsely arrested in Brooklyn, for example, would bring his claim for compensation to a court in Brooklyn. Further, by the same decision of the Court of Appeals, the extent of damages would be fixed by a jury. This procedure, Mr. Edelbaum went on, was a new one, comparatively untested in practice by the courts.

All this was technical, legalistic, seemingly impersonal; but fighting for my rights from inside a prison cell over the years had given me a certain down-to-earth knowledge of the law. I didn't have to be a member of the bar to see that Mr. X, falsely imprisoned for six hours or sixty years for somebody else's crime, stood a better chance of being properly compensated for his trouble by a jury of twelve men—his neighbors, more or less—than by an audience of two legislative bodies, a state governor, and a geographically distant court.

Now came the revelation, and the hope for the future. "One of the best civil attorneys in this city is familiar with your case," said Mr. Edelbaum. "He feels that the provisions of this new decision by the New York Court of Appeals may well apply to you." I could hardly believe my ears—decision of the court . . . a jury to set compensation . . . compensation! I knew it would be long: from the time of the *coram nobis* hearing to the day of my release six whole years had elapsed— six more years—out of my life, not quite a month of Sundays. I knew it might come to nothing. It was only on television that justice always triumphed. And triumphed in sixty minutes. But it seemed reasonable that if society felt free to send me to my death for something I'd never done, it might feel obligated to try to make it up somehow. At least it was worth trying.

Mr. Edelbaum escorted me to the office of the civil attorney, a small, impeccably dressed man with rimless glasses and a very precise way of speaking. He asked me question after question. Why, I wondered, would he be uncertain about my case? He knew the facts and he knew the law. At length the questions stopped and he began to talk, in slow, measured terms. There were risks involved, he pointed out. My name could be blackened all over again; the bitterness of the Foley case that the years had all but obliterated from public memory could be revived, relived; I should be prepared for a certain amount of harassment from cranks—letters, phone calls—who are always attracted by situations like the one in which I would find myself; delays would be inevitable between the initiation of a suit for damages and a judgment on it; and of course there was no guarantee that judgment would be satisfactory when finally it was rendered.

I sat and listened to him talk. Nothing—I knew that already—came easy for Isidore Zimmerman. If the attorney really felt, as Mr. Edelbaum had indicated to me, that the law covered my case—false imprisonment and the rest—he certainly couldn't be accused of trying to sell me on the idea. His attitude implied that the choice—to bring suit or not—was up to me, not to him, and I decided I liked that attitude. At the end of our conference—we might have been talking for three hours—I found out just how right I was. "Why is it, Mr. Zimmerman," he asked, weighing his words as carefully as only a lawyer can, toying with a letter opener, his wrists resting lightly on the brown leather file closed on the desk before him, "why is it, Mr. Zimmerman, that you would be willing to bring such an action at law?" Nothing in his face told me how to answer, but something told me I was on trial. I took a deep breath and said the only thing I could say: "I would like compensation for the suffering I've been through, yes; it was punishment for something I didn't do. But I want it mostly for my people—my father, my family—to try to pay them back." Silence. Dead silence. Zimmerman, I thought, you've said the wrong thing.

The lawyer put down the letter opener, took off his glasses, and smiled. "Wonderful," he said. "We'll take the case."

Maybe there was a silver lining to any cloud, if you waited long enough. I'd been given something to hope for. At the end of a long wait there might be enough money for me to buy Papa a little place in the country, some new clothes, a couple of weeks' vacation in winter when the New York cold settled over the city and made him cough from September to May. With luck there might even be enough money for me to pay my rent. But when the attorney told me the sum he planned to ask in damages, I took a long deep breath: one million dollars. That was worth waiting for.

Meantime, though, I didn't have the price of a movie. It might have been funny, but it wasn't. It occurred to me that the civil attorney's office might be able to help me to a job. If they were willing to take my case, that was a vote of confidence in my future; they were bound to be sympathetic to my present problems. And so they were. They came up with an answer: it would take a little time, but I could get a hack license, and they'd help me cut the red tape involved. Driving a taxi around the city would bring me a hundred or even a hundred and a quarter a week. I could pay Papa's rent, repay the loans I'd been living on, look my fellow taxpayers in the eye, and even see that movie I didn't have the price of. Of course there were formalities: forms to fill out, fees to pay, tests to pass. But it was a beginning—a light showing at the other end of the tunnel. When I left the attorney's office I was flying high.

It didn't last. Checking on what it took to drive a hack in New York, the attorney's office found the provision that would keep Isidore Zimmerman out of work. To be eligible for a hackie's permit, you had to have held a regular driver's license for at least three years. Before I went to prison I'd been too young to drive. Now, to drive a cab, all I had to do was get a learner's permit and an operator's license and wait for three years. I was learning all the time.

Talking with an old friend one night, I turned up fresh grounds for worry. What was my draft status, he wanted to know. I had no idea. When the war broke out I'd filled out a long questionnaire and volunteered, as a Jew, for whatever hazardous duty would make life most unpleasant for Mr. Hitler; but like all lifers serving time I got a 4-F classification as a matter of course. If my status had changed for society in general, it had probably changed for my draft board too; if my privileges were restored, so were my obligations as a citizen. For a time my friend had me actively concerned about going back to prison for draft dodging. A check proved I had nothing to worry about. But if the Army had decided I owed it a year or two of my life, it would at least have added up to a job. I was just as happy it didn't work out that way; to be separated from Papa again after all those needless years of absence would have been hard on both of us.

The problem of separation was one more complication to

my job-hunting. Papa didn't want to let me out of his sight, and I didn't want to go. That meant any job I found pretty well had to be in New York or close by. What would I do, I wondered, if by some unlikely miracle I was offered work in Tulsa or Seattle or Boston? Say yes, and hope it paid enough to take Papa with me? But if he came, it would mean not seeing his other children—Carl and Ida and Louis—and his grandchildren. I couldn't ask him to do that. Say no, then, and go on living off the generosity of others, taking, taking, never giving? Every time I opened a letter with an out-of-town postmark—and the mail kept coming thick and fast—I'd ask myself the agonizing question: is this the job? And I'd live through the agonizing hope: it will be a job, a good one, in New York, one that will let me get back on my feet, start living again, come in from outer space. The agonizing would last just as long as it took me to open the envelope, and then I'd be relieved—or disappointed—again. I never could make up my mind on the proper course of action, but then I almost never had to make the decision. There was everything in my mail but job offers.

The same friend who got me to worry about my draft status told me about unemployment insurance. There'd be a little money coming in, he told me, while I was job-hunting: rent money, money for groceries, carfare. I didn't get off the ground with that one either. With a job history in New York, and the right payroll deductions behind me, I'd have been eligible. Not having worked since 1937, I wasn't: no problem.

—————

The news of my million-dollar damage suit broke in the papers on May Day, after the attorney's office issued an official announcement, and the character of my mail began to change. Up till then the marriage proposals I got . . . well, they were marriage proposals: when all was said and done, a kind of expression of human solidarity, of sympathy, affection, compassion for another human being. I was grateful for them as such. But the proposals that came in now were incredible.

There were women with friends I could marry—"just the girl
for you." There were women with daughters I could marry:
for example, one suggested I marry one of her daughters, a
32-year-old widow with a business of her own—"just the girl
for you"—and become her business associate. There were
women ready to marry me: "Just the girl for you," they said.
And there were also, among the fifty-odd letters I received,
those who offered either their daughters or themselves on a
trial basis: marriage could come later. Isidore Zimmerman
might be unemployed, but he was clearly one of the hottest
matrimonial prospects going.

I got phone calls too. Curiously enough, there were no out-
and-out proposals of marriage by telephone. But there were
plenty of proposals of a less formal nature: thirty-five or forty.
Let me come and spend the night with you, they'd say. Thanks
a lot, but no thanks, I'd say. Then you come and spend the
night with me, they'd say; you won't be sorry. Thanks a lot,
but no thanks, I'd say. It's a little difficult to explain: if you
go shopping, you don't expect to be chosen by the merchan-
dise; and as far as I knew I wasn't even shopping. So I'd
refuse, but politely. So I'd refuse, but politely: it was possible
that some of the offers were made out of an excess of generosity, misguided without being mercenary. Refusing sometimes let me in for graphic descriptions of what I was refusing. "Look, I'm only twenty-eight and I have natural blond
hair and . . ." And so forth. One such caller, to prove the
purity of her intentions, wound up saying, "I'll even give you
money." Thanks a lot, but no thanks. I stayed polite.

There was another class of phone calls, too. First they
frightened me and then they made me mad. I guess they began
when the news of the damage suit broke. Papa's address had
appeared in the papers, and it was a simple enough matter to
dig our number out of the phone book. The phone rang one
evening around seven. "Isidore Zimmerman?" "Yes, speaking," I said, hoping as usual it might be for a job. "Remember Harvey?" the voice asked, cold and unpleasant. I could
imagine the kind of face that went with a voice like that.

"Who is this?" I asked, feeling sure there was something nasty coming. "Well," said the voice, "I'm going to kill you in his name." Then the phone went dead.

I stood there in Papa's living room, feeling foolish, looking foolish. There was nothing I could say, nothing I could do with a dead phone in my hand. I felt a chill. Sure, I remembered Harvey, remembered sitting in court with him day after day, remembered going back to the Tombs with him, sharing a cell with him, sweeping it out with him every morning, drinking coffee and talking about the case, our chances, remembered him across the years saying, "But two wrongs don't make a right, Beansy," saying, "We'll tell our lawyers, all of us, you had nothing to do with it. The Court of Appeals will throw it out, you'll see." I remembered him in the death house, remembered the day we walked down the corridor to the dance hall. Remembered the tune he wanted played on the phonograph—"Did Your Mother Come from Ireland?"— the roses he'd asked them to send his mother at the end, the slur he'd uttered just before they strapped him into the chair and broiled his brains. I remembered Harvey.

An hour later the phone rang again. It's a reflex to take a ringing phone off the hook, and in the hour since Harvey's "friend" called, I'd had a chance to think over what was said and dismiss it from my mind. It was a crank call, and the attorney had warned me about cranks. Whoever it was had probably never known Harvey, and even if he had, there were no grounds for him to kill me. How was I responsible for Harvey's death? I was no child, to be frightened by a voice on the telephone. I picked up the receiver.

The voice was the same. "Isidore?" "Yes." The nastiness was coming again, I knew: I braced for it. There was a flood of obscenity—I never heard worse in prison—all against "the Jews, the dirty Jews." I wanted to strike out with both fists, but how can you strike the air? Then my caller came back to the business at hand: "I'm going to kill you, you dirty Jew bastard, kill you before sunrise." I began to shout into the receiver with more rage and hatred than I thought I could ever feel, and then I heard his laughter, wild and mocking, loud enough to shut out my words, and then the click. The hum of the dial tone. I was standing there, in the failing light of the May evening, feeling foolish, angry, even a little frightened, holding a dead phone in my hand. How can you reason with a dead phone?

It was only the beginning, of course. There were other calls and other callers—there was clearly more than one sick mind in Greater New York City that could get enjoyment from that sort of thing—but the voices always belonged to men. It made me mad, fighting mad, but there was a kind of fear that went with my rage. Who would enjoy this little game at my expense —that was the nagging question at the back of my mind— who but a maniac? And when you dealt with maniacs, it was only sensible to be frightened . . .

Telephone: "Isidore Zimmerman?" "Yes, who's this?" "I'm calling to warn you that unless you drop your suit against the city, it's sure death for you. Sure death . . . do you understand?" Click off. Telephone: "Zimmerman?" "Yes, what is it?" "You're a rat, a pig, a dirty Jew son of a bitch. If you weren't a rat and a pig, you'd have gone to the chair with the others." Click off. Telephone: "Isidore, when you leave the house tomorrow, I'll be waiting for you. I'm going to shoot you down in the street. See you tomorrow, Isidore . . ." Click. Telephone: "Zimmerman, you dirty Jew, we're going to throw acid in your face. We're waiting for you . . . acid . . . burn out your eyes." Click. Telephone: "Isidore, Isidore, be very careful crossing the streets, Isidore. You could be hit by a truck and killed. We'll be watching when you cross the street tomorrow, Isidore. Good night." Click.

Different voices, different hours, too. A call at 4:00 A.M. would wake my father and me, and then another just as we were dropping off again. A call at three in the afternoon and then again five minutes later, and then again five minutes after that. For a while I was averaging thirty calls a day. The bulk of them were sympathetic—or at least not the work of cranks—and I didn't dare not answer the phone. For all I knew, it was the employment agency, the friend, the job offer I couldn't turn down. But even at that, it got so bad I'd hang up right away if the voice wasn't familiar. If there was no sound but breathing on the other end I'd hang up too, because I knew what was coming. Papa was bewildered. I tried to hide the extent of my concern, my anger, my fear, but I couldn't explain away the calls that came in the dead of night and cut into our sleep. The first night it happened repeatedly I decided to leave the phone off the hook; it was the only way for us to get through the night. But we couldn't leave it off twenty-four hours a day. At that rate there was no sense having a phone. So, after three months of harassment, we did the obvious thing and got an unlisted number from the phone company.

The threats kept coming, but they were all in the mail, and we took them in our stride. And we started sleeping nights again.

Days I went on looking for work. Meanwhile, articles about me had appeared in an Israeli paper, the West German, the British, and even the French press had picked up the news. Offers came in from major national magazines to tell my story for publication. The money would have been welcome, of course, but my attorney advised against it, and against appearances on television, with two exceptions. I did get a green light to appear on a TV show called "Who Do You Trust," emceed by Johnny Carson, in August, 1962, and then again on the same show, for which Woody Woodbury was the new master of ceremonies, in November, 1963. Everybody connected with the shows was very gracious to me; the studio audience seemed interested in my story; and as a quiz contestant, I was lucky enough to win $500. I couldn't have been happier with first prize in the Irish Sweeps.

Judging by the number of letters we drew, audience reaction was good all over the country. I got mail from viewers everywhere in the states: expressions of sympathy, of interest in the book I planned to write, advice on "where to go from here," offers of assistance, requests for assistance. Regrettably, no job offers that came to anything. But the letters gave me an idea of the immense power of television: there was everything you could imagine in the mailbag. Some of it went direct to the show, and the producers forwarded it to me.

I couldn't help feel sorry for one of your contestants by the name of Izzy Zimmerman . . . I just out [sic] of the Navy, one of the Reserves called up in the Berlin crisis. If there is anything that I can do for this man, as far as clothes, money, job, or anything else, please do not hesitate to call me up or get in touch. Only too glad to help another one. It's just another case of misjustice [sic] done to another human being. Please tell him of my assistance that I humbly offer.

A girl from Virginia:

I have watched the show the day that man who was in jail for twenty-four years and eight months was on there. I feel very sorry for that man, and I think that every body who saw that show should send a dollar ($1.00) in to him and try to help him out. I think that it is awful that he had to take the punishment for what somebody else did. I think that somebody should try to give him a job so he can get enough money to help his father and get married too. If you would, I wish that you would ask every body that saw the show, to send in a dollar ($1.00) so he can get married. I baby sit, and I would be more than glad to send in a dollar ($1.00) if every body would do the same. Please let me here from you.

In a P.S., she added, "I am fourteen years old."

Then there was the mail addressed to me directly. From a man in St. Louis:

I have just heard your story on the "Who Do You Trust" program. . . . I have also written letters to the state and my congressman. I was shocked to hear about the attitude of the American people toward you.

One of the most touching of all for me came from a widow in Illinois:

I do hope you will soon find someone who will give you a job. I wish you would ask Johnny Carson to help you get a job he is such a wonderful man and I am sure he would be glad to help you. I am sending you some prayers and I hope you will ask God to help you and I know you will get help. My husband died five years ago . . . I wish you would find a Christian Church and join the church and I am sure people will help you in many ways. God has been so good to me . . . He answers all my prayers and I shall ask him to help you get a job . . . I have several shirts I would like to send you if you get a job they would be good enough for you to wear. Let me know if you would want them . . . I can mail them to you . . . They are some I have left of my husband's things . . . I will send you a little Bible in the shirts. I am always so happy when I know I can help anyone to let God help them.

It was signed simply, "Your friend . . ."

There were those who tried to be helpful, but who couldn't help: they don't make the rules. And the rules are tough. I talked to men who told me they, personally, were ready to hire me on the spot, and I believe they were sincere. But it would never work out, they said. It didn't matter that the personnel manager thought I was a good risk, because the first—or second or third—vice-president, who had the last word, would reverse him when he learned the truth, checking over the employee records, checking out my personal history. And if the personnel manager, out of sympathy, ever took a chance on me—falsified a statement, say, or "forgot" to turn my form over to the third vice-president—then we'd both be unemployed when he was found out. And you're always found out.

The situation arose more than once, and on one occasion it really hurt. A friend suggested that, with my first-hand knowledge of criminal psychology—acquired the hard way, during a quarter of a century in prison—I'd be a valuable part of the security setup in some big hotel or resort, where, among the paying guests, there are always a certain number of con men, jewel thieves, card sharps, and the like. Another friend introduced me to the chief of security for one of the world's largest amusement parks. It was in the New York area; the pay was good; the work anything but dull; and I

hit it off just fine with the man who interviewed me. But no
soap. "I think you're the man for the job," he said. "But I can't
make the boss see it my way." That was that.

He didn't make the rules. Nobody makes the rules, but
they're there just the same. The security angle came up again,
with a slightly different twist, as a result of my appearance on
television. The owner of a big resort hotel in the Catskills
saw the show, heard about what I'd been through, and got a
message to me. Drop everything, it ran; come on up—the
place was about two-hour drive from New York—and we'll
give you that job you want. I literally dropped everything,
packed a bag, and left in a cloud of dust. The owner's welcome
was as heart-warming as the invitation: a hundred questions,
a thousand expressions of concern, ten thousand assurances
that Zimmerman's luck was about to change for the better.
I was given a room, free meals, and the run of the place; but
when it came to making specific arrangements for the job, the
owner—still sympathetic, still cordial and full of promises—
turned me over to a brother-in-law, who was to work out the
details. He took me to a little underground room about
twenty-five feet by thirty, a storage room. Farther down than
a cellar: a subcellar, for storage purposes. You couldn't see
daylight there—just a yellow light bulb. My job was to unload
supplies and stack them; my hours were, nominally, from nine
to six, six days a week; and the pay was $137 a month
before withholding. Room and board free. It was clear from
the attitude of my benefactor's brother-in-law that the subcellar was the only place he felt it was safe to keep me. But
it was like going back to prison. The subcellar reminded me
of the box—solitary confinement, where I'd spent some of the
best years of my life. I was buried so deep in the ground that
even the sound of a summer thunderstorm would never have
trickled down to me: the place was a kind of a lab for the
study of stir-craziness, its causes and effects. And the pay—
if I wanted to take the load off Papa's shoulders, I couldn't
afford to work those hours for that money. So, regretfully,
after a couple of hours of nail-biting and soul-searching, I
said No. Brother-in-law's relief at getting an ex-convict off

the premises was something to behold. He'd clearly set it up on a take-it-or-leave-it basis, with the emphasis on the latter. It didn't matter that the owner—still sympathetic, still cordial, still full of assurances—kept asking me if I didn't want to reconsider, and was I unhappy about something, and didn't I want to discuss the matter further. I said No, thanks a lot, and took the next train back to New York.

———

Twenty-five years in prison have taught me a lot. I know things that many a judge, many a lawyer, many a psychologist or penologist are ignorant of—and my life is none the richer for knowing them—but I don't know the answers. Every now and again a friend, an acquaintance, will ask: "How can such things happen? How can such things be? What can be done to prevent them?" I don't have the answers, and if I did, it's not likely they'd be listened to, or acted on.

The problem has been with us for a long time—crime and punishment, Cain killing Abel—and nobody seems to know what to do with it. Realistically, there will always be crime, and so, realistically, there must be punishment. That argument is understandable even to a man serving time, unless he happens to be a hopeless psychopath. But when you consider the next step: how to punish the guilty—let's ignore the matter of punishing the innocent—the complications begin, the problems arise. If solutions exist, they can only be the result of a concerted effort by society to find them, and society isn't really interested in looking. The offender—transgressor, criminal, "outlaw"—is by definition operating outside society, which is embarrassed by him. Anybody who doesn't play according to the rules is a nuisance. And so society, by way of punishment—for "punishment" read "getting on with its collective business"—maintains the transgressor outside: in isolation booths made of stone and steel and suffering, commonly called prisons. To put it another way, society sweeps the mess under the rug. Any housewife can tell you that's no solution.

What is the solution? they ask me. I don't know. If I'm here at all to be asked the question, it's only because—by the grace of God and a few people who wouldn't give up—the system didn't go all the way with me. But the breaking of men is the main function of the system, and plenty of good men, unluckier than I, are broken by it. And when it's over, in the state of New York, they give you twenty dollars and send you on your way. Those twenty dollars don't even begin to pay for the long voyage home.

So if there is an answer, maybe this is the way to start looking for it: with the knowledge that the system is meant to break men, not mend them.

Then there is the knowledge, shattering to a normal understanding, that there are at this minute innocent men in prison; that men have been put to death for crimes they did not dream of committing; that men have served their term of damnation in the hell of prisons for crimes of which they were innocent; and that the future holds no promise this will be changed. Judge Jerome Frank wrote, toward the close of a brilliant legal career:

> If the conviction of an innocent man were as rare as a death from bubonic plague in the United States, we could afford to mourn the tragedy briefly, and turn back to everyday affairs. Unfortunately such convictions are by no means so rare.
>
> The conviction and imprisonment of innocent men too frequently occur to be ignored by any of us. There are too many cases on record to prove the point, and there may be countless others of which we know nothing.
>
> Often . . . the conviction of the innocent is caused, not by perjury . . . but solely by the fact that a jury believes the mistaken testimony of a witness who is entirely convinced that he is speaking the truth. Sometimes the mistake occurs because a defendant, for some reason or other, has not presented his best defense, a defense that . . . might have acquitted him. Sometimes, on the basis of extorted, false confessions, men have gone to prison or their death. Sometimes, too, when the prosecution is overzealous, when evidence is concealed, suppressed, or manufactured, conviction of the innocent may result.

Then, too, there is the knowledge, contributed by Warden

Lewis Lawes of Sing Sing, that "The defendant of wealth and position never goes to the electric chair or the gallows." This is not because people of wealth and position never commit crimes; it is because they can bear the sheer expense of properly defending themselves. That expense can be materially impossible for a poor man to bear, just as alimony payments on the Hollywood scale are out of the question for the average taxpayer. It is no argument to contend that the accused has the constitutional right to be represented by a lawyer, and that, if he has no funds, the courts will appoint counsel to defend him, and that the lawyer appointed may be the most able and the most conscientious in the world. (He may also, for that matter, be incompetent, overworked, and indifferent to the court's disposition of the case.) But even— for the sake of argument—granting him the most sterling qualities, legal expenses, like doctor bills, have a way of ballooning into the stratosphere. Beyond a certain point the best court-appointed lawyer simply cannot finance, out of his own pocket, the proper preparation of a case—defraying the expenses of an "expert" in ballistics, for example, or physically locating a defense witness who has moved to another city or another state—and there occurs in law the same distressing thing that happens in medicine: the poor patient dies in a public ward, and the wealthy patient pays for a team of specialists and survives.

To continue the analogy, the wealthy patient corresponds to the district attorney. He has the funds he needs to provide the witnesses he needs even if they have to be subpoenaed from the South Pole, and he has all the physical resources— investigative, technical, and the rest—that a society of taxpayers is willing to put at his disposal for the punishment of transgressors. Of course money will not make a guilty man innocent, but it can help an innocent man establish his innocence; without money the contest between accused and accuser can be hopelessly uneven. In my own case the six-year lapse between the 1956 *coram nobis* hearing and my release was due at least in part to the fact that the family simply had no more money to spend on my defense. Fortunately for me,

Mr. Edelbaum was able and willing to meet many of my expenses out of his own pocket, and the money he laid out exceeded many times over his original retainer. One answer to this problem might be the institution of the "public defender," that is to say, a public official empowered by law to work just as zealously, and with the same resources at his command, at establishing the innocence of the accused as does the district attorney to establish his guilt. That the principle of the public defender has been endorsed publicly by the present Attorney General of the United States is one indication of its merit.

There are half a dozen other suggestions worth making, and yet valueless until they are acted on: isolate the parole board from politics, so that a prisoner's right to another chance is determined on his merit alone, and not on the climate of timidity or antipathy that arises when a parolee like Wood— who committed a senseless double murder while on parole— compromises by his action the chances of others; give a prisoner—even a lifer—a vocation or a trade that may help him to a sense of his utility as a human being with infinite possibilities; make proper psychiatric help available to prisoners, because a prison is more like a mental hospital than any other institution created by our society, and because, potentially, everybody in it requires help; restrict the number of defendants to be tried at any one time, if only—as stated in a judicial opinion of Judge Irving R. Kaufman, published in the *New York Times* for November 13, 1962—because jurors must "constantly be made aware of the fact that there are separate individuals on trial and that each must be judged solely on the evidence properly admissible against him," under pain of attributing guilt by association; put into practice the preachment of former Attorney General Herbert Brownell that "the primary responsibility [of a prosecutor] is not that he shall win his case, but that justice is done. His should be a two-fold aim—that the guilty shall be 'brought to book' and that the innocent shall go free."

But those are just suggestions. Nobody knows the answers.

It took me ten months to get a job: working as a truckman. Take-home pay averages twenty dollars a day before taxes, and I'm happy to take it home to Papa. I'd be happier still to know there was work every day—or every night, because I work the night shift—but it's like working on the waterfront: one night they need fifty men, the next ten, and you have to be there anyway because they give out the jobs on a first-come, first-served basis. Even in a bad week it's lots more money than they paid me in prison, where I used to get about thirty cents a day for my labor. Nobody knows how proud I am to bring it home, and home is still with Papa: we hear the traffic rattling over the Williamsburg Bridge and the noise of construction—and destruction of the old city around us—jackhammers and bulldozers. If it's home to Papa, it's home to me too, but now and again it saddens me to think how far I am from being able to give him what I dreamed of over the years: a little place in the country and the chance to rest and do nothing after a lifetime of hard work and a weight of worry he never should have had.

But I'm not even sure he'd leave the city. He's lived here a lifetime; his children and grandchildren are here; his friends are here. Living forty-five minutes from Broadway would be, for him, living in exile. When you live with a person—or a city—over the years, you don't see the changes coming day by day. Suddenly the child is a man, or the girl is a grandmother, or the city is a strange city, and all the faces around me are strange. When I look around me at the city I grew up in, suddenly restored to me after my twenty-five years of exile because one day a judge, looking down from his bench at me, said Yes instead of No, I see little that is reassuring, little that is familiar.

There's nothing left of the old block at Rutgers Place—nothing but the public bath, which managed to survive somehow; a housing project abolished the rest. Scammel Street, where the boys' club was, has disappeared altogether: another housing project. And whole sections of Monroe Street have gone somewhere—where do old streets go when they die? Delancey Street is still where it was, and the kosher restaurants—Ratner's, Gluckstern's, Pollock's—remind me of the old quarter as I knew it; but every other street sign seems to be in Spanish now. Twenty-five years change more than the look of the streets. Couples don't walk hand in hand on the Williamsburg Bridge any more; and Pier 36, around South Street, is no place to go with your girl. Anybody walking down by the river after dark can expect to be mugged. Papa's lived here for fifty years, but he stays off the streets after dark; and when my sister comes to visit she telephones from the subway station for me to come and convoy her to our apartment.

Fear walks the streets of the lower East Side, now; I've never seen so many frightened people in my life. In the old days there were fights, there was violence, killings even; but nobody killed old men for the price of a beer or murdered little girls on the rooftops; nobody sold dope to school-children; and a woman could walk around the block on a hot summer night without being raped as a matter of course. There was a code; there were limits people respected. In the old days you knew your neighbor and he knew you: you knew every face on the block even when you didn't know the names.

Nobody knows anybody now; maybe that's the trouble. The housing projects may look better than the tenements from the outside but they're shoddy, shabby, cold inside, full of cold people, fearful people. You don't know the people next door, or the ones across the hall; you don't know the faces that share the elevator with you: all strangers. There are no bars on the window, and I can walk out the door whenever I like; but sometimes the thought occurs that living this way isn't really much different from living in a prison.

It's just a feeling, I know, and it doesn't stay with me long. It isn't so, I know: the gift of liberty is the most precious given to man, and the gift has been given to me. Tomorrow will be better: I know; I feel; I hope. And the lifetime without hope which I might have spent in prison has surely taught me this: that for many men, if not for all, to live without hope is harder than to die.